The Lemay Leveller

by

Erin Summers Norman

Published by COMPLETELY NOVEL – Erin Summers Norman

Copyright © Erin Summers Norman 2015

Erin Summers Norman has asserted their right to be identified as the author of this book.

Cover Art by Matthew Norman
Edited by Elly Hadaway

First published in United Kingdom in 2015 by
COMPLETELY NOVEL – Erin Summers Norman
www.completelynovel.com

ISBN number 9781849148627

Printed in UK by Lightning Source International

www.erinsummers.wordpress.com
thelemayleveller@gmail.com

I thank my husband, Matthew Norman and my son, Alex Norman for their priceless support during the writing of this book. Thank you to my best friend, Rachel Orabka, for always being the voice of reason. Thank you to Elly Hadaway for being an editor sent from God – I could not have made this book what it is without her.

For their donations and support I thank Mike Fisher, Danie Cutter, Amanda Kirke, James Rowe, Bob Shattle, Karen and Mike Taylor and Colchester Soup. Thank you also to those who donated anonymously. I literally could not have done this without all of you. It is with true gratitude that I say thank you to the hundreds of people I cannot list here who have shown me support and encouragement. You are all my heroes.

20% of the profits of The Lemay Leveller will go to Perkin's Family Trust to benefit children.

Into The Ring

We jest that my life began when I was fifteen, as if until that magical year I was simply slumbering through life; closing my eyes to so much around me whilst it all crashed and burned. It's for good reason when in 1994, aged fifteen that it was as if I was struck by lightning and the illumination cast upon everything surrounding me demanded that I steer my life in a drastically different direction. I left my mother's house for good, never having felt at home with her in the first place; determined that from that point onwards I would never again fall under her control. I fell catastrophically in love with Troy Taylor six years my senior. I slept under a bridge, got arrested for the first time, discovered punk music and had completely unprecedented fun.

I was actually born in St. Louis, MO, in 1979, aged zero, coming out squalling six weeks early in the middle of winter. However I'm still not convinced *that* was where I and my fate truly began either.

I'm going to bring everyone down with me on this ride and I won't flinch when it's my turn to have mud on my face. And so here it is: I have made public record the parts of my life of which I am most ashamed and terrified; no longer are my memories locked inside my head. In some ways it would be easy to think I'm acting against my own best interests writing this. It might also be assumed I'm doing it vindictively. Both true and untrue. I have a plan, purpose and reason. I must make good from bad, I'm taking straw and spinning it into gold.

Some names have been changed to protect the innocent, dead and litigious. The rest are left to hold their own.

When I was born I had what most American children reasonably expect to have. I had a mother and a father who had met and married twelve years before my birth, during their years at university after the Vietnam War. A sister, Elaine, was five years old and waiting to greet me. A house, family pets and an extended family, all mine for the taking. Between my sister's birth and mine there had been several miscarriages and one medically induced abortion; gruesome facts that I was regularly reminded of. So mine was by no means an accidental pregnancy; they were trying for a second child and I was the mark of a successful venture. Or maybe I was just the baby that escaped through the net. Maybe they were banking on a boy the second time around.

Whatever the desires of my parents related to my conception, within a year of my birth my dad, a Vietnam War hero and alcoholic, suddenly left my mom and her two children. After that, Elaine and I were only his for a few hours several times a year. My parents were granted joint custody in the court, but it was tacitly agreed that my father abdicated any parental responsibility in favour of overly generous child support payments. That was his choice; he openly found fatherhood repugnant. Nor did my mother relish motherhood; we were constantly reminded of the sacrifices she suffered in being the parent lumped with the children. Her inability to cope as a single parent, and my father's almost complete absence was to be the entire foundation of my childhood. He quickly remarried a lovely lady named Karen. Thankfully I have no memory of life without her. Karen was a blessing, always acting as my father's mouthpiece and propaganda device. Without her, our strained and irregular visits with my foreboding father would have been experiences even more painful than they were destined to be. And I never would have had any prettily wrapped Christmas presents sent from them. Little glimpses of what it would be like to be a child raised by wealthy parents; for my mother, no matter how high the child support payments or her personal income never spared any money on her children. She shopped for designer clothes for herself; she said she had to have the right image to get ahead in the world. We were neatly kept indoors wearing any ill-fitting, uncomfortable and out of date clothing that was donated when she put on the starving single mother routine to all and sundry.

My father's sobriety was gained when I was a very young child, and since I never saw him I never saw him drunk either. The reports of the horrors of his drinking fascinated me. He was already so terribly grim and instantly brought to anger, I wondered if he became like the Hulk when he drank. The alcoholism was used as partial excuse for his neglect of us, but the crux of the matter was that he simply hated children. As long as I knew him he was a devoted attendee of AA meetings, but the awareness of his past alcoholism coloured every moment with him. He could level his steely gaze at me and without needing to say a word I would quake to awaken the beast in him that he was intentionally threatening me with. It was blatantly understood, and even on many occasions literally voiced to us, that he left us to save his own sanity, and any demonstration of feeling or personality in his presence was nothing less than an act of aggression from our camp to his. We were to remain at a reasonable distance. Karen was very peaceful and controlled; she was the perfect consort to my father. It wasn't difficult to see how she would be more calming for a man with shattered nerves than my hyena of a mother and two young girls. None of the adults in question bothered to mince words with Elaine and me. There was no need to, we weren't important enough. We were insignificant pawns without rights or feelings whose circumstances were blatantly laid bare before us.

After the divorce, still in my infancy, my mom relocated the three of us from my birth city of St. Louis to Hannibal, MO, so she could be closer to the support of her parents, who had a lovely old house there. Although we were only two hours away from our dad and Karen, who remained in St. Louis, my sister and I only saw them a few times a year for the ten years that we lived in Hannibal. Each visit lasted only a few hours. It was never enough time to become comfortable in their presence. Karen was a lovely and irreproachably elegant lady; my father was tall, commanding, stern and silent. The two of them formed an intimidating pair to us children during our long anticipated visits. They were like semi-annual reviews of our growth conducted over a tea tray - before we were escorted back out again, hopefully without accidentally raising the hackles of my father in the process, all over the hum of Karen quietly turning the wheels. There was nothing worse than being dropped off in front of our house in disgust after an unsatisfactory visit, when we only saw him a few times a year. No time to redeem ourselves to the father we both secretly craved love from. We were always on our best, most rigid behaviour with him. What might annoy him could be the voicing of a childish opinion which he thought stupid, or the touching of a priceless ornament in his house. It often seemed that he hated the sight of us and we could do no right.

Our lives in Hannibal were much simpler than the militantly organised grandeur of Dad and Karen's house. I always felt as if he was looking at me like I was mucking up his carpet and yes once I was chastised for sitting on a sofa reserved for quality guests. It was like walking in a minefield, trying not to set a bomb off but not knowing precisely where they were hidden. They had a flashy Volvo, Tiffany lamps and designer cats, while I spent my time at home pottering about in my Grandpa's barn that he built with his own two hands. The visits were long anticipated and quickly over, and Karen was easily the pleasantest element of them, being graced with that rare ability of being able to sooth hurt feelings and make torturous social experiences bearable.

During the young years of my childhood my mom and I were quite close. Elaine, a righteous and aggressive example of humanity if ever there was one, hated my mom for her many inadequacies and blamed her for our father leaving. Being five when the event occurred, she had some memory of them living together so the divorce was harder on her. I was neutral since this was how it had been my entire life. Although Elaine often claimed hatred for our mom, and our mom was more than happy to fight her back, making them something like sworn enemies, sometimes the wind would change and suddenly they would unite and come down on me. I was the natural floating ally between them, to be used, befriended or turned on as circumstances demanded. All I wanted was for the constant screaming over my head to stop. Despite this, I was a child, and I wanted to love my mother, I wanted her to love me. I craved her erratic warmth. Even my image of her name, Carol, was a warm and beautiful one. We both loved music and I always thought of her name as a word rather than a more arbitrary name assigned to a human, such as, "Susan". "Susan" couldn't hold its own in a sentence without being attached to a person as a prop, but Carol could. This small difference was impressive to me.

There's a picture of us together, on our deck in Hannibal under the scorching summer sunshine, all bundled up in hot winter clothes, earmuffs, coats and scarves with huge smiles on our faces. That picture stands alone as proof that somewhere, at some time, Carol and I were not sworn enemies. Carol never seriously dated anyone after the divorce, although she had a few offers. She often told me how much she loved my father, and how bewildered and hurt she was when he left her. I was her sounding board, and she kept trying to bounce back, right off of me.

Round One

Elaine was the leader; she always had a clipboard in her arms and a tapping foot. She taught me how to write "cat" on the chalkboard in our garage and rewarded me with a proud, beaming smile. I must have enjoyed her writing lessons because once I got the hang of it, I couldn't stop. Sitting at my Grandparents kitchen table, I wrote Ronald Reagan a letter telling him that he reminded me of my Grandpa. The letter said that I hoped President Reagan didn't get too sad when people criticised him on the news, because morale was important when you had the entire free world on your shoulders. Shortly after, I had a letter back saying the president had read my letter and he thanked me for my support. I felt I had contributed to my country's welfare. When I was fourteen, (still sitting at my Grandparents kitchen table), I wrote a slightly amended version of that same letter to Bill Clinton, omitting the reference of similarity to my Grandpa (for obvious reasons). My Grandpa initially questioned my bi-partisan support and I myself felt a moment's pang for the hypocrisy of it. Everyone I knew declared themselves staunchly Republican or Democrat. I understood the differences between the parties as well as I could and I gathered it was deeply important that you be one or the other. So I gave my Grandpa's question serious thought as he stood and watched me with a coy grin. My answer was that I reasoned both men had a great deal of responsibility, and therefore both men needed as much morale as we could muster now that they were in position. It wasn't as if I had the vote anyway, I was only a child still. When I answered my Grandpa he was amused, and understood my logic, but I had the impression he felt I was throwing pearls before swine. That may have been because he said something along the lines of "Son of a bitch doesn't deserve your letter." Still, I shrugged, licked the envelope and handed it to him to be posted as he wandered into his garage. No reply from the Clinton Administration I will note. I am sure that the former president wishes that he could correct that error and give my letter the full appreciation it was due.

I read voraciously, and it was only a matter of time until I did it criminally. Books were my great passion, but I never had enough of them. I was eight. I found my first and still favourite book about Eleanor of Aquitaine "A Proud Taste for Scarlet and Miniver", by E.L. Konigsburg. I stole it from my elementary school, fuelled by the fear that if I let this precious object out of my hands I would never see it again. I found it on a shelf lining a staircase one day while roaming the halls with a bathroom pass. The cover was a glorious and Gothic depiction of Eleanor on a horse with a knowing expression on her face. Several other characters were riding in the distance behind her. I picked it up and began leafing through. It looked good. I sat down on one of the steps and read a few paragraphs and I knew I had to have it. It didn't matter if it was a school book, a library book or another student's book, the thought of walking away from it made me feel as if the air in my lungs was being stamped out. So I put it in my bag. Thank god I did, too. It spawned an insatiable interest in history that had incomprehensible consequences for me. I had a huge interest in the world around me but that book honed it very finely into the personal lives and political machinations of pretty much everyone who came before me.

Adults loved me for having this quality of being happy – no insatiable, to learn any new information that could shed light on humanity. But the adoration of my elders was very much a by-product of, rather than the object of my obsession. I could discuss many historical events with competency because I ate books for breakfast and I never minded listening to anything anyone wanted to say to me about what they did when they were young. I was learning that history is timeless and governments throughout history are examples to look at and learn from. The ebb and flow of human energy and defeat throughout time are all indications of what must be done now, if only you have the ability to chart your place on the time line; to see where we are, against everywhere we've been.

My mom very obviously felt the strain of parenting us on her own, despite the close proximity of our Grandparents. There were obviously many factors at play in those early years; heartache, financial difficulties and mental health problems. I cannot presume to say that I understand because I was only a young child, but even a young child can hear when it is their shoulder a parent is crying on. On more than one occasion I listened terrified, trying to comfort my mother as she wept and talked of killing herself, wishing she was dead and away from the life of being a single mother. Those words sting and remain rooted in the memory of a child. I remember her dreadful crying jags and tempers like they were yesterday; never enough money, never enough energy, never enough hours in the day. A father and ex-husband who had no love for the family he left; too many checks to balance; too many dishes to wash, too many girls to herd into bed at night; a full time job to work all day. She hated and resented every second of her life as our mother, always feeling that she had been cheated out of the life she should have had. "Bitter" does not do justice to the condition that my father left her in without looking back, and she never climbed out of it. I pitied her greatly but her outbursts set our nerves on edge nonetheless, and her general gloominess was a constant reminder of her misery: namely the children she was stuck with. More than once she recounted the story of my father's leaving, and the moment of his dramatic exit always came right on the heels of my birth. I listened, silently. She carried an aura of instability, and was prone to being utterly miserable with self-pity and anger, but it was largely my mother's angry outbursts that I feared the most – and the equal fury she'd meet in return from Elaine.

Carol used to save the cardboard wrapping paper tubes leftover at Christmas, so that when they were empty of paper she could use them to beat against the stair bannisters to blow off steam. Like punching a pillow, but with the fading screaming memories of Rudolph and Santa Claus echoing in my head. It was a suggestion she read in a self-help book that brought a shadow of fear over every holiday. She seemed proud of herself for trying it, as if she were saying, "Look at me! Aren't I a clever woman, to cope with the horrific load on my shoulders by trying all these novel and festive techniques?" But I was terrified of the rage I saw in her when she went crazy on a cardboard tube. I knew that heaving chest and red face were really meant for me. And I've never looked at a roll of wrapping paper the same way again.

Elaine went through a period in Hannibal when she slept with a ready packed children's suitcase under her bed, with a set of both of our clothes in it along with a few other essentials. Just in case we ever had to leave in the middle of the night, or at a moment's notice, she explained to me. But Elaine and Mom could just as easily change like the wind and befriend each other for a small sunny period, during which time I instinctively slid to the background and silently cooperated with both of them in everything I could, hoping for a continuance of peace in the battleground that was my home. Still, for some reason I could never comprehend, each time Elaine decided to make peace with our mom she turned on me, and then I was bullied by her. So it was, that I could at times be close to my mother, and others to my sister, but never did the three of us work as a functioning triangle, and I often felt that I was the linchpin directing the balance of power. It was a terribly confusing atmosphere to grow up in, that was as much determined by my elder sister as my mother. I felt as if life was a field of land-mines, and I was perpetually praying that my next step would not be my last before an eruption.

Once when I was around five years old I was trying to help my sister rake the front yard, while our mother observed from the porch. I accidently said to my sister that I wanted my turn with the "rape" instead of saying "rake". It was a totally ignorant mistake; I had no idea at all what rape was but I couldn't quite remember how to pronounce "rake", so it simply came out wrong. I wanted to be a big girl and help my sister. Any (reasonable) mother would perhaps kindly correct the child and say "It's called a 'rake' sweetheart but thank you for wanting to help!" My mother was not reasonable. I was bewildered and terrified as Carol came running across the grass towards me, face screwed up in a blind rage. She slapped me hard across the face and said I was a very bad girl for saying a very bad word. As I cried she dragged me by my arm into the house and threw me bodily into my bedroom, ordering me to stay there until further notice, slamming the door behind her as she stomped out of the room. I had absolutely no idea what I'd done wrong but I sobbed for hours. I felt deeply ashamed of myself, and so very stupid. Our every childish transgression was an invitation to abuse and humiliation.

Sometime around the age of six I rather comically stumbled upon my lifelong obsession with music. I received a plastic Fisher Price record player for Christmas that year; I believe it arrived in a large box of presents for us, sent from St. Louis to Hannibal, and it came complete with a selection of Mickey Mouse records. I liked them, they were fun. Mickey's Dancercise was the best. But my mom's record collection from the 60's and 70's beckoned silently from the blue wooden cabinet in the living room, demanding to take a spin under my little needle. When I opened it up there were all sorts of records I could take out and make work on the player in my very own bedroom. What monstrous power! I found an old 45 of the Rolling Stones "Paint It Black" and became hypnotised by it, playing it again and again in my bedroom every chance I could. Before school, after school, after dinner, before bed.

After weeks of listening to the song in every spare moment, I woke inexplicably early on a Saturday morning with a feeling of bleak determination to face reality and end my childhood. While my mother and sister slept on, I began putting all my precious stuffed animals into black bin bags. When I was finished, I dumped them outside to be collected by the garbage men. Once I finished committing this atrocity against my best childhood friends, I returned to my then quite bare bedroom, with the record player in the middle of the floor. I looked at it, and began crying penitent, choking tears. I went into my mother's bedroom to wake her and confess what I had done. She comforted me, retrieved the toys from the garbage and helped me set my room to rights. But that was perhaps lesson number one in the mysteries that sound and unharnessed indulgence would play in my life.

I shared my mom's love of Fleetwood Mac. She regaled me with tales of what a dreamboat Elvis was when she was young. Laura Branigan's Self Control stirred my heart with raw emotion I barely understood despite Elaine saying that she sounded like she had a frog stuck in her throat. I replied that my sister had no understanding of passion. But most wonderfully damning of all was when I eventually inherited my sister's discarded Depeche Mode, Black Celebration tape later the same year it was released. That cassette blew me into absolute smithereens. It explored death, sarcasm and sexuality in terms I had never before heard (quite rightly, I was only seven). Still, somehow I perfectly understood it on a primal level, even if not yet on a literal one. I remember listening to David Gahan singing "Stripped", trying to comprehend if the sex act actually involved some sort of peeling back of the skin, and deciding at that point that I should just stop thinking about it. However I did totally understand the wish to hear someone speaking just for me. It – music and sex and men who made butterflies appear in my stomach - was like a big, decadent, promising cake held just out of my reach and sight, but I knew it was there waiting for me when I grew up. Whatever the potential of that world was, it made me very curious and I liked the way it sounded if the end result was having a man with a voice like that giving his undivided attention to me. For the time being that song was enough but I looked forward to the future with a mixture of fascination, excitement and dread. And a silent prayer that my skin remained intact.

Around the time of my intoxication with "Paint it Black" came a day when my mom and I were organising some books on the shelves. I came across a small paperback with a very gory cover. It was entitled "Johnny Got His Gun" by Dalton Trumbo. I asked my mom what it was. She replied that it was about war, and it had belonged to my dad. When he left us he had left that book as well, and my mother kept it as she kept everything they shared. She said, rather spitefully, that since I was always so interested in my father I should read it. I said yes, I would, and ignored the undertone of her comment. I took the book into my room and sat on my bed with it. I read while playing Paint it Black on repeat in one sitting, too horrified to put it down. I wanted to put it down a third of the way into it but I couldn't. It was my father's – it meant something to him. If he had suffered atrocities like this in war, if this was why he couldn't bear the sound of children, then I was honour bound to finish it and go through it with him, whether he knew or not. I would not shrink from his reality; I loved him and wanted to understand him better. It was a foolish sacrifice for a child of that age to be allowed to make for a man who would never know and never care.

Anyone who has read the book will understand that the horror that came to me was a shock. Many adults have not been exposed to such darkness in literature, let alone very young children. But it was a learning experience. A false one perhaps, for I concluded this was why he was too shattered to love me, and it stored up years' worth of pity in my heart for him that would compel me to accept his abominable treatment with silent grace, never placing blame on his shoulders. Never considering there may come a time when he had to hold accountability to me as he did his fellow AA members and soldiers. I should have spared myself and played with Barbies. It is, no doubt about it, a book made to induce within the reader a horror of war, and it succeeded. Perhaps the children's reading demographic was not its intended market. But it scored its goal nevertheless.

Round Two

During my years in Hannibal the culture of the Mississippi and Mark Twain's legacy of literature left a deep impression on me, a mark that I was not at all unaware of at the time. I knew very well that my fate was being sealed up, minute by minute, and that all the information, feelings, culture and experiences I was absorbing were to form my foundation. The Hannibal of my childhood was still very much small town America, and Samuel Clemens was its undisputed hero. Downtown, which consisted of one long

16

street lined with wooden clapboard and brick buildings, had several small houses and apothecary shops that had been restored to the style of Twain's times. Inside were stiff talking mannequins with pasted on hair, who, if you pushed a big green button on a little panel by the door would give you a speech about what life was like for them in the olden days. It didn't matter that I lived in the town and I wasn't a tourist: going downtown at the weekend and seeing each display, hearing the same speech I'd had memorised for years, was a treat to me. I could always enter into the illusion of being somewhere, somewhen, someone else. I sincerely believed in time travel, I believed walking into the right building in the right circumstances into the right light might enable leaps in time and space. I believed nooks and crannies in trees might lead to fairy worlds, which was nice because my Grandparents house had a lovely little wood and apple orchard on the grounds. Nothing at all was impossible to me. Exiting the apothecary and stepping on to the street of cars always came as a shock, an unwelcome jolt back into reality.

Just beyond Main Street with its pleasant options to escape into the past was the Mississippi River itself, with its mercurial depths. I loved the river for the same reason most people loved it, it was magical, mysterious and full of depth, wonder and potential. It was also horrid and flat and unrelenting but it was there nonetheless and it drew me to it as great forces of nature will draw smaller things to them. Don't you always find that when there's a remarkable, massive, ancient tree in the middle of a forest, you find yourself gravitating towards it, as if it were the goal of your walk? There were huge paddle boats that slowly went up and down the river. One had been converted to a restaurant and sometimes as a treat on a hot night we'd have our dinner sitting on the boat deck and watch the fireflies skit over the water. Elaine and I would dance around and watch the waves in moonlight ripple underneath us. Another old converted paddle boat was permanently moored to the shore and that was actually a McDonalds inside; surely the classiest McDonalds in all the world, and the most exciting to get your Happy Meal from, as it swayed slightly on the water. I loved the feeling of being on the water, I loved having to catch my balance if a larger boat went by and we were rocked by the waves.

I used to watch the long barges push their heavy loads to and fro and think of how timeless they were, but also just a little bit ugly compared to the elegant paddle boats. The trees behind them were magnificent, ancient, tall and full of nests of every kind of bird from eagle to sparrow, and of course, cardinals. Sitting on the banks of the river was its own pleasure; looking down into it for fish and watching logs float by.

I wanted to see romantic fish, tropical fish, fish with feathery fins of many colours that would come to the surface and whisper stories to me of all the exotic lands they had swam to in the hundreds of years they'd covered the globe. The day I realised fish weren't imprisoned by borders I was interested in what they had to say. I was a great fan of my Grandpa's National Geographic magazines. But usually I only caught glimpses of fat dark fish swimming slowly or tiny fish darting quickly away and none of them had a word to say to me. I forgave them for their inferiorities and I was even fond of them too. I've never shaken the feeling that somewhere in that river there were grander fish that simply chose to be elusive.

The Mississippi flooded particularly badly one year, all of downtown was under water. For a small town, downtown was the place where all essential services were located. That meant our one bank was under water too. My mom operated firmly on a cash and a check basis as everybody did then, and no bank meant no money for the whole town. The flood was a crisis in more ways than one. Everyone was very capable and cooperative, and a group of men worked together gathering all the row boats and small motor boats in town. They spent days ferrying people around the lower streets so that they could run their necessary errands, entering buildings by upper windows. My sister and I were rowed into our mom's bank so that we could withdraw money on her behalf. It was all handled with the capability, fun and grace that I have come to expect and desire in times of crisis. The surreal experience of trailing my fingers alongside fish on streets I normally traversed in cars was remarkable and unforgettable to me, as was the smiling man quietly rowing us an extra lap before returning us to our mother. So so! The river wasn't as elusive as I thought it was! It could come to me and consume everything in its path. In which case all I could do was ride it, just like the log. It was an awe inspiring experience of nature triumphing over nurture.

Against this backdrop was the perfection of Grandma and Grandpa, and their lovely old home. If any child was ever blessed in Grandparents it was me. Annie and Jack Cardinal were like a species all amongst themselves in my mind, separate from the rest of humanity by virtue of their divinity. Nobody else was like them; nobody else had within them so many different qualities and virtues, and so little hatred against me and all of humanity. They would have been the first to have scoffed at my sky-high praise, but also the first to understand why I make it, and to allow me to say my peace without undo hypocritical reference to their own modesty. They understood my effusive love perhaps because it came from them and it flowed back both ways; they loved me in such a precious, unprecedented and never to be repeated way, that I felt with them that I was exactly as I should be. When I was with them, the rare and incomparable feeling of being unconditionally loved and safe washed over me as soon as I bounded through their door, only to leave me again as I was driven away to return to my own home. With them I was never afraid. I always knew they treasured the special relationship they were allowed to have with one of so many grandchildren, and I secretly thought myself their favourite. I more or less lived with them off and on for long periods of my childhood, and I never felt like a guest or an inconvenience. They loved having me with them, and their home was more familiar and dear to me than my own.

If ever a couple deserved immortality it is these two beautiful people, who never wished harm on another soul. They were not grand nor were they technically flawless I am sure; reason tells me so although I have no firm proof of it. My Grandparents were filled with something so rarefied and pure that I can only say I felt I was kneeling at the feet of sweet and kind gods, and the gods loved me best of all. It was blessed. However, as close as I was to my Grandparents, they both remained a little mysterious. I always wished I could fill in and memorise every moment that they lived; I never felt I knew enough about them. I was unable to flesh them out much beyond what they were to me in my present: sweet and elderly. Their pasts were vague and sweet shadowy things, suited to my image of them.

Grandma and Grandpa met at a dance in St. Louis in the 1940's. She was fifteen and he was nineteen, and they fell in love on their first dance together. It was so simple, the way they told it, and you never questioned what they said: you only had to see them to know it was true. They would of course have fallen in love at first sight because no other possibilities could ever have existed for those two. One was only surprised that they weren't born married, and I always felt as if they must have felt dreadfully wobbly and lonely before they met each other. Grandpa had grown up on his family farm in Ohio, but was in St. Louis to undertake training at Scott Air Force Base during World War Two. After his training he was due to be deployed to Japan. Grandma, on the other hand, was a city girl, born and raised in St. Louis.

If Fate had played the wrong hand, none of it ever would have happened. Grandma wanted to go to the dance held on the air force base with her friends, but her father said she was too young to go to a dance full of soldiers. She persistently begged until he relented, allowing her to go with a chaperon. Thankfully my Great Grandfather Summers was a liberal man, because otherwise such a beautiful love story would have been lost, and I wouldn't be here writing this down now. But that first night was enough; Grandma and Grandpa felt enough for each other to keep them united and resolved on marrying during the long years that he was away in Japan and she finished growing up. When he returned home, he went not to Ohio, but to St. Louis, and married my Grandma. They set up home in her native town, later to relocate to Hannibal which they had done many, many years before I was born.

It was so easy to picture Grandma as a young girl, she barely gave the impression of being fully grown even when she was in her eighties, although she never lacked gravity and always commanded respect. But that was without trying, she was as open, friendly and kind as a person could be. Being disrespectful to her would have been inconceivable. I was not as good as she was, I was ready and willing to hate anyone who hurt what I treasured, and I treasured my Grandparents.

Grandma retained a delightful girlish quality that emerged in a giggle or a smile or a flirtatious reference to her handsome and dashing husband. Grandpa on the other hand, while he was undoubtedly extremely handsome, was curmudgeonly and cantankerous. And I was absolutely besotted with him. I always had a hard time picturing my Grandpa on a farm in Ohio, it felt too small for him and his intellect. But that farm had been in his family for over 200 years; I expect there were a great many books lying about and my Grandpa enjoyed reading all of them. He had the most wicked sense of humour and a great ability to ask the right questions and say very much in very few words. He easily outpaced most everyone around him, and he and I were famous for our back and forth banter. Unfortunately he also had a sharp temper with fools, also when he felt frustrated because he was unable to convey himself past his speech impediment, caused by a severe stroke. I was never once the brunt of his temper, and in fact I rarely saw him lose his temper, except towards men on the news not doing their jobs properly.

But I have heard that in the post-war years when he was raising his own children and battling alcoholism he was not always as kind. Unfortunately, when my mom was jealous of my close relationship with her father, feeling spiteful and in the mood for unloading on to her child counsellor, she often chose to detail every unkind act he committed during her childhood. I did not want to hear it. My Grandparents were all I had. I had no choice but to appear to listen; protestations would bring screams or smacks. So I trained my face to remain impassive at all times and I allowed her voice

23

to float over and above my head without ever landing on top of it and sinking in. I chose to ignore those things because I knew him as he truly was then and I knew he was good - and I knew even then that she was showing her own true colours by always raining on my parade. Providing me with stories I instinctively knew I'd never burden my children with. Tit for tat maybe, telling me those stories: I inadvertently encouraged her husband to pack his bags and walk out the door and now here I was with her father wrapped around my little finger. Her revenge came in reminding me that what I was left with wasn't all I thought it was cracked up to be, and best of all, I was stupid to fall for it. "So wipe that smug smile from your face" - the final lyric to the endless song.

Grandma and Grandpa had four children, my Mother being the eldest and the only to show signs of constant narcissism and mental disease. Two other girls came after her, and lastly a son named after Grandpa; all four of them blonde haired and blue eyed. They would all go on to produce blonde haired, blue eyed children too, except for my mom. She mated with a black haired man; his genes combined with hers made two very different pieces of work, born black haired like him. The only children in the family of divorced parents, my sister and I stood out in more ways than one.

My Grandpa's passion was painting, and in the 1950's and 60's when he was raising his family, he made a career painting for advertising campaigns, some of his work quite

24

memorable. But when he painted for his own pleasure his work was very different from the stylistic artistic advertising he created for pay. The most stunning piece of all was a dark and moody painting created from his imagination, in so many shades of black that looking at it you were continually stunned that you could see anything at all. But every line was there, every definition meticulously made. It was a depiction of horses pulling a carriage through a brick tunnel in a thunderstorm in the middle of the night. Our vision of the struggling horses and rider is illuminated only by a dim, swaying carriage lantern. The driver, wielding his riding crop, was soaked in his black cloak, but presumably some lucky souls sat dry within. The horse's heads were bent down against the elements, bodies heaving. The puddles and paving stones were magnificent; every chip was there, every dark reflection of light. I could never take my eyes off that painting once they rested on it. I went through a stage when seeing the painting compelled me to stare at it for so long, in an effort to understand all of it at once, that if I was in a hurry I had to avert my eyes from it to avoid its pull. I made up for what felt like a silent insult to a loved one by spending regular dedicated time doing nothing but sitting perched on the back of my Grandparent's sofa so I could more closely scrutinise it.

Its detailed darkness astounded me, but the fact that it came out of my own dear Grandpa, he of the soft wavy white hair and an obsession with Fritos and Werthers Originals, both thrilled and terrified me. It opened up a whole world of possibilities, none of which were remotely average. All of which began on the reflection – who was he, and who was I? His inner life was plainly a harrowing place that only the brave would venture, but it was sensitive and overflowing with emotion; he loved the horses well but their heads were down, their job was miserable. Sheets of rain hit the driver in the face but they all pushed on. His inspired attention to each cobbled stone in the road forced me to consider every hour that my Grandpa carefully mixed Black 1 with Black 2, and Black 3 with some sort of silver of white to make a reflection of water until his efforts achieved mythic status. Why? It was magnificent, but why? Why had he done it, I asked myself? Why this picture, why not a farm scene? My Grandpa existed in soft flannel shirts, faded jeans and solid work boots; he seemed a world away from the scene he created. Why spend day after aching day making tubes of oil into a masterpiece, only to hang it in his own living room? I always thought it should be in a museum and he be hailed the greatest artist of our times. I still ask these questions but I ask them of myself, why write, why create, why live even? I know Grandpa asked it all of himself and it is the cause of our mutual melancholy; we both wish to know that there is a purpose in creation. But the question "Why?" when applied to my Grandpa's painting and my writing is like asking "Why is a weather front?" We can say what a weather front does, and how it develops, but can anyone actually define a reason for a tornado? It simply is, and the onus is on us to deal with it accordingly to the best of our abilities. We slave over our obsessions because they are all that there is within us.

Grandma and Grandpa's home in Hannibal was and is still the house of my dreams and the home of my heart. It was a large, white wooden house with a barn to the side that Grandpa built himself. Downstairs, the barn was a typical example of its kind, housing my Grandpa's ancient truck, tools, and various marvels of mechanics. This we were allowed full and gloriously dangerous access to. But the second floor, inaccessible, was Grandpa's painting studio, and no one was allowed up there without an express invitation from Grandpa. The one defining feature that gave the barn's hidden function away was unusually large windows on the second floor, which he built in so that he would have sufficient daylight for painting.

The house itself was the epitome of warmth and informality. The cavernous living room, with its large stone fireplace, was set down several brick steps from the main hall, giving a feeling of snuggling into a cool, dark cave as you entered the room. Grandpa's old, limping dog was usually curled up in front of the fire, while he sat in the armchair opposite. The kitchen walls were very old brick, typical of a house of that age and so cosy compared with modern buildings. As well as having its own working fireplace and stove, it had a wonderful beaten up old wooden island in the middle of the room with fantastic spinning stools placed around it that I would spin on until I was sick. There were several smaller pokey rooms downstairs that ran one into the other in a seemingly random order, including a well-used dining room housing a table that groaned to accommodate the many children and grandchildren of my Grandparents. If everyone congregated at once that table was declared the adult table, and card tables were set up along the edges of the room as children's tables. When a cousin graduated from sitting at a children's table to the adult's table it was a momentous occasion. All the usual alliances between the many cousins would undergo a temporary shake up of rank in dominance, a game I stayed out of by refusing to participate in, quietly eating my meal alone or circumventing the whole system by eating on my Grandpa's knee. He allowed it and no one dared say no to him.

Up the creaky wooden stairs were the lovely old bedrooms; lovely because I could lay in them for hours and dream of all the girls who'd lain in them in the years before me. Each room had its own special little pieces of furniture, collection of books or paintings. They all held their own special charms but were modestly furnished, taking beauty from their simplicity and offering a view over an endlessly pretty landscape. The sheets were always crisp, soft and familiar; the blankets were all quilts with stitches to trace with my fingers or knitted afghans with lovely knobbly bits to rub. There was always a folded up blanket at the foot of every bed in case you got cold in the night.

There was one bedroom I liked best of all, and I adopted it as my own because I stayed at their house so frequently, and Grandma was very sweet to always make sure it was reserved for me. My sister and I were the only two grandchildren who lived in

Hannibal, and since our mom was often struggling to cope with us, I especially (being the younger and allowed less independence) stayed with our Grandparents. On one occasion our stay lasted for the better part of two months, because my mother had a nervous breakdown and was checked into a "stress centre". It was a blissful reprieve from fights that could never be won, instead immersed in simple activities such as shelling peas, picking flowers for vases and listening to stories from Grandpa.

Grandma and Grandpa's room was beautifully and elegantly decorated with all her pretty little things; perfume bottles, little statues, cross stitch samplers. It had French doors that opened up onto a little balcony that looked over the front drive. The balcony was built with breakfast for two in mind; something I often enjoyed with Grandma. I do firmly remember thinking that having a house with a balcony like that was the zenith of personal bliss, and I should make it my mission to one day acquire the same for myself. But really I wanted it all - the balcony, the creaky stairs, the whole house to be preserved forever, so I would always be able to return to its shelter. I wanted to make that house mine when I was grown up, I wanted to inherit it. I couldn't imagine losing it. I loved it like a pilot loves the sky.

On days the entire family were there the house was bustling with activity, games and cousins bumping into each other in doorways whispering secret codes. But the most magical place to be was the apple orchard, which insulated the lawn from the road beyond the brick walls of the property. It was dense enough that you could imagine you were lost within a wood, but small enough to create familiar landmarks and nooks and crannies to play in. It was of course the ideal place for the annual Easter Egg hunts, which delighted us children. The orchard held ghosts, fairy folk, princesses, queens and kings – anything you could imagine including a tree house I began to try to build myself and was finished off by Grandpa.

At the top of the gravel drive was a cast iron statue of a black man, about the same height as me for a time, before I surpassed him with all my nefarious growth hormone. He wore smart red livery and had his hand extended outwards holding a ring, as if asking me to waltz with and dangle on him all at once, a smile forever on his obscure face. I now know that in days gone by, he was a hitching post for horses, and was in himself intended to represent a slave, but his existence was a mystery to me then. The best reason I could guess was that he was there to be danced with; so we danced and I swung on his arm often. He, cemented in place, didn't move very much at all, or indeed respond in any way to my overtures. I made do as best as I could and twirled around him, expecting what, I know not. Looking back it was the ideal preparation for my dealings with the male sex. And pole dancing.

Of course knowing the house had once been a modest plantation home including its own slave quarters did much for my fertile and historically inclined imagination, which prompted deep thought into the rights of human beings. I developed an interest in the Civil War and all its complexities and battles, an interest encouraged by my Grandpa. Our house and town was not so modernised that I found it difficult to grasp those times. I held a secret hope and faith that somewhere in the house might exist a passageway for the Underground Railroad. I searched every nook and cranny I could find, pushed on every stud in the walls and tested wobbly floor panels. I couldn't accept that our home could have fostered cruelties such as those I had read of. The very walls seemed to exude love, kindness and acceptance. I knew that every girl, irrespective of her birth year, country or skin colour was made of the same stuff, feeling the same feelings. It was not a difficult leap to that understanding, but one of pure common sense. But it was a strong and fervent understanding that instilled in me a sense of the human right to freedom and dignity, and it never left me. I was also fortunate to be sharing the house with two older, doting people who valued life in all its varieties tremendously and would have sharply brought me into line had I ever uttered a bigoted or racist comment.

Outside, the lawn was covered in croquet, lemonade, noise, lawn chairs and boisterous cousins running relay raccs I'd never win. Inside I would find Grandpa, sensibly ensconced in the cool, dark and quiet living room. I would lay my head on his dusty jeans covered knee and he'd try to tame the curls in my hair while we'd have one of our little chats. Long before my time he'd had the strokes that had caused the loss of the

31

fine motor control of his right hand, so he could no longer paint or write; a source of huge depression for him. He was still able to do most of the grounds-keeping, such as wood chopping and lawn mowing, and so I believe he turned towards nature for his comfort. He was often to be found wandering amongst the trees examining branches. His speech was very difficult to understand by those who weren't used to it, which only added to his air of crankiness. To me it added to his charm and uniqueness, I could understand him well enough. He was a doll. But he obviously found the noise of the whole family together too much to take without frequent escapes into solitude. I was quite of the same mind, though not as justified in being so outspoken about it; so I often joined him in his seclusion.

I can see his silky white wavy hair, blue eyes and smiling face as clearly as if he were looking at me right now. He would have been reading a book and watching some black and white movie with shaky film showing fighter planes shooting down other fighter planes. He'd set the book aside on his little side table and grin at me like a devil and I'd curl up like a kitten onto him and he'd tell me his stories of Japan or France during the war. We also talked of the farm he grew up on in Ohio, and his years working as an artist in St. Louis. I remember feeling a jealous curiosity, wondering if when I slipped off his knee and back to the croquet, one of my cousins would slip in and take my place. More often than not, my solution to this green eyed worry was to imitate the American occupation of Japan and stay put to the end of the movie.

Round Three

A terrible and unforgettable day came in my tenth year, when Grandma and Grandpa gathered the family together and announced they were selling their house in Hannibal. They said that Grandpa could no longer maintain the grounds after continued strokes. This marked the beginning of the true disillusionment with my childhood, and all its concepts of happiness and control. I gained a deep and unhappy appreciation of the fact that forces greater than me would act in ways that would steer my life away against my will. I spent my entire childhood hoping things would soon get better; instead it felt like my life was being rearranged in a pattern that I could never flourish in, only survive.

I despised the fact that our beautiful home was going to go to other people – strangers who would never let me in again, redecorate, and put their terrible things where ours should be. I knew every nook and cranny, every room and wall of that house like the back of my hand. In my soul, it was a part of me; it belonged to me, and being cast out of it felt like being thrown out of Eden. I hated the people who were buying it; they were nothing less than criminals in my eyes, robbing an elderly couple of their home. It felt as if the house itself was being burgled and defiled. It seemed savage and uncivilised to sell a home as precious as ours; it wasn't the same as normal houses, including the one I lived in with my mom and Elaine. Those were built a dime a dozen with as much character as a paperclip. Our home was different. I vividly remember scrambling about in my mind for some solution, thinking I could do more - I could weed the gardens or mow the lawns to help out. What was the point of Grandma and Grandpa having so many able bodied children and grandchildren if none of the others were willing to pitch in and help keep them in their home? I said that, I asked that above the din but nobody was listening to me, for once even Grandpa couldn't or wouldn't answer me. I was positive Grandma and Grandpa hadn't thought the issue through. They knew that I hoped to own the house one day, but I was only ten. There were years to go before I could think of buying it; the house would be destroyed before I could lay my hands on it again. No one was listening to me. A huge chasm of horrifying and endless possibilities opened up before me, upon which I teetered on the edge, understanding that I would *never* be able to reclaim my beautiful home once it was abandoned.

But there was nothing I could do, I had no ability to puppet master my elders and my voice carried no weight, despite the fact that I felt I cared more than almost anyone else involved. My Grandparents began work building a partially underground energy saving house on my Aunt's land, located in the isolated countryside. It was off a long dirt road in a small town, population a couple of hundred. My Grandparents new home was built by our own family members, even I hammered some nails. Once the house was completed a false earth hill was built around the sides and back to entirely cover the roof, a nod to the environment by my Grandparents.

I wanted to hate that house but it had its charms, and after all, it was still where my Grandparents were. If they were by some twist of fate housed in Hades I would have been eager to move in with them. Though I never stopped aching for the old house, the new house in the country was begrudgingly charming. By climbing up the hill around the house you could stand on the roof and look out over the front drive and countryside beyond. It was my favourite place to be. Sitting on the grassy roof of that house was some consolation for losing my favoured home, so I inevitably came to love the underground house as well. The spinning stools were still there, with the painting and the blankets at the end of the bed. It was cosy in the way that only Grandma could make a home be. Grandpa never let the log burning stove go out in the winter and the smell was divine. However it wasn't long before I realised that they had in their old age moved away from an active town with friends, amenities and a hospital, to an extremely isolated location, hours away from anything or anybody but a busy daughter living a quarter of a mile down the lane. I suppose they wanted total quiet in their final years, and there certainly was no better place to achieve that. But I worried for their health and wellbeing.

When I was all grown up, more or less, I moved to England. On a visit home to see my

Grandparents in their final months, Grandma told me not to go and see the old house, the first and dear home in Hannibal. She said the house and town had changed so much for the worse that I'd be upset by the sight of it and she wanted me to remember it as it was. But by that time I was weary and wiser than I had been when I danced with my iron man on the drive. I wouldn't have been overly surprised if our beloved home had been turned into a crack den, I expected no less from life. But some perverse desire made me disobey her for perhaps the first time in my memory, and I went anyway.

I'd been told that Hannibal had undergone an industrial building boom in the many years of my absence, but when I saw it I was shocked by the change. Much of its old world charm had been rubbed away. The loss of the house and the innocence that went with it had occurred years before though, and that was my pain. I already knew it was all irretrievable. Hannibal bore little resemblance to the town of my childhood. It was busy and unfamiliar. Main Street was unfriendly and I couldn't imagine any quaint little boat rides taking place for little girls if it flooded. As depressing as driving through the town was, predictably the worst part was seeing the house. A crack den it may not have been but destroyed by neglect, yes, it was. My dancing man was gone and Grandpa's barn had a tattered old basketball net hanging off it. House and barn were covered in peeling paint and the driveway was full of broken down trucks and cars. I didn't go inside and I didn't want to. The outside looked like hell enough.

Surprisingly, the death blow wasn't to be found in the house, but on the land. I nearly fainted on the approach seeing that the entire apple orchard was gone. So was the rest of the land around the house but for a small lawn for the current residents, hemmed in breathing noxious air. In place of the most tranquil patch of earth I'd ever known stood the ugliest apartment buildings I'd ever seen. All my Easter egg hunts and forest dens obliterated for shitty little cubed prisons plastered in billboards. Our grand house with all its quiet dignity was dwarfed in comparison to those monstrosities. It was robbed of the only setting it could ever have been at one with. I was dizzy seeing it, I had to look away. The windows of those apartments were eyes of reprehensible faces I must avoid meeting at all costs, lest I lose my shaky composure right there, in front of the gawking imposters sleeping in my Grandmother's room. As usual, I probably should have listened to my Grandma and saved myself the sight of our home looking so ill used. If the land had to be developed I would have almost preferred to have seen the whole plot burnt to the ground so it could go in peace.

I had lived an entire life since the days I called that house home. I stood in the gravel drive with a frigid and frozen smile plastered on my pale and clammy face for the benefit of the current residents. My mind was racing and calculating the damage done and I was trying desperately to pull myself together. My husband was standing on the other side of the car watching me. I was thinking, it really is impossible now! I'll never get it back. I'll never get away with bulldozing all those apartment buildings and

I'll never get those perfect damn trees back now they've been cut down. All the money in the world couldn't return what had been lost to me. I experienced a white hot rage and grief so complete that I could have collapsed into a fury right in that moment. But I had to say thank you to the residents for allowing me to gaze at their house, get back in the car and politely make my exit. As we drove past the apartments I had a strong urge to spit out the window. The only thing I could do was swallow the hurt and anger I felt. A feeling that I was deeply familiar with.

Round Four

Shortly after Grandma and Grandpa left Hannibal my Mom also decided she needed more out of life than the town had to offer. She had been a single mother of two daughters for 10 years and Hannibal had very little to offer a vibrant woman in her 40's. And of course her parents were having to abandon ship, so there really wasn't much keeping her there anymore. My Mother had taught English to high school students, she was very well educated, but intellectually frustrated. St. Louis had a far superior job market and more social opportunities – and of course my dad still lived there. We – especially I – believed that if we were in the same city we would see more of him than our twice-annual visits. The natural place for us to go was back where I'd been born.

It must have taken some courage for her to move to a relatively unfamiliar area with

Elaine and I, where we had no real contacts, in the hope of a more promising future. It certainly took courage from us girls and a lot of energy from all three of us. My Dad, as usual, remained absent in the moving process; it never would have occurred to him to do anything to help smooth the transition. Still, St. Louis was lovely and exciting, and as cities go it had a nice genteel feeling mixed with a satisfying, cosmopolitan sense of hustle and bustle. Of course St. Louis is also on the Mississippi River. In a way I felt I'd only moved to a different neighbourhood, down a very long road that I was extremely familiar with; I still had my old watery friend to visit when I could get away. When it flooded very badly in 1993, instead of sharing in the panic felt elsewhere in the city, I fondly reminisced about the floods in Hannibal. Everyone, city wide, was asked to volunteer to go to the Arch, River Des Peres and Jefferson Barracks to sandbag, and we did, which I thought was a great deal of fun. St. Louis was huge and shiny and modern and the Arch was a wonder to marvel at. I rapidly formed the opinion that the Arch is magnetised, and anyone with St. Louis in their blood has some of that magnetic compound within it, compelling them to return again and again, drawn by a silent humming made by the stainless steel giant. Perhaps it was an experiment in the 1960's when the Arch was being built and space was the final frontier.

The apartment complex we moved into was called Marlborough Trails. It boasted a huge swimming pool and long winding shaded corridors that linked its many buildings together. My new friend Jenny and I travelled the whole complex from one side to the other using only these half outdoor, half indoor corridors to get from her apartment to mine. It became a challenge to see how far we could go without stepping foot in the full sunshine; a talent we would be grateful for in the blazing hot St. Louis summers. While searching for the best route from Point A to Point B, one apartment along the way quickly came to our attention. It had one occupant, a man in his 40's. He spent his waking time within his apartment stark naked with his front door wide open onto the dark corridor we traversed. We crept past his door in disbelief, trying not to look at his stomach churning, white body. Unfortunately his apartment was right in the path between mine and Jenny's so every time we went from one to the other we had to pass his awful open door and see him from the corner of our eyes, ironing or watching TV naked. It was expected that we worked ourselves up to a run as we approached his door so we could fly past it at great speed and not stop until we made it round the bend breathless. To do anything else indicated we found his nudity appealing, which would have been an appalling thing to admit (as well as an untruth). I never questioned his wanting to be naked but why he insisted on leaving that door wide open was mind boggling to me. I remember thinking at the time what a waste it was that he was so hairy and unattractive. If anyone was going to be an exhibitionist why couldn't it have been someone pleasing to see instead of this pale, bumpy, drooping man who did nothing but iron all day and watch TV?

I began to rapidly mature living in Marlborough Trails, and not entirely for the better.

At fifteen, Elaine had become a very headstrong teenager, just as I one day would. She and mom were (as mom put it) "butting heads", and quite violently at that, like crazed billy goats on methamphetamine. Their relationship crept from volatile to open warfare. When they were in a room together it was like two sets of scissors slashing at each other fighting for the right to cut some cloth. I was inevitably caught in the middle of every fight between them. Neither of them fought fairly nor did they think of anything beyond their own points, to be made as violently and dramatically as possible. Living in that apartment was like being in a cage with two alley cats screeching at each other, with me in the middle mewing for milk. I hated it. Nobody ever cared in the slightest about me as an individual or how I might be feeling. I was left to furtively make peanut butter and jelly sandwiches then escape back into my room in an attempt to stay out of it all. The sounds of their screams reverberated on my walls and I stared straight ahead listening to music. When it got too much I'd run out and try to mediate. Sometimes it worked, sometimes I became part of the problem.

The same year we moved to St. Louis, when Elaine was 15, my Mom ventured to go out of town for a weekend retreat geared towards stress reduction. If those aren't famous last words, I don't know what are. She chose to take this little vacation (by herself) during a time when we were also queuing at food banks for groceries. My mother's income combined with the large amount of child support my father paid should have sustained us just fine, but my mother was addicted to shopping – for herself. She left us home alone with Elaine in charge, despite the fact that the two of them couldn't say a civil word to each other. We had a fully stocked kitchen and phone numbers to call in case of emergency. But Elaine, with all the wisdom that one has accumulated by 15 years of age, delved into our Mom's jewellery box and took the spare set of keys to her car, left parked in the driveway. Of course taking our Mother's car was not only disobedient to an extreme, but it was also illegal since my sister did not hold a license. We'd both been taught the rudiments of driving on our Grandparents land, but she was not experienced. Understandably I suppose, the temptation of that car was too much for her to resist. Elaine had it all planned before Carol even left the house. Elaine and her friends wanted to go out driving for the night, and they *were* taking the car, wise or not. What they were not taking, was Elaine's little sister. Elaine didn't think I should be left home alone, so she dropped me off at a local roller skating rink on her way out, heedless of my distressed protests from the back seat. I was quite terrified she would come to harm and in addition I didn't want to be dropped off in a strange place alone. Not to mention I couldn't skate and had no money. But Elaine would not be thwarted; she never would be when she wanted something, she was ruthless. I was ejected from the car and told she'd be back for me later. They drove off. It was night time, it was dark. I went inside.

I spent the night at the rink in various states of awkwardness, anxiety and terror. Everyone was part of a happy family group, and I was outside of it all. I felt acutely alone and embarrassed by the stares directed at me from time to time. I became

paranoid that the people who worked at the rink would demand I leave if I didn't pay

and skate. I found a quiet booth in the corner and curled up in it, trying to make myself

as invisible as possible, and dwelt on the troubles that were facing me that night. I

knew Elaine was damned one way or another, and I wondered how far down with her I

was going to go - if I'd even get home alive at all. Which I was beginning to doubt.

Would I be kidnapped? Thrown on the street? Would Elaine be killed in a car crash,

would we both be, on the way home? What would our Mother do?

As the night wore on, skaters began to filter out and the music stopped playing. The

roller rink was closing and Elaine had never come for me. I was faced with what I had

feared, the owners were asking me who I belonged to and how I had come there. The

police were called, and before long they arrived. I knew nothing of what would happen

to me.

I knew then that the police were collecting me from the rink, but I was not expecting

that they would already know who I was when they got there. The officers told me that

Elaine had indeed been in a very bad car accident. The car had been totalled, so

crushed that the police had to cut Elaine free from the car using the jaws of life. As

they loaded her into the ambulance, she said her little sister was at a skating rink.

When the owners of the rink called the police to report me two and two was put together. I was being driven to the hospital; they had already called our Mother, who was on her way back to St. Louis. But she was hours away still. I felt as if the world was imploding beneath me as I climbed into the police car. I wondered if I alone would watch my sister die before our Mom arrived at the hospital, if Elaine was that badly hurt. I felt mortally responsible for what Elaine had suffered. I felt that I should have done something drastic to prevent her from going out that night, I had been too quiet about my misgivings. I finally understood that all the fights between my Mom and sister weren't the cyclic things I'd come to believe them to be. They were going somewhere very direct and very bad indeed, and I was going with them willing or not.

Round Five

Our Mother arrived and the storm cracked over our heads. Elaine came home from hospital, suddenly seeming much younger to me than she had before. She was battered and bruised all over, whiplashed and wearing a neck brace. No sooner was Elaine settled at home on our sofa did our Mother begin screaming threat after threat of punishments at Elaine. Elaine slumped on the couch weeping defencelessly, suffering no doubt from her own physical and emotional trauma as well as our mother screaming and bearing down on her. Their fights had often become physical before but I couldn't believe my mother would dare hit Elaine while she was in this condition. Despite wishing that my mother would show Elaine some compassion, it became immediately

44

obvious that our mother's fury and hysteria were rising in equal measure and Elaine was in danger. I covered Elaine with my arms and begged Carol to let Elaine recover and sleep for a few days before anything more was said of punishments or what she had done. I said that I would take care of Elaine entirely on my own, that Carol need have nothing to do with her. She agreed. Afterwards, when Elaine and I were in her bed, she cried into my arms, weak and helpless as a newborn kitten.

Of course I knew my sister had done an unbelievably stupid thing, but I pitied her a great deal. She knew how terribly wrong she had been. No matter how our Mother chose to punish her, she was already paying miserably for what she had done. Her friends had been injured as well, and everyone was pointing a finger at her. I myself had been deeply traumatised by the whole event, but nobody gave me two seconds of thought. My shock was overrun by the need to stop this crisis destroying us. I did everything I could to mend the breach between a very reluctant mother and sister and was often the brunt of both of their tempers. Around this time Social Services investigated our mother but nothing came of it.

Eventually the incident blew over but still no one thought to address the trauma I had experienced. It seemed to be the unspoken rule in our house that I was nothing but an afterthought, easily forgotten. I had then only lived in St. Louis for a matter of months, I was ten years old and I had been dropped off in a public place and left for hours. I had almost a premonition that night at the skating rink, convinced I would have to sit alone in the dark car park hoping someone would think to find or help me. I didn't have to face the dark that night, but the entire scenario was building to a point where I actually *would* have nowhere to go to in the middle of the night *but* a car park.

Although my Dad and Karen were now only twenty minutes away from us, they still mysteriously failed to materialise even in that moment of crisis, to take an active part in our lives. No increase in visits or disruption to schedule came when we arrived in St. Louis. All the years that we'd been in Hannibal I had rationalised that he was so far away it was just too difficult for him to see us more often. When this excuse no longer applied, I began to ask myself serious questions about my Father and why he behaved as he did towards us... as if we did not exist. Why were we still only seeing him a few times a year? Mom was quite clearly falling apart from the pressure of raising us, Elaine was blowing herself sky high as she entered her teenage years and I was trying to form a bridge between them when I should have been having a childhood. Where was he? He *was*, where he is and always had been. He lives in a beautiful, serene brick house within a gated community in the most expensive area of St. Louis. But I was allowed to go there on invitation only. His life was not subjected to the constantly moving turmoil that mine would be; at least his outer life was not. I cannot speak for the inner, nor do I care to.

Our apartment in Marlborough Trails had a small patio in front of it, to the left of which was a bare patch of earth that no one had ever touched. The other side of that was the patio of our next door neighbours, a retired couple whose name now escapes me. I shall call them Mr. and Mrs. Foul. In the original draft of this book I called them Mr. and Mrs. Smith. It didn't sit well with me though; surely there are many good Mr. and Mrs. Smith's out there in the world and I shouldn't assign such characters to their name. Naming methods aside, I decided to turn the ugly patch of earth between our two patios into a flower garden as a past time. I began haunting the 'outdoor' aisles of grocery stores and doing aimless digging. My scant knowledge of gardening had been acquired at my Grandparents houses, but it amounted to little more than seeds were good and some bugs were bad. Nevertheless, I was hopeful that with a bit of hard work I could turn that ugly patch of dirt into something quite beautiful.

Being a latch key kid I was often home alone while mom was at work and Elaine out with her friends. Mr. and Mrs. Foul took an interest in my attempts at gardening during the after school hours that I was alone. I was hopeful of finding familiar ground with them, based on nothing but the fact that they were old and my track record with old people up to that point had been excellent. They often supervised my planting and gave me cakes, and gradually the plot of earth between our two patios began to resemble something fairly decent looking. I was becoming accustomed to receiving praise for my efforts, not only for the gardening but also for being so eternally charming.

One day Mrs. Foul was out at the hairdressers and Mr. Foul said he had a present of a huge pot of chrysanthemums waiting for me. He asked me to come indoors with him to get them, and I hesitated, wondering why he didn't just bring them outside to me. Almost as soon as the thought entered my mind, I felt a stab of ingratitude for questioning his kind gift. Deep in my mind were vague warnings about predatory men, but I was a young girl of great conscience who made rapid comparisons in the blink of an eye. I thought of someone ever being suspicious of my own dear Grandpa, and my mind recoiled in horror. I followed him indoors.

When we entered his apartment, I was surprised to find that the flowers weren't in his living room. He told me they were downstairs, which I found confusing, but accepted. As he led me into the basement my heart began to pump like prey. I became aware that I was doing the wrong thing but the tact that had been drilled into me since birth forbade me to turn and run when an elder was leading me on my way. I knew then that he was going to hurt me but I was too afraid to try to stop him. I was afraid of what damage he might do to the rest of my body if I wasn't fast enough to escape. I could be killed, beaten, locked up and tortured. I would be too clumsy trying to stumble up the basement stairs and out the front door, with him behind me. I felt stupid almost, dazed, burning with fear and premature shame. I was afraid of the humiliation I would face if my intuition was wrong and this was all as harmless as he was portraying it to be, how could I explain why I wanted to run away? What if there really was only a pot of chrysanthemums waiting for me in his basement? It seemed safest to go along with whatever was happening and then try to get away as quickly as possible. My mind froze suspended in that acute state of panicked awareness while my obedient legs continued to carry me further into his basement, just the other side of my own, which was then my bedroom. I looked at the separating wall longingly for a moment, wishing I could morph right through it into the safety of my room. A little sofa was pushed against the wall. Next to the sofa was a table. Sitting on the table was a very large pot of chrysanthemums.

I reached towards them with relieved, trembling hands and thought for a moment I was going to escape my fate. As I said a hurried thank you and turned to the stairs he grabbed me firm by the shoulders and told me I must thank him properly for his gift. Or else he would tell his wife that he had given me flowers, and she didn't like it when he gave gifts to other pretty ladies. I was extremely confused then, wondering if by walking so compliantly into his basement I had actually become a willing party to something like adultery. Added to the fear of harm I was feeling came another dread, that of having done wrong yet not knowing how or where. All I knew was that I was somewhere I shouldn't be and it was a very bad place. I did the wrong thing by trusting him and then by being too afraid to run when I realised my trust had been misplaced, this would reflect on me.

All sense of shame soon vanished into mute terror as he forced his quite disgustingly engorged, purple penis into my mouth and throat until he came. It all happened so fast and his grip on me was so strong I didn't know what was happening until it was almost over. I was flooded and gagged on what, I didn't know, my mind snapped. Finally I was released and as I stumbled up the stairs and out into the sunshine, he chuckled behind me. Later that day, he left the pot of chrysanthemums on my patio for me, I saw it when I peeked out the blinds. I didn't know what to do with them but I was sick at the sight of them and I didn't want to touch the fucking garden ever again. I poured bleach into the pot of mums and took a fork to the flower patch I'd been creating.

The dead flowers were left there in that space between the two patios as a constant reminder of that day because no one else bothered to tidy them away. It looked trashy; like a failed endeavour I hadn't been quite up to scratch to seeing through. That was the assumption that all the adults made, tsk-tsking me for giving up on my gardening project. I had to walk past Mr. and Mrs. Foul almost every day to get in and out of my apartment, most of the time I was alone within and frightened, thinking of him just the other side of the wall and thinking of me. Only one time after the incident was he mentioned in conversation with my mother. We were pulling up in our car, and I saw him sun bathing on his patio and shuddered. My mom said to me "Has something happened with that man? Has he done something to you?" I said haltingly, "Yes, yes he did." My Mom sat for a moment, looking at him in silence. I wondered if she would call the police, I began to feel palpitations of terror, what if no one believed me, and I had to live next door to him! Then my Mother said "Well. Get used to it. That's what happens to pretty girls." She sighed and got out of the car. We went inside, nothing more was said.

I have a strong memory of my internal world at this time that I feel is important to point out, because it shows just how differently children think from adults and just how dangerous those misconceptions can be. It's a good example of how the effects of early childhood abuse can lead into an endless cycle of abuse later in life at the hands of others besides the original abusers. In the aftermath of the assault by Mr. Foul I spent almost all of my time huddled in my bed alone in my room. Sometimes I couldn't stop reliving it, other times I'd drift off into an imaginary world to try to erase the memory. Many times I relived it with the purpose of finding the point at which I was to blame, looking for the moment when it would have been within my power to stop it from happening. Despite the fact that I couldn't think of anything I could have known to do better or differently, I still blamed myself. I was ten years old and he was in his sixties, but all I felt was that I was no longer pure and that what had happened had been a very, very bad thing which I was deeply ashamed of and must never tell anyone, or they would despite me.

Within this confusion, I remembered the incident with Carol five years earlier when I'd accidentally mispronounced "rake". I had said I wanted my turn with the "rape". By the age of ten I knew what rape was, and I knew what I had experienced was something like it. Those remembered words rang in my ears with fresh mortification. It seemed to confirm that I'd asked for it, that I'd labelled myself the type of girl that sort of thing was done to. It didn't matter to me that the words had been said when I was five years old in another part of the state, out of earshot of Mr. Foul. I'd still said them and somehow the label was visible on my forehead to those who wished to capitalise on it. I'd said I was willing to take it. And Carol had been so furious at me for it, because this was the result of saying that word. I'd always nursed a wound over that incident, but when I remembered it in the wake of Mr. Foul I believed both that she had been right to punish me so harshly for saying the bad word and that he had correctly identified me as a bad girl who he could do that to without consequence. That is how I felt then, that is how easy it is to abuse a child. A child in the wrong hands can get to the point where she doesn't believe in her heart that beating a five year old for mistaking a word and forcing a ten year old to suck a sixty year old man's cock are not grievous crimes.

Children simply do not think the way adults do, nor do they understand the complications and subtleties of life and society. A huge motivation for writing this book is to remind as many adults as possible how vulnerable and easily confused children can be. If my experience makes one parent more diligent in nurturing and protecting their child then exposing my humiliation is worth it.

Round Six

Shortly after I had the misfortune to try to my hand at gardening, Elaine began babysitting for a three year old boy called Edwin. She took me along with her, and Edwin and I began playing like two best friends. Edwin called me Cha-Cha; he was unable to say Erin and that was the replacement he chose. When Edwin's mother, Marsha, returned, she and I took to each other just as instantly. We were like two jolly souls who'd long missed each other. Marsha asked if I could babysit instead and Elaine was happy to hand the job over to me in order to pursue her social life. I became a regular visitor to their house, during the day, evenings and overnight, and it wasn't long until the pretence of babysitting was dropped and I was treated more like another child of the family. Marsha asked my mother if I could stay over regularly and my mother said yes, so before long I even had my own lovely little bedroom and routine at Marsha's. It was a wonderfully freeing atmosphere, one in which I was respected but allowed to be a child. Marsha was a social worker, and she was absolutely deranged, in the most wonderful way. I adored her. She was like a magnificent bird of paradise with outrageous plumage, wonderful and intimidating all at once. She struck you so forcefully as a presence that it was impossible to be unaware of her when she was near, and it was a pleasure to bask in her brilliance. Everything about her crackled excitement.

Marsha had flaming red hair, the whitest skin I'd ever seen, scarlet red lips and bright flashing turquoise eyes. She always wore big earrings and she had the deepest southern accent I'd ever heard. In addition to Edwin she also had an older daughter from a previous marriage who was a beautiful and intelligent cheerleader - with a boyfriend! - Perfectly embodying all of my young ambitions. Marsha was a wonderful mother, though I'm sure her eccentricities were not always universally appreciated. Her husband was a dreadfully boring and stifling man, who gloomied the room as soon as he stepped foot in it. I don't know what his profession was but he seemed bred to be a tax man. He wore wire rimmed glasses, a bad comb over and always a frown for his exuberant wife.

Marsha was working on a novel in her spare time; she had a large sheaf of typed papers that she kept in a box under her bed. She once allowed me to read excerpts of the manuscript, which was very adult in content. In it was a scene in which her main character had oral sex forced upon her while on a date with a man. Of course it affected me greatly although I never spoke of what happened to me, I merely expressed obvious empathy for the character. It led to a conversation between us. I asked her "If a man wants sex so badly, why doesn't he just go to a prostitute, or anyone who's willing? There must be enough women who are! Why inflict pain unnecessarily?"

Marsha replied "Rape isn't about sex, it's about power." An answer so simple but so surprising, echoing in my ears while I slowly digested the truth of it. She once she told me what sex with a man would feel like. It was part birds and the bees talk and part warning to not expect too much when I lost my virginity. She said "Honey, sometimes it feels nice, but most of the time it's just like gettin' poked with a pencil!"

My eyes must have been round as saucers wondering how something like a pencil could possibly justify the orgasmic scenes I saw hinted at on television if the poking went on where I thought it did. I had seen Pretty Woman but been told to close my eyes in the piano scene, and been banned from watching Flashdance. None of that gave me the impression I had anything to dread, so long as my mother wasn't in the room. Nor did I think of poking pencils when I caught the hint of love and pleasure David Gahan made me curious about in Black Celebration. My experience with Mr. Foul, on the other hand, was dreadful, but that I kept locked up inside myself, never to be told to anyone. It was still etched in my body's memory, never to fully go away. I hoped what happened with him was an aberration, unknown to others and never to be repeated. I still held out some hope that one day a man would love me and unlock this mysterious part of me that combined my heart and body. But when I added my experience with Mr. Foul to the idea of a pencil poking my intimate parts, the concept of sex between a man and a woman became rich in potential horrors. As well-meaning as Marsha's speech was, it conjured too many disturbing images to even begin to enumerate here. They began with fleshy pencils protruding from automated panels hidden within the male body and ended with my kidneys being ruptured. I was finally beginning to wonder if the whole charade of female sexual pleasure was one great Hollywood exaggeration. Was it actually nothing more than something so desired by men and women *alike* that it was willed into existence as an idea, but that was in truth a mirage? It seemed that women neither relished sex nor had any reason to. Instead they focused on and magnified the positives while averting their eyes from the negatives. The juxtaposition of pleasure and pain surrounding sex overwhelmed me. I was full of the urge to hurry and grow so I could determine what sex was - good or bad.

I was truly dismayed at the thought of sex being one great lie. It was the biological equivalent of discovering that there is no Father Christmas. Thankfully I was at least partially wrong and Marsha was also lively enough to point that out in due course. For reasons best known only to her, the moment she chose to enlighten me about the female orgasm we were in her car at the drive-thru window of McDonalds. Marsha was intent on explaining to me the most efficient way for a woman to achieve orgasm. She said it was no good leaving it up to the man to make sure you had one, and regardless I would want to be able to have them when I was alone. The mere concept of orgasm itself still being a mystery to me, I could once again do little but sit open mouthed and nod at the correct intervals to maintain an image of intelligence. Always with Marsha, the rule was: try to keep up and pay avid attention.

She took pauses in her speech to pay for and collect our food from the boy at the window. As he and I both listened, a captured audience, she began to list on her fingers:. "You can get one from a man's tongue (but they don't do that much), his fingers, your fingers, his penis." (roll of the eyes) "Or maybe even a woman doing all that if you're into that kinda thing, but most likely just your own fingers. So make sure you practise at that lots!" Upon completing this explanation, she gave me and the boy at the window a blinding smile. And drove off! I imagine I wasn't the only young person to get an education that day.

Marsha was equally relaxed about nudity and frequently walked about her home naked, which disturbed her daughter's boyfriend a great deal, and amused Marsha even more. I learned to laugh at both of them and blink an eye at neither. With my mother, my early developing breasts were mocked in suspicious tones, as if I had summoned them for the purpose of engaging in general sluttery. With Marsha I learned to look her in the eye and hold long conversations about art and ethics while she was stark naked. She took me along with her on a road trip to visit her family in Kentucky, and I waited in fascination to see if the grass would indeed be blue. I brought a soil sample home in a glass jar to compare it to the colour of Missouri earth. I had tremendous fun and felt loved for the first time since parting with my Grandparents in Hannibal.

Once during a stay at Marsha's lasting several nights in a row, she surprised me by phoning my school and telling them I was sick. We went to the art museum instead. It was lovely to have that space and quiet amongst all that beauty. Everything at my home was in league with chaos and rage. Probably because of that, I found a great sense of peace sitting in the museum; the contrast was beautiful to me. Afterwards we went to lunch at a proper adult bistro. It was overpriced with stupidly tiny portions displayed on ridiculously large plates showcasing sauces squirted in gratifyingly poncy zigzags. It was great. Marsha presented me with a beautiful coffee table book full of impressionist pieces of art. It was beautiful, and I treasured it. During the long lonely years ahead, the colours, scenes and feelings depicted in that book never let me down; they always gave me somewhere to set my mind when it needed a resting point. In the years to come my life would be so turbulent that I didn't manage to keep many of my belongings into adulthood, but I still have that book, and I still enjoy it as freshly today.

In it there is a double page sized image of Woman with Chrysanthemums by Edgar Degas. When I first saw it, it took my breath away, because the lady in the painting looked so much like my Grandma - only as she must have been when she was the age of the sitter; before my time. It was intriguing and odd, because I always read the expression of the woman in the painting as that of attempting to suppress distress or irritation, as if she is waiting for someone or something and she's suffering for the pause. My grandma's features were reflected in this artistic mirror, but in the face of a woman who was neither happy nor at ease. I knew my grandma to be a ray of sunshine, but the expression of her likeness was so compelling, it led me to think of her as a woman in her own right. Someone who had lived and loved through World War II, raised four children and shared in the joys and hardships of each of their lives. The painting was like a clue to her inner soul, the way my Grandpa's dark painting was a clue to his. Staring at the picture was compelling. It felt almost naughty, as if I were spying on her private life when I should have been in bed. To give Grandma and her beautifully sunny nature their due credit she remained in my heart always insisting on finding happiness wherever she was. Even with all my newly discovered wisdom I struggled to picture her languishing in despair for long. As well as the book being a wonderful memento of Marsha, it is also in a way a relic of my Grandma so it is doubly blessed for me.

My time with Marsha could best be described as one of looking liberation squarely in the face, warts and all. It certainly did much to lift my depressed spirits and for that I am eternally grateful. There was nothing and no one else in my life at that time to fill the void left by my shattered family and broken spirit, and any time I was left alone for a significant amount of time I would inevitably begin contemplating suicide. Marsha, perhaps sensing this, ensured that at least this one latch key kid was not left alone. I'm prone to withdrawn stages of muteness and shyness, but I was far more so as a child. The aspect of my character that a few years before had become hypnotised by playing Paint it Black on my Fisher Price record player had become imperceptibly dominant after my encounter with Mr. Foul. I badly needed someone like Marsha to draw me out a little and allow me some childish laughter. There were times, as I was growing up, that my own laughter shocked me and sounded harsh to my ears - more of an unpleasant cough or bark than a merry sound of joy. It came too infrequently, and my voice would emerge hoarse from silence. Marsha was valiant and admirable, yet vulnerable too, and I understood her very well. I don't remember what happened, why we stopped seeing so much of each other. I believe a lot was going over my head with her frowning husband and they were in the midst of a separation.

Round Seven

Elaine became pregnant. My nephew, Nathan, was born when I was twelve and Elaine was seventeen. His father, Elaine's boyfriend was the consummate Metallica loser, and abusive to boot; Elaine was sensible enough to leave him before Nathan was a year old. After a brief testosterone fuelled period of harassment and abuse towards Elaine, "loser boyfriend" finally disappeared, not to be heard from again. He was immediately replaced with new, lesser loser boyfriend and monumentally, we left Marlborough Trails apartment complex, away from Mr. and Mrs. Foul. We moved to a tiny house in a row of four.

Like all cities, St. Louis County has many small suburbs within it, each with their own subtle place on the social ladder. Marlborough Trails was in Afton, a predominantly white middle class area with a reputation for athletic schools. The new tiny house was on the Afton border of a cheaper and slightly more run down area called Lemay. The times, they were a changin'. Lemay was less affluent but it felt like it had a pulse; every street corner was alive with a beat box. And, as I'm sure the reader will appreciate, I was not sad to leave Marlborough Trails behind. Mr. and Mrs. Foul had by that time declared that, as I was approaching my teens I had lost the charm of youth. In fact I could even be downright rude at times and I let the garden run to shambles. No, the move didn't bother me at all. By this time I was already beginning to work on feeling less and being harder, trying to find who I was supposed to be within all the chaos surrounding me. And I was happy to look for those answers on the canvas of Lemay. It fired my imagination in a way that carbon copy Afton never could have.

It was around this time that my Dad took my sister and I to the infamous Gateway Arch for a visit. Karen was noticeably absent, which alarmed me a great deal. For as long as I could remember my father happily used Karen as a buffer between him and us, and he was by no means the only beneficiary of that arrangement. He terrified me, and with good reason. He was a stranger to me, yet if ever we had cause to walk in public together he steered me like a car with a vice like grip on the back of my neck and angry reprimands for incorrect steps uttered through gritted teeth. And that was his most mild behaviour. Visits with my father were so agonising they almost require a book of their own to fully describe; each movement I made was scrutinised, criticised by a man employed to put the fear of god into seasoned soldiers. Karen's absence at the Arch frightened me, both for the lost protection and the questions it raised. I was terrified he would tell us that they were divorcing. That was my first and only thought, and I remember panicking, thinking that I would never be able to suffer a lifetime of visits without her.

Although Elaine, my Father and I went through the motions of touring the Arch, going up in the egg and visiting the museum, it was obvious the entire time that he was rushing us through it and his mind was elsewhere. When all the boxes were ticked, he took us to sit on the grass under the Arch. He lit a cigarette, then so did Elaine. Aware of the pack in my pocket and my formidable father watching my every move, I pulled out a cigarette and lit one myself. I'd started smoking at Marlborough Trails shortly after the incident with Mr. Foul. After a few furtive weeks of attempting to hide my new habit from my mother I decided it wasn't worth the effort. I sat her down one Saturday morning and said "Mom, I smoke. I'm going to smoke no matter what you do or say so I suggest you just accept it now. I'll smoke outside but I'm not going to stop smoking. There's no point in trying to hide it from you." She listened, nodded and carried on being lost in her own thoughts.

Unlike the insouciance I displayed with my Mother, I was blatantly terrified of my Father. But I was determined to start showing a minimum of backbone with him, and I wasn't going to sit there smokeless while he and Elaine blissfully puffed away in front of me – not when in absolutely no other way was he involved as a normal father in my life. My attitude towards him had changed since we moved to St. Louis. While we were still in Hannibal, it was easy for me to justify his absence by blaming it on the distance. But now that we lived only a twenty minute drive away from him, one that was so simple even I had already memorised the route, I was angry that he continued to be an absentee parent while our lives were falling apart. I was beginning to see him less as a tragic war hero and more as a failed and selfish individual and in very small baby steps this began to be reflected in my behaviour towards him. Lighting up boldly in front of my military father at the tender age of twelve was provocative. It was an action begging to see how far he'd be willing to interfere with my freedom in the name of parenting. He both passed and failed the test by doing exactly as I expected: absolutely nothing beyond a raised eyebrow and a telling Gallic shrug. I was granted total freedom by both parents. A victory to any pre-teen, surely. And a crushing blow to a child desperate to feel she was treasured, worthy and loved.

Elaine was in her early pregnancy so babies were very much on all of our minds. But baby mania was centred on Elaine – I did not expect it from Dad and Karen. They had already been married for over ten years without any brothers or sisters arriving for me and Elaine. My Father could not tolerate children. They had animals, and they had them in a way I'd never known anyone to have them before. I had grown up with animals in all sorts of places and in the country I fancied myself something of a fairy sent to love the wild animals I found in the woods. At our home in St. Louis we had cats, and we loved them like little treasures; like equals or siblings really. But Dad and Karen's pets were viewed by them to be a breed apart from mere common animals, and indeed they were. My Father's home was full of pampered pure bred Maine Coon cats that each cost more than was spent on me in an entire year. They all had fine pedigrees, odd names and individual temperaments that children like us could never hope to understand. After the cats, Karen gave my Dad a golden retriever called Yankee, who became the great love of my Dad's life, second only to Karen.

There was never a question that when I entered the house it was the pets who came first, not the human daughter who occasionally intruded on this vision of perfection. My Dad once joked to me when I was around twenty that if he had to choose between saving a drowning Yankee or a drowning Erin, he'd have to save Yankee, because Yankee was just... well... his Yankee! His baby! "You can swim!" he said & chucked me under the chin. Then there was a long awkward silence when we both took in the hard edge of truth in his voice. I remembered that an element of truth exists in most humour. Element be damned, his truth was a meteor. By then he had fairly literally thrown me into the gutter so that he could devote his life to canine care, so the joke fell flat.

And so it came as quite a shock that sunny day under the arch after we all lit our cigarettes when my Dad said "Well kiddos, I've got something to tell you. Karen wants a baby and we can't have any, so we're adopting one. His room's all ready, everything has been arranged. We hope you'll both be really happy for us." There was a moment of recognition, of upsidedownness, of grasping the understanding that he was jettisoning us further away from him. It was a realisation as deep and profound as the river we sat alongside, but on its heels came a feeling of excitement for Karen. How she must so want the baby, and how wonderful that she would have it! My first instinct after the initial confusion was to feel very sad for her that she couldn't have children of her own, and not a little guilty that the love of her life had wasted his seed on me.

All of these thoughts came piling upon each other faster than my brain could catalogue. Then in one moment of crystal clarity I understood why Karen was absent on this one and only visit, ostensibly to pass on the good news of her baby... She was being spared the ordeal of being present when the hard truth of their news sank in. She didn't have to look into our understanding eyes or hear the deafening silence as Elaine and I absorbed this news. That he already had two children *whom he had entirely ignored,* and now he was going to buy a new one to please his beloved wife. A child – a boy, of course - who would be raised as truly his. More his than we who were genetically linked ever could be. It was tragic actually. He didn't actually care at all if he had a child, he only wanted Karen to be happy, it was all for love of her.

Up to that day we'd all lived in a polite silence agreeing to pretend that my "Dad" didn't want to see us because of the emotional scars he bore from the war. I had already begun to understand this, but now it was made absolutely clear to Elaine and me that we were his discarded mistakes. Karen wasn't there in order to spare her the small pain of watching our elusions fall away. She was complicit in the neglect and replacement of us and she knew it. For a moment I felt nothing but pity for my future younger brother.

I felt the grass beneath me and knew that I was not allowed to react to the full range of emotions I was feeling. So I forced myself to try to focus on my pleasure for Karen, because I knew that underneath her quiet and polished demeanour was a deep well of maternal love. She simply didn't want to waste it on her husband's children. Still, she had been the kind face of my Father for my entire life. As it turns out my father and Karen lost the baby when the birth mother changed her mind at the last moment, but for me the shot had been fired, and it struck its target. I wouldn't forget that they prepared a nursery for another baby but refused to let me explore their house beyond one room.

Their heartbreak was obvious and upsetting and I pitied Karen greatly for losing her baby. Nevertheless the entire incident caused me to make a slight mental adjustment in my relentlessly forgiving attitude towards my father and his wife. And a day would come when my father would make choices that would cement this new understanding.

The timing of Lawrence and Karen's attempted adoption couldn't have been more poignant, given Elaine's pregnancy. Bitterness and resentment oozed from the two of them towards Elaine who fought back with every ounce of pride and vigour that she had. They even approached her about adopting her unborn son, Nathan. Her answer was more along the lines of "Fuck off and go to hell, you destroyed Erin and I, you won't destroy my son…" than a mere "no" (understandably). It resulted in an almost decade long estrangement during which Elaine had no contact whatsoever with our father and stepmother and I was made to be a go-between yet again.

Round Eight

The day my father announced to us that he was planning to adopt a baby was the first time he fired an arrow successfully into a chink in my armour, wounding me right in the place where I kept him as a distant but treasured hero. Up until then I'd spent my childhood years silently suffering the total lack of his attention but steadfastly continuing to defend him against his very bitter ex-wife and eldest daughter. All the while I remained positive that if I was only patient enough, in the right circumstances he would pull through for me. I couldn't believe he could love me as little as it appeared, the reality of it was too horrific to contemplate, and I mistakenly accepted the excuses offered to me as apologies. My policy with regards to my father was to give unrelenting love and patience in spite of the nothingness and anger that came in return from him. I was wrong. He was never a hero to anyone but his military comrades and he would never be mine, no matter how severe my need.

My Mom and sister often expressed frustration and anger with me for my loyalty to a man who rarely materialised or gratified our needs. Once, when we still lived in Hannibal I sat by the window all morning, waiting for him to arrive for a visit. I was full of nervous agitation and wanted to see him the very first moment I could until the last. My mom didn't like seeing me there and angrily told me to leave the window, that seeing me there made her sick. My sister poked fun at me for being so naïve. Even then, when I was so young, I could understand how grating it must have been for my Mom to see me waiting for sight of his Volvo on a Saturday afternoon when she was the one there day in day out. But I couldn't help it. When I was that young I thought every single twice yearly visit might be the one during which he would finally look me in the eyes and truly love me, make himself a part of my life. Of course Lawrence was unaware of my loyalty and the general mockery that went on between Elaine and my mother, and ironically he blatantly favoured my sister over me, whom he hardly acknowledged. I suppose he had at least lived with her for five years before he left after my birth, and she was an older "tomboy". She could disappear into his workshop and play with tools while it was thought best to leave me browsing rose catalogues with Karen. That was how every single visit went when we were young. Elaine had been taught to be bold while I had been moulded to be the peacekeeper. I lived in awe and terror of my father and when he (rarely) addressed me I became overcome with muteness or stuttering which clearly disgusted him.

Despite all this I persevered in my affection for him, repeating to myself the few stories I knew about his past, most of which I learned from my Mom. He had a suitably tragic background to combine with his stoic exterior and thereby allow him all his unpleasantness towards us. It was this that I clung to for justification of my dismissal. Indeed, I tried to make his abdication from parental responsibilities into a mere side effect of his nobility and sacrifice; he had suffered a great deal in the war, and therefore indirectly so did we. It was practically my patriotic duty to forgive him all.

But when he invited a new baby into his life he was no longer exempted from parenting due to incapability. In truth it was the children he had with Carol whom he was incapable of fathering. I tried, quickly, to cover up the damage done to his reputation inside my heart and mind but I could not. I began to put pieces together that I had not wished to see before and from that point onwards he became something more predatory and dangerous than the misunderstood hero. Something deeper had begun to creep into my unconscious. I was beginning to view him with a sort of horror. It was as if he was standing high above me, breathing pure oxygen whilst coolly watching me suffocate to death below.

My mother was my only source of information about Lawrence and his family; I truly cannot express how little he spoke to me. I heard stories of his heroic war deeds, lauded in every newspaper in the United States at that time. But I heard much that a child does not need to hear about their father. I could have done without knowing how much my Dad enjoyed the prostitutes in Vietnam. I was often left wondering if I might have half a dozen half-Vietnamese siblings living in poverty. I thought that if indeed there were any siblings in that far away land, I would like to tell them not to worry. He didn't love or care for his American family either, it wasn't anything personal. I could have done without him casually talking over the dinner table about the "seek and cull" missions he led, ripe with guerrilla warfare detail. Neither of my parents ever stopped to assess or care for their audience when they had a mind to vent about themselves. I was, however, interested in my relations on his side, who were totally unknown to me.

What I knew was that my father's father was so unpleasant to his son that he drove him out of their wealthy New England house and into the Vietnam War. We eventually had something of a clue as to why Frank, a long-time executive of Chrysler, preferred

Lawrence's sisters to him. Though I hasten to say, this is a clue, not an excuse. In my late teens my Father's mother died. When Lawrence was sorting through her belongings he discovered a different, older copy of his birth certificate. It did not have Frank's surname on it; Frank was not his father.

Lawrence's mother, Violet had become pregnant by, and also apparently married to, a foreign soldier, who for some reason was on the East Coast during World War II. At some point after my father's birth, the soldier returned to his native country. Violet and Frank immediately married, and a new birth certificate was created with Frank's name on it as the father. The truth of Lawrence's parentage was covered up in honour of the respectability expected in those times. Regardless of the means by which Frank applied his name as father to my dad, he did so, and he shouldn't have held a grudge against my father for his own choice for all of his life. Suffice it to say, when this news was discovered in my teens, I had already become so detached from any concept of belonging to my family that it seemed like even my surname was a cruel joke. I had Frank's surname, and he wasn't even related to me. It was another ironic nail in the coffin of my concept of family. I gave up using my surname and since I had often been called by both my first names I thereafter went simply by Erin Summers.

Lawrence enlisted in the Vietnam War when most young men were dreading receiving the draft. When his obligatory two year term in Vietnam was up he shocked once again

71

by voluntarily re-enlisting for a second term, cementing his military career. I felt an enormous amount of pity for him when I was a child, wondering how bad life at home must have been for him to prefer life at war. I didn't know Frank. I received a cheque from him every Christmas but that was all. Still, I hated him for not being kind to Lawrence and driving him into such a terrible place. I blamed him for Lawrence becoming the man he was, the man who could not love me. I saw my father as a young boy only wanting love and not understanding why he was rejected. I could relate to that child.

My dad was amazingly successful at war; he was brave almost to a reckless degree and fiercely loyal to his men. He was soon promoted to a Captain in the US Army. My mom was proud of his most famous war story, and told it to me many times. My father's platoon was ambushed. Most of his men were dead or wounded badly enough to be left for dead under such heavy fire. My father too had already been shot in the chest but he was still up and fighting. A medical helicopter landed while the platoon was still under fire. The medics reached my dad, but he refused to go with them. Three of them wrestled him into the helicopter against his will. It was important to save the Captain, or for that matter anyone who could be reached. The helicopter took off. The medics, assuming the struggle with my father was over, released their hold of him. He promptly jumped out of the flying helicopter. He refused to leave his men while they were under fire.

Back on the ground, Lawrence took out enemy after enemy while he laboured to drag all his men to a safe, defendable location, until there was no one left for him to defeat. In the process he'd taken another bullet. The medics eventually came back and collected his entire platoon. Although many had died, at least their bodies would be returned to their families. Lawrence was justly credited with saving the lives of all those men who otherwise would have been left behind. The act made national news in America. Violet was sent newspaper clippings of the story from all over the nation, with personal notes of thanks from the parents of some of the men my father saved. He was a hero.

Hearing these stories from as young as I can remember made me think more about war than I'd wager my peers did. I saw how war might be necessary but my understanding of the political origins of the Vietnam War was not as complete as my understanding of the realities of it. No one ever bothered explaining to me why my father had to kill all those people. But I did understand World War II, in which my beloved Grandpa fought, and I understood Hitler had to be stopped. I began to see the difference between the soldier on the ground and the politics behind the lives he would take, but I could also clearly see, etched over every inch of my father, that each man and woman would have to live forever with the actions their own hands and feet carried out. War became a complicated issue that I spent an inordinate amount of time attempting to understand.

What was justified? At what point did you say it is right to fight for something? These thoughts drove me onwards as I grew older and began to fight my own personal war against injustice. As a matter of fact, this book could be seen as an act of war; a war waged by many to protect our children and give them something more than what we ourselves had.

Eventually my Dad was decorated by two United States governments. He was awarded the Silver Star, Bronze Star, Purple Heart, Combat Infantryman Badge, VN Cross of Gallantry with Palm, Parachutist Badge, Ranger Tab and Jungle Warfare Badge. He commanded one of the few, elite units to be awarded the highest honour given to a military unit, the Presidential Unit Citation for "extraordinary leadership and exceptional valour." He left the war with a whole slew of opportunities that he had not had before Vietnam. It made him. After the war he taught marksmanship, military strategy and leadership at West Point Academy.

In my eyes, the legacy of his war was knowledge that he was a hero for some, that he'd jump out of a helicopter for some, but never for me. There were reunions held in his honour, newspaper clippings, letters of gratitude and beautifully mounted medals on the walls of his sombre study, all acclaiming his greatness. It was that appreciation he craved; not that of his young daughter. Lawrence's primary interest in me began and ended with the required monthly child support payments to my mother. I was little more than a legal financial agreement. What he never seemed to understand though was that if he had just once lifted a finger in love for me, I would have offered him loyalty down to the last drop of blood in my body in gratitude, even more than he received from those whose lives he saved in battle. But the fledgling loyalty I was born with and nurtured so heavily could only sustain so many blows, slights and insults. So it slowly withered and eventually died altogether.

On paper, my dad had the makings of a romantic hero. But he would never be one to star in my novel. I was stupidly slow in understanding that. As I grew more mature, my hope turned into resignation, until finally, I simply despised him.

Round Nine

In my early teens I had a totally fresh and unregulated mind and it's safe to say that while I was taking in every detail around me, no one was taking the slightest interest in my development. Therefore I was forming my own conclusions and making my own decisions and mistakes. I was a child living off the fruits of an urban wilderness and I had a taste for freedom as well as survival. Rarely did an authority figure attempt to exert any influence on me, but if they had I would have been deeply suspicious of them.

It became obvious that first my Mom, and then without undue surprise, my Dad, seemed to accept and expect an exceptional amount of independence from me. Their hands-off parenting was both the yoke which bore me down and the knife I cut my bonds with. I began to read dangerous, thought provoking books, especially the works of Voltaire. I began to form an idea of my rights.

They expected me to be a self-watering pot, which was all very well so long as the status-quo was maintained. If I was to be ignored, beaten, insulted, left to feed myself and hold my psyche together all alone, then I wanted independence in return. It made perfect, logical sense to me. I was constantly told I was not wanted, that I should have been drowned at birth. Again and again, every problem I faced I faced alone. I reasoned they, primarily Carol, couldn't have it both ways. I was fourteen, at an age when even children from happy families are prone to rebelling. I had no restrictions to rebel against but at least one parent who was constantly spoiling for a fight. The result was that I drew a line in the sand and began to fight back against my mother, insisting on my rights and intent on making her understand how badly she was hurting me. To sum up: It was a declaration of war. No longer would I go silently into my room when she said I wasn't worth the oxygen that kept me alive. I'd stand and fight her back until I couldn't stand anymore from the blows my body took. More than once I was left slumped on the living room floor simply because she became too exhausted to carry on. Those were little victories for me, I hadn't quit last.

Of course she had struck me several times when I was younger, but when I began to fight back with words instead of running away and hiding it simply added fuel to her fire. Before I knew it I was pushed down a flight of stairs into the musty damp basement, where my bedroom then was – the second bedroom in our apartment having been converted into a spacious closet for her designer clothes. The door slammed as I tumbled down, hearing the click of the key in the lock. It wasn't the only time I was locked in that basement. Carol claims to have no memory of these incidents. I do.

On one memorable occasion she had me trapped between her battering arms, like a body caught between the blades of the windmill. Blow after blow rained down on my head, back, chest - anywhere she could reach and I could not escape. In a quick moment when she paused for breath I made my escape and ran downstairs into the basement. I had collected discarded mattresses and therefore my bed resembled that from the Princess and the Pea, six mattresses high.

She stormed down the stairs after me. I scrambled up my many mattresses for safety, where she couldn't reach me. She grabbed at me and I shuffled further back on the bed away from her grasping hands. In frustration she began punching the cheap wood panelling that covered the wall. It shook the wooden shelf covered in my precious ceramic ornaments that hung above my fairy tale bed. The shelf and all its ornaments crashed down on my face. I was left screaming and bloody with a broken nose and black eye. She paused in shock. The first words out of her mouth, face red and contorted with rage, chest heaving, were that I wouldn't be taken to the doctor so to clean myself up. To this day, a bump in my nose serves as a reminder. A flaw in my face where once I felt lovely.

Although many of our fights did end physically, it was the things she shouted at me that were unforgivable and unforgettable, though she has apparently forgotten. She said I was hateful, that it was impossible to love me, that no one ever would love me because I was so vile. She said she should have drowned me at birth. Yes, that one I heard many times. She said I was a liar, a manipulator, a girl with no morality or conscience. My lack of a proper feeling of love and respect for her defined me as a freak of nature, an aberration. She said that no matter what it took she would break me. She would break me. You should read those words as if blasted from a megaphone. I heard them time and time again as her arms flew against my body. I'll admit that when I heard them they broke my heart entirely, but they also drove me to continue fighting back. There was very little that I could control in my life, but myself. And I vowed she would never break me. There were times when I thought I was drowning under it all, losing my sanity, perhaps being broken. But I hated that feeling and I fought back against it as hard as I could, fighting her with my words.

Round Ten

When Nathan was born I fell madly in love with him. I was there for every moment, from throwing Elaine her baby shower to his first steps. Our parents didn't offer her much help with regards to providing for the baby so I began dumpster diving in our apartment complex to find his first stroller. I fixed its wheels and cleaned every inch of it and proudly presented it to Elaine, who was grateful despite its origins. I sewed his baby bag and quilt in my home-ec class and bounced him on my hip. Sometimes we shared a room, and I cared for him through all hours of the day and night while my sister completed her education and worked a fast food job. For the first time, I knew the sweet smell of a baby's newborn head and every gurgle he made was precious to me. I loved him with what was truly a maternal love, but I never wanted to be in competition with my sister. There were times, when he was very young, that the violence of my emotions and love for him caused me a great deal of pain, because I was not his mother. I had limits to how much influence I could have with him. I soon learned that I had to love him more selflessly than that. I loved him so deeply, I often felt a physical pang in my heart when we were separated, and indeed I still do.

During this time it was natural that Elaine and I became closer. I began to be included within her circle of friends, even though most of them were already much older than Elaine. We frequented the local pool hall, where I quickly learned to play while fending off unwanted advances from men twenty years my senior. Elaine and I had as much freedom of self as each other as far as our mother was concerned. As long as we cleaned the house every day we were left to do as we pleased. If Carol came home from work and there were dishes in the sink there would be hell to pay and another ugly scene. Sometimes she came home from work looking for a fight, in which case no amount of housework on our parts would prevent a blowout.

When she wanted attention she sought it using us, brutally. I remember when she photocopied my diary – I had written about a crush on my sister's friend. She passed it out to a dozen adults from the single parents' support group she attended. One day, I waltzed in the door home from school and there they all sat ready to confront me for being a slut, in my written imagination. Nothing can convey the humiliation of that day.

By my teens I had come to see myself as nothing more than a business transaction and my general viewpoint was increasingly nihilistic. Considering that one of my jobs was to balance my mother's cheque book, that wasn't a difficult leap to make. The money went in each month, and then the money went out. It was spent on either basic household essentials or on the constant improvements to her wardrobe that Carol required. Despite the fact that many items in her closet still had tags on them, she always needed new clothes. If not clothes, then she deserved a treat, a 'pick me up' for herself, because life was so hard. Another weekend away. Indeed it was hard to make

ends meet. But she made it so.

"She" (That would be the harried, angry woman I saw in the evenings - the one

shouting about check books, dirty dishes, crashed cars, pregnant daughters, useless men

etc etc etc) received money for me each month from "Him". He would continue to pay

her a set amount per daughter until we each reached eighteen years old. The amount of

our worth had been determined between them; she received two payments a month for

each of us girls. One was the payment he was required to make by law, which went

through lawyers. The other payment was a private transaction she petitioned him for,

simply a check from him to her written on the same day each month. Just like paying

the electricity bill. No doubt the reason that he went above and beyond the minimum

amount payable was in part to appease his guilt over the total lack of attention he paid

us; we could never argue that he hadn't provided. She went to him over and over again

saying there wasn't enough money for our family of three women to live on. So he

paid, but never bothered to take the slightest interest in whether or not any of that

money was actually filtering down to his children, beyond contributing to keeping a

roof over our heads.

He simply threw money at the problem. But of course, he was essentially only paying

his ex-wife in order to avoid hassle. His children lived in a state of having to express gratitude for their very housing; we had no extras and were screamed at regularly to grovel for the essentials. Our heads were filled with rants about how much of a drain and a burden we were to our single mother. When this gradually became obvious to him over the course of our semi-annual visits it did not compel him to act in any way, he simply asked us from time to time if things were any "easier" with our mother. We said no, he shrugged and carried on.

The concept of actually being loved and cherished by my parents never occurred to me. I surveyed my life and surroundings and surmised that I was both a valuable commodity and an object of exploitation. I didn't like it. I wanted to be treated like an equal partner and if I was going to be exploited I wanted to be the one to profit from it. Capitalism at its best, in the bosom of the American family home.

The turning point when relations between my Mother and myself went from tense to untenable was when Elaine and Nathan left St. Louis and moved to Florida with Elaine's future husband when I was thirteen. It was a huge blow to me, not only because I lost my only ally and my cherished baby, I also lost all access to the only social life I'd ever known, the one I shared in as Elaine's little sister. It was only Carol and I, rattling around the house together, which created a nuclear situation.

Carol, possibly out of fear, decided that was the right time to exert her authority, but of course she had no real idea how to do it without driving me further away. Her method, if she ever had anything so coherent as a method, was rather merciless tough love. This, combined with the sudden disappearance of the historical troublemaker (my sister) was a recipe for disaster.

Her interferences in my life were arbitrary, cruel and inconsistent. There were days when I woke up bruised on a concrete floor with a cockroach on my face. Great discipline is required to train yourself to wake up with a tightly closed mouth to avoid inhaling a disgusting insect. So many times she said that she would be better off if I died, if I had died at birth instead of surviving being born premature. An aberration of nature. A slap across my face here or there. A wish that I'd be raped to teach me a lesson. Mired in the grief of losing Elaine and Nathan, I was suddenly required to do so much extra housework that I barely had time for homework or rest. I could go on. Suffice it to say her methods of trying to regain parental control after taking almost fifteen years off didn't endear her to me. Our screaming matches surpassed the ones she had with Elaine's by a long, long mile. Every agonising day made me stronger than I was. It became more than the sum of its parts, there was no doubt that it was a battle between she and I, and nothing but nothing would appease her except my complete subjugation. All that time I defended myself with words and when necessary by blocking blows with my arms. But the moment was coming when I would strike back harder. We both knew it, and we knew when it finally happened the game would change forever.

Round Eleven

I became a teenager during the grunge years, and a new and deeper immersion in music coincided with my newfound determination to control my own life and refuse to accept my mother's treatment. To be myself, without compromise whatever the cost was my goal and I had a full soundtrack to flex these new muscles to. In 1994 there were plenty of rebellious sounds to inspire me, both new and regenerating in the punk scene I began to gravitate towards. From my mother, I knew Elvis, Fleetwood Mac, various bits of classical music, and the classics from the 60s revolution. From my sister and the pool hall I knew heavy metal, rap and 70's classic rock. My tape of Depeche Mode's *Black Celebration* prompted a love of Britpop. After my sister left St. Louis, I had no friends at all so I spent all my time in my bedroom reading the classics and philosophy books borrowed from the library while listening to anything I could get my hands on. For fourteen, I was a well-rounded musical sponge who did nothing but read books all day. A classic dork with no friends.

During the shady years between Elaine leaving at thirteen and my life changing at fifteen, I began to write seriously for my own pleasure and escapism, filling up notebook after notebook; but the proud interest I once took in academic achievements had vanished. Quite frankly, I was tired of no one noticing that I was making straight A's. I was tired of doing all the work for nothing. For years I had been a straight A student, but now the entire system seemed irrelevant and insignificant compared to my home life. I was as keen on learning as ever, but I had no interest in modern education, and I no longer cared about percentages on tests. I largely abandoned school pursuits, as I began to understand that it was unlikely I'd be able to complete my high school education. The way things were between Carol and I it was crystal clear that I'd be leaving home at the first opportunity, the same as Elaine had. School was less important than my living accommodations, and that is what I was concerned with securing.

I read Voltaire and studied Nihilism, which seemed to add up to the dawning understanding that my existence was rudderless and futile. All I cared about were ideas; they were all I filled my mind with and nothing else. I wanted to learn about and discuss life with others, and study history on a significant level rather than made to simply memorise facts for tests. I wanted to hear, see, taste and judge everything myself, first hand. It's a feeling that many teenagers will be very familiar with and many adults will remember.

Why should I dance to the tune of the education system, and why should I dedicate four hard years of my life just to graduate high school? I viewed it as nothing more than the gateway to a good university and I knew very well I could simply leave school and take the GED test for the same qualification. And with what money could I pay for university? Life had not taught me that I might be one of the lucky few to get a full scholarship. Where would I live while I completed a degree? The overriding theme that played in my mind when I considered school and my future was that I was not going to be able to live at home much longer, I just knew it somehow. The fights with Carol were shocking and getting worse and she'd already begun threatening to kick me out. Equally, I was wishing I could live elsewhere. The days in my mother's house were numbered, and it was absolutely crucial that I got a job to support myself. My spider brain had already seen it all, and it was doomed.

I knew from the beginning my parents would be lending me no hands when it came to money. I was totally on my own. I surmised that in all likelihood the most I would be able to afford would be a few classes at our local community college, which was little better than an advanced high school. I knew what my prospects were. Crap. And on the off chance that all the necessary things fell into place to allow me to go to university, I doubted if I could get a degree in thinking or listening to music, which appeared to be the only things I was any good at. I simply determined, using the logic I had at that time, that I would be better off putting my energy into finding a way to provide for myself, rather than into getting good grades at school.

When I was fourteen I met a girl named Eliza who had the same taste in music that I did. We were both obsessed with Nirvana (this while they were still playing live), Sonic Youth, Pixies, Jane's Addiction, KMFDM, Tori Amos, The Cure and so on. We started talking in class one day because she was wearing a band t-shirt that I liked. She wore her differences like a badge of honour, while I felt disfigured by mine. She was kind as well, and I instantly loved her. I was capable of being criminally shy, but she was very confident in her own skin, an attribute that gradually spread to me. I learned a lot from her about being myself. I began to realise that if I accepted what I had and worked with it, those things would be assets rather than hindrances. I had a way with words, I could identify any song within five seconds of sound and give you every fact about its creation. I was odd and damaged but I could shape those things into a reputation, an aura of power, that would remove me from the trap of abuse and misery I was living in. Eliza had a group of like-minded friends, and thanks to her, they also became mine.

And so it was that many things happened at once. When I was fourteen I began a campaign to leave my school before the legal age that you could drop out, which was sixteen. I also met someone who would change my life forever – but I shall leave that to one side for a moment. I made it clear to the school officials that my parents did not object and until I was legally released from school I would abstain from any work at all. There was a long battle as they tried to coerce me into complying but my mother had certainly taught me one thing: Stubbornness. I said to more than one teacher whom I liked very much that they weren't to take it personally, I simply had other needs and plans for myself. I would not participate in school.

I felt a strong change coming into the wind, and I chose to lean into it rather than fight against it. Looking back I still feel as if each terrifying step was predestined. Even most of my new friends thought I was mad, although they stood on the side-lines applauding. But I had an instinct that a storm was brewing that I would have to deal with as an adult, not as a schoolgirl. I distinctly remember feeling like a fly trapped in honey.

When the appalled school counsellor informed me that I had gone from the honour roll to scoring a triumphant, magnificent 0% in every subject, I reminded her that I'd made my intentions clear from the beginning of that school year and I had succeeded in what I had set out to do. I suggested that the teachers make better use of their time by focusing on the students who intended to stay in school, and if it bothered them that I read and wrote in class instead of doing assignments then perhaps I should be excused from attending. And so it was that they finally gave up and allowed me to divide my time at school between swimming and working as a library assistant, as well as attending all four lunches that were served to the school population of two thousand students. That was how I spent my final days there. I do wonder sometimes why none of the school officials thought to report our family to social services. At the time it was certainly an unusual arrangement, the only one like it at my school at least, but few people ever thought to ask why. Those who did were told the truth and still responded with apathy.

In that final year of school, they did insist I participate in the dreaded annual MMAT test. Nowhere to hide; every student is meant to be in a chair with a test in their hands, state requirement. The purpose of the test: to tell the state how well their schools are performing. It doesn't affect your grades, no matter how well or terribly you do, but participation is compulsory. I used to always come out in the top one percent, but this year was different. It probably wasn't wise of them to make me sit for the test since my stance on schoolwork had by then become infamous and the results would only reflect on the school.

The format is one book full of multiple choice questions and another full of corresponding numbered circles to be filled in with your answer using a number two pencil. You must have two number two pencils on your desk at all times, one to use and one for spare and one pencil sharpener just in case. You continually flip back and forth between the two books, first reading one then answering in another. It was always stressed to us that we must not go outside the lines in our circles with our number two pencils, because the results were scanned by computers, not humans. Every god damn year we were given the same speech as if we didn't have the dreadful process forever seared in our brains. Clearly all of that sounded like a whole lot of work for nothing, just a big fat waste of time and energy to me. However, I was trapped in that building and I had to sit in a chair with everyone else. My solution was to spend my time filling in the circles of the second book to make pictures. I made a sail boat, the anarchy symbol (how original!) and a bubbly fish.

Round Twelve

There was one exception to my near-complete apathy towards school. Mehlville employed a history teacher, Mr. Wilson, a man in his 30's who was hands down the most popular teacher in the school. He was a history teacher, and far more passionate about his subject than about rules and regulations. I rued the day they handed out classes and didn't give me him as a teacher, I was sure no one would have appreciated it more. I often left my post at the library or paused in swimming endless laps across the pool to sneak into his class. He had a habit of sitting on his desk while reading to his class, and although the class usually started out raucous and rowdy, before long he could reliably capture a rapt audience. I was so grateful that finally someone was speaking sense. His words had value because they were based on the human condition and driving at something I could actually grab at, run away with and use somehow. He also gave you the impression that when he looked into your eyes he was actually seeing you and understanding the true meanings behind your words.

Once, he stopped me in the hallway, and asked me how things were with me, and how things were at home. No one had ever asked me that. I couldn't meet his eyes and lie to him but I was suddenly embarrassed of my circumstances and at a loss as to how to explain them. My eyes shot from his face to his tie to the floor and back again and I mumbled that I was fine, just having a difficult week. I didn't know how he could tell that my life at home was hell, but somehow he did, and I was pathetically grateful. I had the urge to throw myself in his arms and ask him to adopt me. I imagined he had a cool apartment with wooden floors in South St. Louis with a spare bedroom I could make my own and then sadly kissed the thought goodbye.

Mr. Wilson gave a speech about the Holocaust to the entire assembled school. He was as eloquent as always, every word sounding in the audience like the low notes on a piano. His subject was the various badges the Nazis made people wear to designate their ethnic and religious status. He elaborated about what each badge meant, finally mentioning the pink triangle that homosexuals were made to wear. That was the point in his speech when he said that if he had been living there at that time, he would have been made to wear the pink triangle. And that was how he came out, to the principal, his fellow teachers and students alike. It took a moment for his message to sink in. He continued with his speech but the silence that fell over the audience emanated from the back where the Principal stood. Then a furore arose, and Mr Wilson was escorted out.

After that everything in our school went very quiet and Mr. Wilson was suddenly gone, presumed fired. But no, he hadn't been fired; he was merely suspended while the school board reviewed whether or not he was suitable to continue teaching. There was a huge uproar of protest, not only from the students but also their parents. Only a *very* small minority of people grumbled that homosexual people should be banned from teaching or speaking of their sexuality. Several petitions and a few South County protests later and Mr Wilson was reinstated to his position. However, it was with the proviso that he speak of homosexuality only if it were strictly relevant to the approved lesson plan and never in personal reference to himself. Essentially it was a gag order, as all of our other teachers were able to casually speak of their home lives, but at least he wouldn't lose his job, and crucially, the students wouldn't lose him. Mr Wilson returned to school after his time away, but by then I was more or less homeless and hadn't attended school in several months.

I had already left school by the time Mr. Wilson was reinstated to his job, having met my Romeo and being too busy with him to bother attending anymore. But occasionally I felt nostalgic for the old place and had the urge to return. I made a habit of sneaking into the school via a gate at the furthest side of the football field, and then going in through an inconspicuous door in a deserted hallway. Once I left school it was technically illegal for me to be on school grounds. Mr. Wilson turned a blind eye when I snuck into his classroom, never noticing me in the back row as I listened to him speak. I think we both saw some black comedy in the fact that I had staged such an impressive and sustained campaign of passive resistance to prove the point that I had the right to leave school, but as soon as I accomplished it I had no qualms about breaking and entering the building to attend classes.

The final time I went back to the school after his reinstatement, I wanted to speak to him to say thank you and goodbye. My life was quickly moving on and I wasn't going to be sneaking into class anymore. But as I went down the hallway towards his classroom he saw me and shook his head no. A moment later the Principal joined him, and they entered the class together, the door closing behind them. I realised things would be very different for him now that he had been under such intense scrutiny, and after all I'd made my choice when I decided to leave school. I didn't envy him going into that lion's den but I was proud and grateful that he did it. He was a wonderful teacher in the truest sense of the word; teaching by example and there to be an ally to any hungry minds he found.

I barely knew him except for these small observations that hundreds of other students would have shared but I felt very deeply that what he did was right, not obstinate. If it still creates such uproar for a teacher to simply declare to his students that he *is* homosexual, then we haven't sufficiently evolved beyond those Nazis principles, the very ones that the school government had gathered us together in that assembly to condcmn. It made no sense. I was also very grateful that he allowed me to learn a little something when I desperately wanted to, even though he knew I'd be taking no test at the end of it to reflect the school's accomplishment. It must be wonderfully ego stroking, as a teacher, to have students sneak into your lectures rather than out of them!

Round Thirteen

School and home unravelled simultaneously, the fights with my Mom were reaching new and exciting peaks. It might seem with hindsight that getting an outrageously inappropriate boyfriend was the obvious next item to tick off my list but I was blindsided by him; absolutely, blissfully star-struck and nearly in a state of silent hyperventilation under the unexpected scrutiny of his gaze. He was never part of my plans, however vague and sketchy they were, I never would have dared to aim so high. It never occurred to me that I, only shortly before, friendless and locked in my room listening to music with Medea pacing outside, would capture the eye of this god. The man at the top of the pile of all St. Louis disgruntled youth. The Elvis, the James Dean, the Sid Vicious. The one you knew of by name only, and half suspected everything you heard of him had to be myth. Before meeting him, I thought of him more like an idea that everyone knew *of*, but it was so good it couldn't possibly be true.

Our paths never should have crossed. I was nobody but a stubborn drop-out. I was invisible almost all of the time. When we met, in that first crucial moment I went scrambling about the frantic staircases of my mind, I knew there was a girl there who could look him in the eye, who could be good enough for him, but I had not the faintest idea how to find her, and no expectation that he would see her if I did. Realising that he wanted to keep catching my dazzled eyes and pinning me to the wall with his, despite the fact that he was so much... more than me, was baffling. It sent me scrambling up more of those staircases right into the attic, there to assess my new protagonist from a better vantage point. He was fascinating and absorbing and I had no idea why he singled me out for his attention. I only knew I was dead grateful. He was my every dream and better.

At twenty-one, Troy Taylor was almost seven years older than me, but his experience made him seem even older than that. Equally, for all my invisibility, I seemed much older and more sombre than fourteen; I usually passed for an easy seventeen. He was effortlessly authoritative, and at a solid six foot two he made me feel like a china doll when he touched me, a physical sensation reinforced by his often surprisingly delicate care of me. He was a stunning combination of fine and rough; his facial features were clearly etched with strong cheekbones, full lips and dreamy eyes. His face always made me think of a medieval king who started out looking quite noble and grand, but had ridden into one too many battles to ever appear truly civilised again. He was beautiful in the way only a man can be, a terrifying beauty that takes nothing whatsoever away from masculinity. Rather, this beauty actually adds an air of menace to what might otherwise be mistaken as merely a brutish beast, one dimensional and therefore easily conquerable. There was nothing easy to conquer in Troy, as I would learn at great cost.

His head had been shaved in the not too distant past; the hair was growing back soft and scratchy. Most of his body was covered in tattoos. He had teardrops falling from one eye and a spider's web stretching out the corner of the other. The four knuckles on one hand read – NAZI - the other – SKIN. He almost always looked a little sad and far away, unless some emotion actively imposed itself on his face. His skin was beautiful. He really did glow in a way I've only seen in a few people. No matter what he covered himself in, he could not be sullied. He looked like a fallen angel infused with superhuman strength. He was awe inspiring. His physical presence was such a strong part of him that it is necessary to describe. Inside he was every bit as charismatic as he looked. He was a natural leader, caretaker, and thinker.

His physical beauty and strength was powerful, but it would have meant nothing if he hadn't had the mind and heart to go with them. Belying the tattoos on his fingers, he loved people and he was driven to achieve justice wherever he could. He was intelligent, although he too had left school when he was fifteen. He could handle himself impeccably in matters of logic and reason and had a curious mind about the workings of the universe. He was funny and witty with wordplay. He amazed me with his ingenuity and ability to handle dangerous and difficult situations quickly and efficiently while remaining completely unruffled.

The night we met I was staying over at Eliza's house. It was towards the end of my campaign to drop out of school. I rarely slept at home anymore, choosing instead to stay at Eliza's on a semi-permanent basis. The night was balmy, and wanting to get out, she and I walked to our friend Lucy's. It was hot and there were fireflies out. We didn't expect anyone else to be at Lucy's, but as we walked down her road we saw Troy and his friends sitting with her in front of her house. It was immediately obvious from his appearance that this was *the* Troy Taylor I had heard so much about, but certainly never expected to meet. I didn't even know Lucy knew him; their connection was that her childhood friend and neighbour, Ralph, had grown up to be Troy's raging alcoholic dunce of a faithful sidekick. Ralph was best known for trying to shoot up Formaldehyde, for which I shall always sincerely love him; he created much amusement. He was also as loyal as a dog to Troy and therefore, by extension, myself eventually.

The sight of them as we approached made my stomach tie in knots. It was unexpected, and I was afraid of making a fool of myself in front of the very Troy whom everybody worshipped. There were also about four other boys, either sitting on Lucy's lawn, porch or perched on Troy's car drinking whiskey and shouting back and forth to each other. When we arrived he was on the porch. Lucy introduced us but I was blinded by the porch light shining behind him; I could barely see his face but he could see me. It made me uncomfortable so I looked away. I felt totally out of place with these people who were listening to old punk music I didn't know and drinking what I didn't drink. I resolved as soon as I arrived that I'd be best off if I pulled my "invisible girl" act and simply covertly memorise every action he made.

My plans to remain inconspicuous were shattered when Troy came up to me and started a conversation leaning up against his car. I had chosen that spot because it was the furthest away from him on the porch, because he made me uncomfortably aware of myself as soon as we met. Leaning on *his* car felt strangely intimate and pleasurable, even before he appeared, but when he stood so close to me, it was as if we were swallowed together in a dark bubble, excluding everyone else. I couldn't stop wondering why he was bothering to talk to me, and why he had walked with intention past other people to join me. I even remember asking him why he was with me instead of all the other people there, in answer to which he just laughed. Our introduction was awkward and bizarre but because neither of us knew how to skirt around the awkwardness without instantly verbally acknowledging it, within ten minutes we were well on our way to being fairly obsessed with each other.

I didn't know any way to speak but to be blunt and transparent, he was more evasive but equally honest. It was an instant and electric connection that clearly fascinated both of us. We seemed to know each other, as if recognising a long lost acquaintance, but it made no sense. We did not part once the rest of the night nor did we speak to anyone else, much to the annoyance of everyone else there. To anyone but the two of us our conversation would have seemed implausible; we spoke so fluidly so quickly. I heard a small voice in the back of my head saying to me "you are speaking too truthfully and randomly to him, stop it now or you'll never see him again!" and another saying "get away from him, he will break your heart!" but every sound and word he uttered compelled a response from me. We went from idly speculating on aspects of life to quizzing each other like interviewers and then to soft laughs of fast affection. We understood each other and each other's respective lives, joys and pains instantly and effortlessly without needing every detail - it seemed like only a matter of time before every little detail was filled in. That first conversation was like launching a boat into the sea; it set a ride in motion neither of us could escape, tossed about by tides and praying for calm waters.

When Eliza and I had to leave Lucy's to return to Eliza's he drove us back. He said he wasn't ready for our night to end. Eliza and I went inside while he parked his car around the corner, then he walked round the back of Eliza's house where he spoke to me through her bedroom window until sunrise – much to Eliza's annoyance. Our conversation was a continuation of the one we had been having at Lucy's, but in the quiet first hours of the day while Eliza slept in her bed behind me it became more intimate. It was tender, not sexual. We exchanged stories of our lives up to that point, almost trying to assimilate as much information about each other as quickly as possible, as if that one night were sand falling through our fingers. His life and childhood made mine look downright spoiled but he understood the great struggle I was involved in, and we instantly wanted to make the other suffer less.

We could only see each other by moonlight, Troy once cursed a cloud for covering our light source; all we could hear was the chirping of crickets everywhere. He looked at me, again and again, with a face full of radiant love and adoration, as if he'd never seen anything like me. I could see it but I couldn't understand it; returning it was easy. No one had ever looked at me like that in my entire life. We laughed a little bit over one thing or another and I could see he looked glowing and happy when he laughed, like a careless boy. He stood the entire night so he could be at eye level to the open window I leant out of; our faces close and hands tentatively touching. Yet the entire night, we never kissed; only talked. There really isn't any explaining it. It was an instant connection so strong that it derailed every other idea either of us had been entertaining of our respective futures; we didn't have to say it but it was clear we were linked from then onwards. I still don't understand it except to say, perhaps what is meant to be sometimes feels like magic. It delighted and baffled me in equal measure.

He left around five in the morning so the waking neighbours and Eliza's mother wouldn't see him, leaving instructions for me to wait for his return later that day. I lay down in bed, but couldn't sleep, only replay the night again and again. I wondered if he would come as he said he would, if it would all be forgotten or I had somehow misunderstood him. But around ten a.m. he arrived to collect me in his awesome red seventy-nine Catalina. We both adored that car and I thought it was fitting that his car was made the same year I was born.

Despite the fact that we seemed to instantly fall in line with each other in quite a remarkable way, I still wasn't sure why he was so interested in me. It simply seemed too strange to be true. I got into his car that morning unsure if he was to be my new elder brother or my boyfriend; it was a distinction we never fully clarified that left me in desperate anxiety. But while the car was still parked in Eliza's drive he turned to me and said, "Well, come here then," pulled me over to him, and we kissed. It felt like an answer to the question I hadn't been brave enough to ask, and it was the right answer too. He was mine! I was his! It happened suddenly and unexpectedly but life without him was already incomprehensible. It was the most exhilarating and perfect kiss; in it I felt victorious like never before, yet blissfully open and safely vulnerable. I had built layers of armour around myself for so long that I had begun to think no one would ever truly touch my heart. I felt too damaged. It was the same for him. He pulled back and looked me in the eyes while he held my face, searching, then smiling, and kissing me again. We could understand each other with the smallest of movements. We were both elated and felt encapsulated in love together.

He drove me to his house. We held hands the entire way and he kissed me at every stoplight. When we got there he made breakfast for us, and sitting down to eat together we experienced our first awkward silence. I was overcome with the feeling that I had just jumped off a cliff, and I looked to him, trusting that I had not been mistaken in my faith. I was acutely aware from the beginning that my heart was bonded to his, and he was an almost frighteningly compelling person. I didn't know what would happen, I only knew it would. I was afraid, he understood. Every move he made reinforced the promise that he would soon make to me; that where he had a home, so did I. If we knew one thing it was that we were together and we always would be. It felt like the beginning of the rest of my life. We were linked, almost immediately, by an invisible chain that tightened uncomfortably during absences from one another and fizzled with energy when we were near.

I noted in the daylight while we twined fingers that there was a disturbing dichotomy between my passionate defences of the rights of someone else's gay teacher, and falling in love with a man who had the words "NAZI" and "SKIN" tattooed on his knuckles. I even mentioned it to Troy, who quite understood. It's rather like being a vegetarian whose favourite coat is made of baby bunnies. During our talk the night before he confided in me the origin of those tattoos, and the pain he carried for bearing them. Although I wasn't yet sure what all of his specific moral ideals were yet, I knew we were on the same general wavelength.

I don't feel comfortable telling Troy's life story or exposing his indignities. This is mine, and he has the right to rest in peace. But I can say he was abused and given very little choice as to what did and didn't happen to his body at certain stages of his life. He was not a Nazi or a Skinhead, but he was certainly a criminal, which I didn't mind beyond a concern for his safety. I'm sorry if it sounds hypocritical, that I'm trying to justify loving a Skinhead Nazi. But it wasn't as black and white as that, nor were his opinions on humanity. I refuse to condemn him simply because it might be expected of me by people who never laid eyes on him. He deserves amnesty and I know he would have joined me in the fight for equality. That's all I can say about those two tattoos. Ultimately, it mattered very little. He was the kindest person to me, Erin, recognising me as a human being worth fighting for and he is still one of very few I can say that about unreservedly. I could forgive him anything and he often gave me good reason to.

Troy was moody, influenced very badly from a young age, but good natured at heart.

He felt shame for some of his tattoos, and a simultaneous feeling that he had to live up to them. He had black friends who he cared deeply for, but yet he watched KKK propaganda videos in other company. At those times he became withdrawn, sullen and angry. He lived like he didn't give a damn what anyone thought of him, he would be his own man no matter what. That included bravely and silently bearing guilt for words written on his skin without explanation or apology – more than likely anyone who gave him grief over them would have been given the middle finger. It does take bravery to bear the results of abuse on your skin without apology. People who met Troy in person were compelled to make up their own minds about him; he divided and also united many people, but he was certainly not full of evil. I believe it's obvious that my love for him was unquestioningly unconditional. I had already begun teaching myself how to hold my head high against abuse; I'd begun to fight back in carefully chosen battles. But Troy taught me how to live without apology and how to fight for myself. I would not be alive today without learning those lessons so painfully well.

When we had political conversations, which were often, I learned that in truth he was an ardent anarchist and nothing much more. He believed in total autonomy and the right to fight for the things he cared about. His ideal was something like extreme devolution but with radical, somewhat socialist changes to society as a whole. He wanted freedom and specifically economic equality taken to its fullest extent. He hated the police and with good reason. Police violence in Lemay is notorious and we were all victims of it at one point or another. Racist police violence has since shed some international light on the St. Louis police force, but it was a reality for us long ago. It was well known that a blow job would save a woman from a speeding ticket and those arrested were often beaten insensible. Troy tried to keep everyone under his aegis safe from the violence that was common in our area, from children to bikers to the waitress at Steak 'n Shake. Many of those people came to him when they needed help rather than going to the police. Victims were both afraid of mishandling by the police and retribution from the criminals who rarely seemed to go punished. A quick roughing up involving everyone involved was too often the only real result of calling the police.

The blinding light of Troy faded all else in my life into total insignificance. He eclipsed everything merely by existing with me. Even when we weren't together, he gave me courage. When I was in my mother's house, deep in the hell of our fights, the knowledge that he was my ally gave me strength just as it was waning. Suddenly I wasn't remotely alone anymore. I wasn't undefended or drowning under all those smothering words. Anyone who hurt me now would have to answer to Troy for it. It stiffened my spine like a back brace, gradually teaching me how to stand up straight without the aid. When I wanted to run out of the house, knowing that I had someone to come and take me away gave me the chance to escape to sanity. He was my saviour, my champion, my stable point who never, ever took anyone's side but mine. He was there at a moment's notice, I only had to call him and then I knew the minutes were ticking down until we would be together again. Trapped no longer. I was his top priority and he couldn't bear to see me hurt or upset. Even when we weren't together I felt safe and warm and loved because I belonged to him and he belonged to me. I was at such peace with this conviction that ultimately it didn't even matter to me if he regarded me as more lover or sister, in all truth I was every woman to him and he was every man to me. Joining up with Troy ripped the fabric of my life apart; I stepped through the gaping hole left and into the wasteland beyond, into his life and my future.

I became so used to basking in his brightness that the dimmer glow cast from everyone else made me feel as if I were walking blindfolded when he was gone. Fights with my Mother were becoming more vicious as I began to visibly change from a cringing little girl into a confident, even arrogant young woman. Any chinks I'd ever had in the armour that shielded me from my Mother had been mended, forged in the melting hot metal of our rage. I had nothing but hatred and contempt left for her. She could go fuck herself if she thought I was going to continue providing slave labour for her when she got paid to keep both me and my absent sister, which is exactly what I told her. I would not tolerate any more swipes, insults or punishments without retaliating by putting the fear of god right back into her with my precise words, legal threats and steady calm. I loathed her, and it was my intention that she felt it. The advent of Troy accelerated that, because she knew she'd met her match in him. Nothing would hold me back when he was at my side, we made each other unbeatable. I was spending most weeks at Eliza's house, only returning home to repack a suitcase full of clothes during the hours that I knew my Mom would be at work. Our days were our own; we lounged in a blissful and languid state. It was a wonderful time for us, with so many days spent alone together. Soon enough I would find out what it really meant to be the girlfriend of the man everyone wanted a piece of.

That fragile living arrangement with my mother finally came to an end during one chilling confrontation when she and I agreed to have nothing more to do with each other anymore – at all. It happened for a good reason. For the first time ever, I hit her back. I'd spent days with Troy and had come home briefly to repack my bag. She picked a fight over him, generally insulting him and our relationship. I fought back. He was the one thing I wouldn't let her take from me. One thing led to another and before long she had struck me several times. As usual I was arguing back with words until finally I realised that more than anything else in the world I wanted to beat her back. So when she pushed her red distorted face into mine, screaming wishes for my death, I punched her as hard as I could in her stomach. It was the first time I'd hit someone purposefully in my life, and I did it with every bit of strength I had.

She doubled over and for a moment I felt horrified at what I had done. For a second the mother I craved love from flitted across my mind, and I was sad that I hit *that* mother. Then came the even more frightening thought that she would turn me over to the police. I had called the police on her several times during our fights but each time I was told to obey my mother without any further investigation. I knew I would be viewed as the wrong one, no matter that I had already been hit several times that day on top of the verbal abuse. It was my word against her and the authorities always took hers.

There was silence in the room as she looked up at me with pure hatred in her eyes. I said I thought we should talk. She said she agreed. We both knew exactly what we were going to say. She told me to get out and not come back and I said I would gladly do so. Almost as if very little out of the ordinary had happened she sat down and drafted a contract saying she was no longer responsible for me in any way. It was titled "Minor Emancipation". We both signed it. I asked if that meant she would be signing over Dad's child support payments for me and she told me to go to hell.

I went into my room and took a last sad look around. I had two suitcases and a trunk with a padlock on it that I could pack. I filled them with as many essentials as possible; clothes, books, notebooks, Walkman and tapes and a few pictures. I'd bravely got through the fight with my mother without crying, and I was determined she wouldn't see me shed tears over leaving her home. But in truth it was awful knowing that there was no doubting any longer that my family was ruined, and I was being ruined with it. What on earth was my life going to be? How was I going to get through it? In a daze I paged Troy after packing, putting in the code we used that simply meant "come pick me up". I knew he wouldn't call back but I trusted he would come and get me. So I carried my three cases out and piled them one on top of another in the road in front of Carol's house. I sat on top of the cases, back stiff and straight, refusing to succumb to the tears stinging behind my eyes. I saw Carol watching me from the window and I would not allow her to know how very close she *had* come to breaking me. It was being able to get out of that hellhole and go to Troy that saved me; I don't know what would have happened to me if he and I had not met. Carol and I were already well on our way to the place where she was going to kick me out before his time, she'd been ranting about it since I was twelve.

I was taking a huge risk assuming that he would take me not just for a few days at a time but virtually permanently. Although Troy was actively supporting me in the war against my mother we had never discussed what would happen if I was kicked out of the house. He knew it was an issue that often came up in my arguments with her and usually when I talked about it he just looked very solemn and quiet. We had no agreement to live together and I didn't know who else might be willing to take me. I could only sleep at Eliza's so much before her mother wanted to see the back of me. But he didn't let me down. Fifteen minutes after I sent my page, he drove up, audaciously parking horizontally across my mother's driveway, sending a glare towards the window she was watching us from. He'd seen and understood the situation as he approached: me sitting outside, waiting on a pile of suitcases. It wasn't exactly rocket science.

For the first time since the fight began I began to crumble. I wondered if I'd overestimated him, if now that I was more of a responsibility than a pleasure I would push him away. Again, he rose to the occasion. He got out of the car, walked towards me and wrapped me up in his arms. I started shaking with sobs. Understanding my pride, he used his body as a visual block between me crying and my mother watching from the window. He walked me to his car, told Ralph to get in the backseat, and sat me down in the passenger seat. He strapped me in, told me to wait there, and went back to load my cases into his trunk. When he was finished he got in the car and immediately drove away before anyone could speak. Eliza was there, she and Ralph were asking me what happened. Troy answered for me, knowing I was beyond words. His answer was "Erin doesn't live with that bitch anymore, she lives with me." I crumbled in relief, gratitude and sobbing. Ralph was making an excited song in the back about Troy and I being Sid and Nancy and getting married. Troy told him to shut up.

We drove mostly in silence, first dropping Eliza and Ralph off at their homes and then arriving at Troy's house. I was acutely aware that now I was officially a homeless burden to everyone around me, especially Troy. I resolved to be as little trouble as possible, to make it easy on anyone who helped me. After carrying in my cases, much like that first morning, Troy made us food. And as we ate together in silence this time, we were both contemplating the fact that now for all intents and purposes we were living together as a couple. I think I looked as bad and as scared as I felt, which is why he came around the table and knelt down by my side. He kissed me and held my hands and told me that he was happy I was finally out of that house and that we would find a way to make everything work. He told me not to be afraid and to trust him. And I did. He was my final lifeline, the only remaining safety I had access to. That night as we fell asleep together in his bed he said everything I needed to hear. He said if he had a home I did too, and that was everything.

I realised that as we drove away from Carol's house I felt broken and daunted, but vindicated. My mother had always said no one would go out on a limb for me, that no one could love me because of how horrible I was. She was wrong; I had just proven her wrong. Troy was going out on a limb for me, and he wasn't just "somebody" either, he was magnificent, ten times the human being she could ever have hoped to be.

Round Fourteen

There was still a huge hill to climb and the first steps were taken the next morning when I met Troy's family over breakfast. He lived with his mother, her husband who was his biological father's brother (Troy's Uncle/Stepfather), and his sister. Like everyone, they seemed unwilling to deny Troy anything, and they raised no objections when he introduced me and announced I too would be living there. But I was not made welcome and I knew enough about his family already to know I had to be on my guard in his house if I was ever left without Troy's protection. I tried to be a gracious guest and cause no hassle. I'd had a lifetime's practise pretending to be invisible which came in enormously handy when I became homeless. However I needn't have been afraid of his relations. In all the time that I stayed there, we rarely saw his family members. They seemed only vaguely aware of and not at all interested in the young girl ensconced in Troy's bedroom, which was exactly how we wanted it to be.

Troy's house was a little wooden, half falling down thing in Lemay, complete with required porch and banging screen door. Only someone who grew up in Lemay can properly understand the beautiful, delightfully carefree, apathetic and tragic times that can be had in those houses. The cast of characters surrounding Troy was as colourful and rewarding as he deserved, but one especially notable extra was his ex-girlfriend. She liked to drive slowly past his house and stare at me intensely. Troy usually gave her the finger and scowled on such occasions, and bundled me inside the house or car as soon as she appeared. He made no concessions to her vanity, and in fact was quite crude to her, but she remained undeterred in her devotion to the cause of ousting me from my position of girlfriend and taking it for herself. Her name was Samantha, but Troy and his friends simply referred to her as "Big Head". When Eliza and I asked why she had that particular nickname Troy coughed, there was much laughter, and he explained it was because they all thought her head looked overly large. It didn't seem to make sense to me and I said that although I couldn't like her I thought her head was a normal size. Troy just kissed me and swiftly changed the subject by changing the record we were listening to, which was a little habit of his.

Much to my shock, horror and dismay, Troy made it clear from the beginning of our relationship that he would not be having sex with me because I was too young. I vehemently disagreed with him, saying that if I was old enough to do everything else I was doing then I was old enough to do that, but he would not be budged, and in fact refused point blank to debate the issue with me. He let it be known that *one day* he and I would consummate our union but refused to clarify when. It felt as if I simply wasn't that appealing yet, too adolescent for someone with so much more experience than me. I wondered if I was more of a long term investment for a man who wanted a woman and not a childish girl. If that was the case, did I irritate him as I was then? I felt woefully inadequate, rejected and bewildered. I wanted to be losing my virginity soon with the man I was seriously in love with. But he didn't want it. All the terrible things I'd heard about him, all the girls he'd made quick use of. He clearly enjoyed sex. And he clearly loved me enough to scrape me off the ground and give me a home, but he wouldn't share that part of himself with me. In fact we never did anything more than hold hands, kiss, and cuddle in bed while fully clothed.

I felt shut out in the cold from my god, and I couldn't understand why he was doing it. The only explanation he ever gave was that I was too young. Something I can look back on now and think was perhaps part of his character, so intent on not taking advantage of anyone who was vulnerable. But I didn't have that perspective when I was fifteen. I heard "You're too young" and I felt "You're not sexy enough". There was no moving him so I gave up arguing, but held hope that he wouldn't make us wait too long. I wanted to marry him, and by default share that only with him. It was an issue that neither of us would budge on.

For the most part, from that point onwards, where Troy went I went. Although things would go no further we kissed and were very affectionate with each other. We slept in the same bed, ate the same food. Suddenly I had an entirely new group of people to fit in with, and not all of them were pleased to see their leader becoming so domesticated. Settling in with his friends was difficult. I was the object of resentment and I knew that in certain company every move I made would be repeated to Troy in an unflattering light. Of the many people regularly around us, Eliza, Lucy and poor drunk Ralph to a lesser degree were the only ones I trusted. Everyone else had one reason or another for preferring a single Troy.

There was no question that Troy and I were together, but given the semi-communal way in which we lived there was also no one left ignorant of the fact that he'd said he wouldn't have sex with me. It was a perfect point of attack from those people who couldn't bear our attachment. About six weeks into our bliss of living together I was sitting alone on Troy's porch having a cigarette, when one of his friends came outside to join me. I felt instantly wary because I knew he didn't like me and somehow was connected to Samantha "Big Head". He didn't waste any time. As soon as I said hello to him he replied that I shouldn't feel too overjoyed for being Troy's new love, because he still went to Samantha regularly to get fucked. He laughed at the look of dumb shock he saw on my face, and went back indoors, job done.

It was an utterly devastating revelation that suddenly made perfect sense. The pain was physical and took my breath away. I sat shaking on the porch chair, lighting cigarette after mindless cigarette. I never felt a huge sense of anger towards Troy; I instantly felt stupidly naïve for daring to presume that he could have been satisfied for so long by me alone, especially when we weren't having sex. The thought had crossed my mind more than once that he might come to regret his impulsive declaration of intending to house and protect me. But now I had nowhere to go but to him. The revelation was more humbling than infuriating, as it might have been. I felt like I'd overstepped myself in assuming that he should be faithful to me. Of course he would have wanted sex, and we hadn't been having any so he would have been unsatisfied. I cast my mind back to every time he'd left me at Eliza's for a few hours, and realised he had likely been

115

dropping me off so he could go to her. Had he been counting the minutes until he could offload me? If he felt like that, how could he possibly want me to be around him as much as I was?

Some time after my informant left me alone on the porch Troy came out. I didn't greet him happily as I normally did. He asked me what was wrong and I said "I know about Big Head now. Samantha. If you're fucking her you should at least have the grace to call her by her name." He stood rigidly for a moment that seemed to stretch into hours. In that moment I assumed everything we had shared was over, and I would be immediately moving out. Then he placed his hand on my head and said he was sorry but that I was to understand that she didn't mean anything to him so I shouldn't take it personally. He said he had to have sex and she was "embarrassingly willing". His words. As I was beginning to argue that I was willing too and I was his girlfriend he cut me off with the same answer I was always given, "You're too young." No. He told me it didn't mean he didn't want me but we had to wait until I was older. He said he couldn't go that long without sex but he swore he was in love with me, and he asked me to try to understand. I was choking in silence, I nodded. He asked me to go back inside with him. I thought for a moment. I knew that going back inside with him was silently agreeing to this arrangement. My pride, hurt, love and fear all collided inside me with an almost nuclear level of feeling that I had to keep tight reign of. But I went back inside with him. I would have made the same choice even had, for example, a friend offered me a home and I no longer needed Troy for security. It was dysfunctional and goes against the grain of everything I have learned as an adult. As I write these things I can hear all the potential insults that could be lobbed at me for choosing him again. But it just didn't matter. The connection between he and I was stronger than the element of her. Being with Troy was like living on a runaway train, both thrilling and paralysing.

We didn't really speak of it again and I no longer tried to make him change his mind about sleeping with me. I found it repugnant to beg for what he was freely giving her. My family had taught me to hold my feelings close to my chest, to smile when I was dying inside and to expect very little. I used all of those "coping methods" to close my mind off from the issue of Big Head. Troy's "friend" who told me the good news on the porch was given a punch in the face and declared persona non grata with Troy for some time, but other than that nothing changed. I never saw Samantha but for her occasional slow drives past the house and on those occasions I refused to acknowledge her presence. Troy continued to poke fun at her, quite conspicuously sometimes as a means to reassure me. He wanted his friends to recognise the same distinction between she and I that he did but in truth most of them resented me a great deal for what they saw as a softening in Troy's character since we'd been together. He was caught between vigilante punk chaos and a first attempt to play house and be a responsible man with something like a family of his own. Samantha's character and looks could be ripped to shreds, three men in the room comparing notes on the sex they had all had with her, but the few careless times one of his friends let a sarcastic insult against me drop he unceremoniously told them to get out of his reach and sight, one minute laughing, the next deadly serious. It was a curious position for me to be in, on the one hand valued greatly and on the other shamefully relegated to a place that required tremendous patience, humility and humiliation. More than once I was reminded that I wasn't the one getting him off, only never in his earshot. I chose to keep those comments to myself rather than report them to him each time. I wanted to earn respect for myself by taking the higher ground with as much grace as I could muster.

His behaviour with regards to Samantha was despicable; it certainly made a dichotomy from the relatively gentlemanly attention that he paid to me. I wondered if she had ever been to him what I was then, someone to be cared for and valued. Had she fallen from my position to this other one of simply servicing him and being the object of derision, or had that always been her lot? I would never ask all those questions, but I was resolved that as much as I could control it, he would never feel that way about me. I would refuse to be as desperate as her; I would never again express my desire for intimacy between us. I would simply enjoy each moment we had while pretending very hard to be indifferent to what he was doing when he came and went. I was equally determined to never become more of a burden to him than I already was by putting limitations on him that would make him dread my company. My nerves made me worry at times, but I still had an unshakable faith that Troy and I formed one complete unit and all of these complications would be worked out in due course. The last time we discussed intimacy between us he promised that one day we would be fully together, and at that point he would be faithful to me. I chose to believe him, and hope for that unnamed day when we could be together as equals in love.

I reasoned that if he went to her for four hours, he was with me for the remaining twenty so I was clearly the one whose company he preferred. But in truth, each time he left me with any of our friends and I knew he was with her I paced the room like a caged beast, becoming increasingly irritable and randomly insulting those around me. There was always a profuse amount of alcohol on hand, so I would take drink after drink as I became full of rage that I lacked the sex appeal needed to make him want to fuck me while someone like her was the one he chose to open himself to in that way. As very insecure as I was, even I couldn't deny that I was considered obviously prettier and more pleasant than her. I could close my eyes and see him doing it with her, knowing he was with her right in that same moment that all his friends were watching me becoming more and more tense. I wondered if he ever uttered words of tenderness and love to her when he was caught up in the moment. I ached, physically, each time I was separated from him. I was constantly trying to understand what she had that made her sexually acceptable that I lacked. I suddenly decided her head was indeed abnormally large and added it to the list of reasons he shouldn't be going to her when I was waiting for him.

Maybe Troy had a soft spot for her because of their history together, I wondered. In that case I could never compete; they were the same age and had been fucking when they were seventeen and I was eleven. Yet he couldn't say enough how much he couldn't stand her, he said she made him sick. I never understood. How could he sleep with me nightly, our bodies entwined in trust when we were at our most vulnerable, and still not be tempted to choose me over her? It defied everything I understood about the male sex, so I looked only to myself to apply the blame. It was obvious that for whatever reason I simply wasn't tempting enough. But then why keep me all the rest of the time, why go to all the bother he went to for me?

I actually wanted to interview her at times, to ask her why she thought he liked to have sex with her but spent his time with me. I wanted to ask her how it felt to have sex with him every few days but otherwise be banned from his company while he and I lived together. But she looked like she had a mean right fist and not the type to take things scientifically. More than anything else, I wanted nothing to do with her; I wanted to try to pretend she didn't exist, which trumped my curiosity. She was poison from the moment her existence wound its way into Troy's life as a wannabe groupie. In addition to robbing me of what was mine it was also plain to see that all she cared for of Troy was his reputation and the status she would have as his girlfriend. She wouldn't give a damn about him if she wasn't able to gain from him in some way, whereas I truly loved him, for himself, who he was. It would never be me screwing every one of his friends on my downtime. She may have wanted to be his girlfriend, but she wasn't; I was.

The worst effect of my new knowledge of Troy's sex life was that for the first time he and I began to deal delicately with each other. We tried harder to ignore it, tried harder to recapture the ecstasy we shared before I learned the truth. We both knew our relationship had taken a blow but we were both quietly determined to overcome it. I lived in fear of forfeiting my position as his beloved, cherished girl, always wondering if by putting a foot wrong or being absent in a crucial moment I would lose him forever. It added yet more terror to my feeling that I had to behave perfectly at all times. I constantly strove to better myself in every way and never ever lose my face in public so that no fault could be found in me.

I tried to be as appealing to Troy as possible, without fawning over him and making an idiot of myself like I saw so many others do. I tried to find that delicate and particularly female balance of being both available yet still someone worth working for. I had no intention of failing the acid test of his desire whenever he chose to spring it on me. I loved him with every atom of my being. But I was also now dependant on him, with nothing left in the whole world but an extremely hostile mother whom I had sworn in writing never to depend on again. He held his cards so close to his chest I never knew what he wanted from me or for how long I would remain this mysteriously favoured plaything and companion. The imbalance of power between us, once it became so glaringly obvious, disturbed both of us equally. The feeling of having the sand shift gently under my feet began in earnest. I've fought against it ever since, frantically piling down brick after brick in an attempt to remain on solid ground.

Round Fifteen

A night came when tensions were high amongst Troy and his friends, though no one would say why; Troy had forbidden everyone in the room to "talk about it". I didn't know what "it" was but I knew enough to know he needed me to sit quietly with him, not question him. He was in a foul mood, and everyone was trying to stay out of his way, with good reason. We sat alone together in a room for a while, but anger emanated from him so strongly I dared not speak to him. I only lay a hand on his leg and felt a small victory that he allowed me to comfort him at all and not exclude me entirely as he had all the others. I didn't know why he was so angry, but it was obviously building up an inferno inside him that must eventually explode. After an eerily quiet time he announced to everyone gathered in Ralph's basement that it was time for us to go. A few of us got in his car and I sat next to him as he drove, wondering where we were heading. It was already around ten at night. The car was winding through the residential streets of Lemay, until finally he pulled up outside one unlit house that I was unfamiliar with. He parked his car and told everyone inside to stay where we were. He took something with him as he stepped out of the car but it was too dark for me to see what. I watched him through my window as he strolled up the lawn of the house. Some of the tension in me dissolved as I wondered if it was the house of a friend of Troy's because he looked so casual. Suddenly he moved so quickly I missed it with a blink, but the sound of shattered glass broke the silence. At first I thought he'd shot a gun but as he walked back to the car and I saw him empty handed I realised he had only thrown a brick through the front window.

I turned to him, open mouthed as he opened the door and sat down in the driver's seat. He smiled tightly and kissed me. I looked from him back to the house and saw that lights were coming on and heard a man was shouting. I looked back to Troy, mutely begging him to hurry and drive away, but he kept to his normal, casual pace: seatbelt on, turn the key, change the gear, check mirrors. We drove away with what I think I can call a communal feeling of having a head full of helium. The car was full of the sounds of slightly hysterical laughter in the wake of our shock. Later that night Ralph told me that the house's owner had reportedly raped a thirteen year old sister of one of Troy's closest friends; that was the only additional information I had.

Troy drove us to the house of someone who I had seen once or twice but didn't know well. He was amongst that mysterious "other" group of people that Troy spent some hours away from me with. We went there for one purpose, and it was Troy's purpose: to get as fucked up as humanly possible. Throwing the brick hadn't calmed the beast inside him. Troy was not taking any bullshit from anyone that night, and everything he did had an edge to it. He wanted non-stop and dedicated consumption of anything on hand, and he wanted me at his side the entire time. He kept his grip on my hand when we entered the house and told me not to leave him for the rest of the night. We arrived and without any small talk Troy told his friend to make ready the goods and sat himself down on the sofa, pulling me down next to him. There were already several people scattered about the room in various states of consciousness. We were drinking the usual mix of vodka, whiskey and beer, as well as smoking joint after endless joint.

Eventually everyone else had passed out, and it was only three of us left passing bottles and joints: Troy, the house's owner, and me. I concentrated hard on keeping pace with Troy even though I was easily half his size with only a fraction of his experience with seasoned intoxication. Troy's friend was sprawled on an armchair across the room, Troy sat at the head of a sofa and I lay stretched along its length with my head in his lap. I was looking up at the ceiling fan circling around and around, to his face then back to the fan. I looked at him several times and he smiled back into my eyes, and bent down to kiss me, which filled me with a warm glow. When Troy passed me a bottle I drank, when he passed me a joint I smoked.

This went on endlessly until my body couldn't move anymore, it had gone to a strange and still place and its parts felt like rubber. I tried to cry off, mumbling that I'd had enough, but that drew an immediate reaction of annoyance and denial from Troy. He said again that he wanted me with him all night and he meant it. Even his friend told him to let me be, that I'd had more than he thought I could handle, but Troy told him to shut up and insisted I keep taking what he was giving to me. He was crazed in his intoxication. It started out as him showcasing his pride in how much I could take, despite being a girl and small. My desire to merit his pre-emptive pride propelled me forwards though I felt a mild sense of alarm and foreboding. The friend, our passive observer, passed out in his chair and finally it was just Troy and I awake on our sofa, both of us more intoxicated than alive.

I didn't feel I could have any more, drink or drug, but he was intent on continuing. I kept trying to mumble to him "no more" but he seemed genuinely angry at me for that. Even in my half aware state I found this mildly alarming because up until then I had been immune from his anger. I couldn't move my body from where it was, the rubber of my limbs melted into molasses and then solidified into lead. I could do nothing but lay there, still as a statue, and when it was my turn to inhale he held the joint to my lips, said "suck" and I did. When he held a bottle to my lips he said "drink" and I did. He was not himself, not in a state to realise what he was doing and I was not in a position to be able to reason with him.

This carried on for an indeterminate amount of time, during which I became fully mesmerised from watching the ceiling fan above me spin on its endless cycle round and round, with its whisper of a rhythmic wind. It became all that I could sense; all else fell away. I began to feel something like a cool breeze leaving my body, beginning at my toes and slowly going upwards. I could do nothing but lay there silently observing the feeling; one like an air conditioning vent being gradually pushed upwards inside that leaden body which would not move. The space it passed through, vacating all within, was left empty, pointless, unfeeling and paralysed. I recognised a pattern as it went up my legs past my knees. I thought vaguely as it left my stomach and I could no longer feel anything below my waist, "oh no, it's heading to my heart!" It rose steadily upwards and I felt the last easy pump of that organ slow down. The cool air continued its course up my neck and ears and I thought once again, "oh no, it's going through my brain! I'm really in trouble now…" Still I could not move my lips or open my eyes to try to alert Troy. Before I had time to dwell on that fact, the cool air left my body entirely, and then I understood that the cool air was "me" because I was within it, floating above the leaden flesh below me. I saw my body so still on Troy's lap. I looked down and realised I was nothing, I was a wisp, I was simply my mind and nothing more to me than a brush of air. I saw that I was near the blades of the spinning ceiling fan, and I flinched away from them instinctively in true fear that I would be

126

caught and shredded.

Taking my wary eye off the ceiling fan for a moment, I looked down from my ceiling height and saw Troy holding the joint up to my lips once again, saying "suck", but I was no longer obeying. He was getting angry with me like before and he shook my shoulders. The "me" floating above him shook my head, knowing that his actions were futile; my body lay below me, unresponsive to Troy for the first time since we'd met. I saw him shake me again, watching him as he sunk into the understanding that I could not be woken. He said my name and slapped my cheek; the look on his face now was one of dawning horror and remorse. I felt a terrible pang for the guilt he would feel when he realised what had happened to me, and what his part in it was, and I wanted more than anything else to protect him from that. More faintly, in the back of my mind I felt for Eliza, my Grandparents, even my Mother for a moment. But those thoughts were like mere transparencies alongside the very solid anguish I saw in Troy as he held my head and continued to try to rouse me with tears welling in his eyes. I distinctly remember thinking that it was still within my power whether I let it go with a sigh or a struggle, and in a time that felt as if it stretched to eternity and back, but could only have been a split second, I debated which to choose. It seemed I was so close to the chance to die and I wondered if I shouldn't take it while I could. I knew the odds of me having a life free from strife were alarmingly low and I wasn't particularly looking forward to my rather bleak future. I was not so in love with life to immediately run away from the chance to end it. But now Troy was openly crying over my face, saying my name in tones I hadn't heard before, and I could never have left him like that.

I summoned all of my energy like sucking in air before blowing out candles and dove like a swimmer back into my body, instantly coming up spluttering and choking for air. I felt as if I'd been beaten senseless, but I was there! Bruised, gasping and being crushed by my boyfriend's arms around me. Troy dropped to his knees and began apologising profusely for making me keep up with him, and then it was his head in my lap, while I sat dazed, stroking his head automatically but unable to utter a word. He picked me up and carried me into his car, then drove us home. He carried me up the stairs, put me into bed and climbed in with me. He held me while I slept, just about dead to the world but not quite.

The only significant reflection I made upon this incident came the next day, when I re-examined my memory, hardly believing what I had felt and seen the night before. If it was all true, then I had hit upon a disturbing notion of death. I learned that there may be times when I could say "not yet", but that meant the reverse was true as well – I may one day be able to choose to die. I tucked the knowledge away like a cyanide pill, and then moved on with my life. I would have to continue to judge the distinction between the two like a balancing act, because suddenly a whole new level of decision making appeared possible. Once again I felt that Troy and I had opened up a new dimension between us. I tried to explain to him what I saw up at the ceiling fan but found myself too tired to make myself clear. I wondered where all of this was taking us, but could think of nothing. Taking a pragmatic approach to the puzzle, I reasoned that it hardly mattered if I knew where we were heading, we were going there regardless! I had but to sit back and allow life to happen.

Round Sixteen

Life with Troy was in full swing and he and I were going from strength to strength as friends and as a couple. We felt indomitable and unconquerable together. One night Nine Inch Nails was playing at The Fox the same night as The Melvins was at Mississippi Nights so Troy and I parted company only long enough to see our respective shows. He was coming to The Fox to collect me after the concert. After the show I went looking for Troy. There was a crush of a raucous crowd spilling out into the lobby. I was frightened that it would be hopeless trying to find Troy while I weaved my way through the bodies looking for him.

However I was saved from being lost when I spotted two people who literally stood heads above the crowd: The Enigma, who I had just seen on stage in the opening act of the Jim Rose Circus, and Troy. They were on the other side of the room comparing tattoos. I made my way towards them, inwardly beaming at the sight of my gorgeous boyfriend. He was there for me, and he was the best, the finest man in the building, Trent Reznor included. I was never as proud as when I reached his side and his arms enveloped me and he kissed me warmly, letting me know he'd missed me too. He introduced me to The Enigma, who was very polite to me and said I must be something special to have such an awesome boyfriend. Troy and I beamed at each other. I never heard myself referred to as Troy's girlfriend without feeling a thrill of pleasure that momentarily made me speechless. I was rather star struck by Enigma and even more embarrassed over the compliment so I only mumbled a few words of thanks. Troy and Enigma said their goodbyes, exchanging contact details and Troy escorted me to his waiting car. We still had a whole night ahead of us and we were ready to be together again.

Round Seventeen

Living with Troy – and his almost inescapable entourage of friends – plunged me into a world I'd not even imagined before. My outings to the pool hall with my sister seemed positively angelic compared to how I was then living. No longer was I experiencing life through books and music alone, I was living it first hand in all its lawless glory. Fifteen years old and escaping from scrape after scrape by the seat of my pants. In other words, I was rapidly evolving into the timeless and borderless street urchin, intent on survival and entertainment by hook or by crook. I was blissfully free from my

Mother and even the tortuous semi-annual visits from my Father. I felt for the first time that I was in total and sole possession of my own mind and body. The only person who I was deeply concerned with was Troy, but he felt more like a male branch of me than a totally separate being, so his presence in my mind was never an intrusion. Our home was the whole world, Lemay, the streets, his car; wherever we were we were at home within ourselves and with each other. Being totally independent and free of obligations, rules or adult interference was exhilarating. I would never be willing or able to tolerate living with my mother or indeed anybody who tried to exert much authority over me again after that first taste of total, anarchic freedom.

Troy and I had no creature comforts, but we were entirely our own masters and our time belonged to nobody but ourselves. Our purposes were to enjoy ourselves, keep out of sight of the authorities and meet as many basic necessities (hunger, sleep, warmth) as possible. It was blissfully simple, deceptively simple. Every day brought a new adventure, whether it was scavenging through the dumpsters behind the Lemay Salvation Army or spare changing at a driving range. I absorbed Troy's wariness of encountering officers of the law because we were both in breach of it living as we did, and my greatest fear was being removed from him. The law would (astonishingly) fail to appreciate mine and Troy's authority. Together we scaled more than one chain metal fence in dashes from the police through strangers' backyards and public parks, Troy chucking me over when I couldn't keep up.

One night around four in the morning, we crept into Troy's house, as always unsure if his family members would be there or not. After ascertaining that we were alone in the house Troy sent some of his friends to sleep in his sister's empty bedroom while he and I went into his, collapsing from exhaustion in bed. The next morning I woke alone, startled out of sleep by sounds from downstairs of shrieking laughter and smashing glass. Experiencing the awful feeling that I had slept through all the fun I quickly made myself presentable and rushed downstairs, wondering what could possibly be happening. Everyone else was awake before me, and having a whale of a time too, taking advantage of a most unusual situation under Troy's General Grant style of direction.

Something inexplicable had happened since we'd last been to Troy's, something uniquely suited to the twilight zone that is Lemay. We'd stayed at Ralph's the night before and apparently at some point during the day of our absence Troy's Uncle/Stepfather had emptied the living room of its entire contents - furniture, objects and carpet, taken to place unknown. But the truly incredible thing was that he had also smashed in the room's wooden floorboards leaving nothing but a huge jagged, gaping hole into the basement below where only days before sofa, family photos and television had been. No explanation had been left or was apparent for this sudden architectural crisis. The splintered floorboards that had once lain neatly side by side could now be seen in a pile on the basement floor below, just where they'd landed when smashed in. There was nothing like a neat line made around the perimeter of the room, where some small amount of floor remained. It was simply… a broken absence of floor. I looked to Troy for explanation but he just shrugged and handed me a plate to throw down.

This unexplained household phenomenon was most surreal, and being Troy he was unable to let it pass without causing further mayhem. Walking away from something like that would have been unworthy of us. Troy provided an assortment of kitchen materials that he confidently stated his mother no longer wanted and we made short use of them, chucking the crockery into the basement below for the satisfaction of hearing it smash. That was the sound that woke me. I quickly joined in after recovering from the shock of the sight. Troy also produced several folding chairs, which were set up in the safest areas of remaining floor. After a while I was given something for breakfast and took my place sitting down, enjoying watching the chaos around me.

Troy brought his record player down from our bedroom and we had a lovely day to the soundtrack of *Saturday Night Fever*, The Smiths, Dead Kennedys, Sex Pistols, Misfits, The Buzzcocks, and so on. After a long run of the most manic punk he had, Troy put The Cure "Kiss Me, Kiss Me, Kiss Me" on for my shattered ears. Troy had a beautiful collection of vinyl and he handled his records like lovers. We sat around looking down over the gaping hole, drinking and eating chips whilst throwing the remaining bits of crockery into the basement below. Troy playfully handcuffed me to a garden chair and pocketed the key in a bid to tease me, but actually I didn't mind it one bit. I had a drink, a pack of cigarettes and Troy, so I was in no hurry to go anywhere. We loved sparring with words together, forever teasing each other senseless and using everything and everyone around us as fodder for debate or humour. I was slightly alarmed when a campaign was raised by some of the others to get the key to my handcuffs off Troy. This caused a scuffle that got rather too heated, landing my key on the basement floor below and leaving Ralph dangling by his arms from the edge of the floor. All in all it was one of the most innocently fun days of my childhood. And in the end we all thought it best to vacate the premises before nightfall, lest the Uncle should make a sudden return.

However if we're to speak of awkward things to wake up to in Lemay I would be remiss in leaving out a glaringly bright morning several weeks after the incident with the floor. I had the worst hangover I'd ever had in my life, and that includes the day I woke up after going one on one with a ceiling fan. As I gradually came to, my eyes tried to focus, struggling to open from the crust. My head attempted to orientate itself on the pillow and in the room, and unconsciously my hand reached out beside me; Troy was gone. The last thing I remembered was him laying me down in bed in the early hours of the morning. I had assumed he'd come to bed with me but it seemed he'd gone out again. I frowned. As my vision finally began to clear, I saw Samantha Big

Head sitting next to my bed, watching me sleep. My first thought was that she was there to murder me.

She was glaring at me, her arms and legs crossed and tapping. My second thought? I'd like to murder Troy. I'd never spoken to her before. The house was utterly silent and it was apparent that we were the only two in it. I wondered how long she had been watching me sleep. I slowly sat up, never once taking my eyes from her face. I was grateful that she quickly broke the silence because I was utterly at a loss for what to say. Or should I even try to speak, should I just make a dash for the door? I had no idea how to proceed in this bizarrely awful situation.

"Troy was called away on an emergency. He told me to drive you to Ralph's." Her jaw was working, clenching and unclenching. I exhaled. So she wasn't there to kill me. And if she tried Troy would at least know who did it. It was marginally better than my first guess, which was that she had snuck in after seeing Troy leave. Both my relief and fears must have been plainly visible on my face, for she said next, "Don't worry I'm not going to hurt you. Not that I couldn't." She looked me up and down as though assessing a lame farm animal. She continued, "I could break you in two if I wanted but Troy would kill me if I did anything to you. But don't push me. Come on, I don't want to babysit you all day."

I got up in terror, rage and humiliation, but seeing no other choice I did as I was told, quickly grabbing my bag and walking down the stairs behind her. As I walked behind her I asked myself what Troy could have possibly thought was worth this. I registered the obvious glee she felt in knowing more of Troy's whereabouts than I did. I wouldn't be learning any of his secrets from her.

We got into her truck which was parked outside and my feeling of choking panic worsened. The slightly crazed look that was always present in her eyes now claimed her face entirely, making her resemble, oddly enough, Carol. She was the loosest of cannons and I was locked in a moving vehicle with her. She drove fast and recklessly, berating me the entire time for taking her man from her, for being young and stupid and a thousand other things. I was seriously beginning to wonder if she was going to deliver me anywhere alive. I thought about trying to open my door and jump while the truck was at a stoplight, and I believe I might have but as it happened, by pure chance we hit nothing but green lights. All I could see looking out my window was concrete whizzing by. She had a sick little half smile on her face and started telling me in vivid detail how beautifully Troy made love to her when he left me. I tried not to hear, tried not to be sick. She reminded me of how many years she'd known him; said that his separation from her would never last because they had history. I was nothing but a flash in the pan.

As she spoke her driving became increasingly dangerous. She mounted corners in her turns and slammed on the brakes at every chance, only to quickly accelerate again. I gritted my teeth and clutched onto the door to brace myself but said nothing in reply. I had a long experience with tirades of verbal abuse and I knew silence was the ultimate weapon against it. Every word she uttered was a dart aimed at the place within myself that I held dearest, but through an almost supernatural force of will I managed to remain expressionless. This had the same effect as it had on Carol, which was to frustrate and infuriate her even more. But I would not be drawn in. I knew if I allowed myself to protest or fight back in any way there was a good chance I'd come out of the situation the worse for it. My only power came in controlling myself with an iron will.

As we approached Ralph's house the truck hardly slowed at all. I noticed and was alarmed thinking she meant to push me out while it was still moving. Finally it lurched to a halt, bumping into a telephone pole on my passenger side. I was jerked so suddenly that I only narrowly managed to stop my head from meeting the dashboard. "Oops" she simpered, smiling with teeth bared. Indeed, I'm sure I looked quite green and rattled in my head, so she had good reason to be proud of shaking me. A screaming instinctive voice within me demanded that I leave with some small piece of dignity intact. I paused for a moment before speaking or moving, collecting myself while she gloated. Then, for the very first time, I looked her squarely in the eyes. I smiled, and said "Thank you for the ride to Ralph's. I'll be sure to tell Troy you did exactly as he asked." She went white and made as if to grab for me, but I already had my door open and was half falling, half jumping out of the cab.

Round Eighteen

Despite all the fun, the reality of being fifteen and almost homeless was sinking in. Troy was not able to take care of me all the time, nor was he willing. In the beginning of our relationship he avoided going anywhere without me but as we settled into something like a routine together it became obvious that he needed to do some things alone. Since we were living together I didn't begrudge him these times away, which was fortunate because if it had been otherwise I would have been miserable. Each time he went out without me he had to find somewhere to put me in his absence, usually Eliza's or Ralph's. I couldn't stay at his house without him, he said it wasn't safe.

Typically his solo outings were nothing but afternoons here and there but sometimes he'd know that he'd be gone overnight and in that case I'd sleep over at whichever house I was at. I preferred Eliza's for obvious reasons but actually Ralph (when not surrounded by a gang of people egging him on to idiocy like the village idiot) was surprisingly sweet company as well. So many nights he and I lay on two single mattresses laying end to end on his basement floor, our heads pointing to each other, and he would tell me how much Troy loved me, tell me not to take the issue of Big

Head as hard as I did.

When I stayed with Eliza we sat up all night watching MTV and old black and white movies or just listening to music and talking. She filled me in on gossip from school, I recounted to her my days spent with Troy. Then I'd go to sleep on the awesome pallet we made up in her walk-in closet. She had so many pairs of Converse shoes I used to fall asleep trying to count all the stars. I hadn't always slept in the closet at Eliza's, but since I'd left home and school for good it was a precaution we began to take after her mother asked several unsettling questions about my precise place of residence. My greatest fear was being handed over to the authorities and put into either a youth rehabilitation centre or some sort of foster care. I was horrified at the thought of being lifted out of the only life I knew and could reasonably expect to control, only to be deposited elsewhere that would be little more than a cage of red tape. I didn't want to be taken from Troy. I believed to the core of my being that nobody on earth had any rightful claim over me and I was entirely free to live where I pleased, with whom I pleased. My parents were the only people who could have ever made a claim on me and we mutually didn't want each other. It would be nothing less than kidnapping if I were taken into anyone's custody but my own. I was recklessly and totally in love and though my future remained grey and hazy I was confident that one step at a time Troy and I would get through my adolescence and his mysteries. So long as I had him, I had my home.

The year wore on to autumn, an endless round of larking about enjoying the delights of Lemay, until one balmy night when Troy needed to be off without me. A Big Head night, a brick through the window night, a drinking night, I don't know. He left me with a smile and a kiss, but before many hours had passed I received a message ferried to me through a series of Troy's friends. He had been arrested (for what I never knew) and would be spending the night in jail. I was told not to worry and to stay in one of my usual spare places and wait there until he came for me the next day. There was a problem though. Troy had left me with Ralph intending to be back before nightfall, and on that particular night I had no back up place to sleep. Eliza was away overnight somewhere else. Ralph's Mom had cottoned on to the fact that I was not living at home and declared she would not allow me to sleep over anymore to avoid involvement in any potential trouble I carried with me. She was adamant that I must leave his house by midnight.

Not wishing to show my distress, I pretended that all this subterfuge to excuse my existence wasn't hurtful, but in truth it was almost unbearable. There were so many times that I felt like nothing more than an unwanted parcel being passed from one pair of hands to another. The worst thing though would have been for me to show how alone and increasingly broken I was feeling. I could not remember a time when any perceived weakness in me would not have been joyfully exploited to hurt me more.

So it was that I decided to be left alone at the twenty-four hour Lemay Steak 'n Shake while I thought of what to do. I was facing my first night of sleeping outside and suddenly, outside seemed too big and dark. After several hours sitting in Steak 'n Shake nursing a pot of coffee I began to be frightened by the enquiring looks being thrown my way. I cast my mind about and quickly dismissed sleeping in the cemetery across the road as too frightening and Troy's back yard as too dangerous. There was only one secluded place that I knew I could remain out of sight in and that was underneath a small bridge near Ralph's house. It was a couple of miles away and sewage ran down the middle but by climbing up the slanted concrete walls either side I knew you reached a ledge several feet wide, directly underneath the road above. It wasn't a lovely prospect to walk that far alone in the dark and then sleep under a bridge, but it was the only idea I could come up with.

I sat in Steak 'n Shake and watched the clock tick to midnight while I tried to work up the courage to begin walking to the bridge. But suddenly the long walk down Lemay Ferry Road seemed infinite. I quaked; I didn't want to go there. What if I wouldn't be alone there? I didn't want to sleep on concrete. Suddenly I desperately wanted my own bed, and I would have given all but Troy to have one that belonged to me permanently. A bed and four solid walls! These simple objects we so often take for granted, and they were all I prayed for. I wanted it so badly that I took a risk which was, for me, far greater than that I took when I left my Mother's house for Troy's. I fished around in my pocket, produced some quarters for the payphone and I called my dad.

Round Nineteen

I'd had his phone number memorised for as long as I could remember. Still, every time he spoke to me he gave me his phone number as if speaking to a new acquaintance and I patiently listened without contradicting him. I had even set it to a tune in my head. But never before had I called it unsolicited and rarely had I called it at all. Certainly in my wildest dreams I never thought I would call him in the middle of the night asking for help. My resolve to call and ask him for help had been strong while I sat at the table in Steak 'n Shake. But as I crossed the dark parking lot to reach the payphone my nerves quickened and I began to reconsider the potential merits of sleeping under the bridge. I stood and deliberated one last time and you know what I remembered then, before dropping the quarters in and dialling his number? I told myself I was calling a man who was willing to jump out of a helicopter to save lives. Surely he wouldn't turn his own young daughter away and make her sleep on the street. It would be mortifying for me but he would come. After all, I'd never asked him for help before. This was his chance.

I'd never put a foot out of line from what he wanted from me. I never made a single unwanted peep. Surely calling in one parental chip every decade and a half was my due? Still, we spoke so rarely that he didn't even know that I hadn't been living with my Mother for so many months, which meant there was going to be a lot of explaining to do. There was an expectation from my father especially that I would be responsible and clever and succeed, where my sister was deemed to have failed by conceiving and dropping out of school at sixteen. I felt I had to live up to that. But living with my boyfriend, homeless *and* a drop out by fifteen really took the biscuit. I'd gone miles further and faster than the recognised dedicated rebel of the family. These sorts of bold actions were never expected from me.

As these thoughts raced through my mind I decided it'd be best if I quickly gagged them. I couldn't do what seemed to be my only other choice – walk the miles to that bridge and then sleep under it all night long. I simply had to ask for help. His phone rang once, twice – I resisted the urge to hang up while mentally forming the case I was about to put before him.

My regal, impenetrable Father finally answered the phone and he was already angry at whoever had the temerity to dial his number at that time of night. I felt slightly dizzy. Gathering my courage about me I introduced myself and began by apologising for calling him at such a late hour. Then I tried, badly, to explain to him exactly what I

143

needed and what was happening. The silence on his end of the line indicated nothing but growing contempt and fury. Stuttering as I always did when speaking to him I tried to explain the contract Carol and I had written and why. I said I had been staying with my boyfriend. I rushed in that it wasn't as bad as that sounded, knowing he would assume I was having sex which certainly would not help my cause. I explained that a crisis had happened and this one night only I had nowhere to go, nowhere to sleep. Could he please, please come and get me and let me stay at his house only until the next day? I reassured him that Troy would collect me as soon as he was able, or my father could drop me off back in Lemay the following day. After several awkward minutes of me putting my case forward while his silence rang in my ears like blows to the head, I finally summed up, asking if he would please come and get me and please let me stay the night in his house; his beautiful Arts & Crafts house, full of antiques in a gated community. I had never been welcome there but I was asking anyway.

I finished my brief and desperate speech and there was a long, crackling silence on the line for an uncomfortable, punishing amount of time. I thought for a second that perhaps the line had gone dead. Then he asked me why I was calling him instead of my mother. The first sucker punch of the conversation, delivered. I had thought I'd explained that but I tried again saying she and I couldn't have anything to do with each other anymore, that it was far too dangerous and I hadn't been living with her for some time. His response was that if I had a problem with my mother I should speak to her

144

about it. I was floundering. I wasn't asking him for advice on dealing with Carol, which I knew to be a pointless endeavour. I was asking him to help me right then, that night, and it was not looking like it was going in that direction.

He had known for years about Carol's temper and how Elaine and I suffered. During our semi-annual visits he often casually asked us if she was any better though he never replied when we said things were as crazy as always. He himself often said he left her largely because she was impossible to reason with. He was asking me to do the impossible and clearly setting himself apart from the situation. Gathering all my courage I said that I couldn't go to her, that she wouldn't let me in anyway and I badly needed his help because I had nowhere to sleep that night. I asked once again if he could please come and get me. He laughed bitterly and said "You really expect me to drive all the way across St. Louis because you've got yourself in trouble?" Second blow. This wasn't heroic at all. Self-loathing began to consume me. This was my fault, I shouldn't have called him. Now he would never think I was good enough for him. Fifteen years' worth of working to try to impress him all ruined after one terrible phone call. My eyes closed against these thoughts but he continued driving the knife even deeper with one small sentence that effectively ended our conversation, permanently: "You know I never even wanted to be a Father. This isn't my problem."

I held the phone in my hands but it dropped slightly down from my ear. "Oh." I said, stupidly. I mumbled another apology and hung up. I'd made such a complete fool of myself defending him against my mother and sister for so many years. And he did not and would not ever love me. My mother said I was unlovable, she said she should have drowned me at birth, she called me the anti-Christ. Why, why did they have me? Twelve years married, trying to conceive for the last four of those finally resulting in me. But I was utterly despised and both of my parents made it clear their lives would have been immeasurably better had I never existed.

Like a sleepwalker I mechanically put one foot ahead of the other to head to the bridge. Cars honked at me, passing men offered me money for sex as I picked up my pace and ran past them. One man pulled over and offered me a lift which I declined. I reached the bridge with aching legs and back. I scaled up the wall and rested my body along the ledge under the road, feeling it shake above me and hearing the roll of tires overhead. I tried not to dwell on the irrational fear that the bridge would collapse onto me under the weight of traffic I heard above. I reminded myself countless times that hundreds of cars drove over that bridge without incident twenty-four hours a day, mentally slapping myself across the face. I huddled myself into as small a ball as I could manage and prayed that no other homeless people would be joining me that night, it was a popular location for rough sleepers. I thought of all the people driving over me with the cars they could afford and the houses they were heading home to and wondered what they would think if they knew a young girl was curled up beneath their road. Would anyone help me? Or would I just end up a statistic. At least when I was fighting with my mother I knew how to fight back. There was nothing I could control about this situation.

The sewage drained down to a dark and winding overgrown path under the bridge. I knew where it went; if you entered the network of tunnels and followed them long enough you would end up at a deserted quarry. I'd spent my thirteenth summer breaking into that quarry every day by walking across a hundred foot long railway bridge. The buildings were abandoned, but two horses lived there. I was drawn to them, and the space the quarry gave me when I was the only human in it. Eventually I was caught breaking in by the owner, but after apologising and explaining that I was there because I loved the horses, she offered me the daily job of their grooming and care. Through the quarry and later with Troy I'd spent countless hours exploring the sewage tunnels under South County. The network often created a sort of underground shortcut from one place to another. A lot of people used that needle scattered path, most of whom were junkies. I hoped none would come along that night. Sleeping wasn't really an option. It was too difficult to stop being watchful for someone approaching. The concrete I was lying on was too hard to do anything but bruise my protruding ribs when I tried to lie down. I waited in a state of alertness and discomfort while trying to project my mind into a dream world, far, far away. I thought of Troy sitting in a jail cell. I wondered if the police had hurt him, or if he'd been hurt in some

147

other way. I wondered if he was thinking about me, how he would react when he discovered how I had spent my night. I also resented him the safety of jail.

By the time daylight came I was grateful for it because I was sore and restless. I was impatient to find some friends and then be reunited with Troy. I wanted to put the whole horrible night behind me and get back to the life I had become accustomed to. But there were other factors at play that night, which I knew nothing about. Elaine had returned from Florida some weeks before, and on finding her little sister missing from the family home was not as complacent as our Mother. She set about trying to locate me herself, and came up with some damn good leads. Namely, that I had been spotted at Ralph's house, right next to my bridge. This little bit of information landed in my sister's lap right around the same time that Troy was being arrested. She phoned the police with it, shortly before I phoned our dad for help, reporting me as a missing runaway and giving Ralph's street address as the best starting place to search for me.

And so it was that when I came blinking out from underneath my bridge, stiff and eager for food and drink, I was greeted by three police cars, lights on and officers with guns drawn walking towards me. My heart sank like an anchor. There was no way I could run away from these police, they had me not only cornered but also broken with exhaustion. I said a silent "I'm sorry" to Troy for letting us both down. My night of bravery was for nothing in the face of these higher powers. I immediately realised that it was unlikely I would be back with him any time soon. One of us arrested the day after the other, but my arrest would be handled very differently from his. As soon as I realised I'd be taken into custody I knew it was essential I did not mention Troy. The last thing I wanted was to have him charged with kidnapping a minor. For an endless amount of time I would be questioned as to where I had been all those absent months, but every time I just shook my head and remained silent.

As they handcuffed me and told me that I'd been reported as a runaway, I actually laughed out loud. A runaway! The day I left my mother's house she had written and signed a piece of paper (no doubt since destroyed) saying she was absolved from all parental responsibilities for me and then held the door open while I packed! Only hours before I'd asked my Father, who held joint custody of me, for shelter under his roof and I was denied. I was no more a runaway than they were parents. That night signalled the end of the life I had known and hoped for.

My mind went blank with panic as I realised the police were driving me to the locally infamous and dreaded Highland Hospital for bad children. It was one very small step down from juvenile prison, the main difference being Highland offered "mental health help" and was paid for by health insurance. In reality it was a storage facility for those too bad to be accepted in their homes but not bad enough for juvi. It was the most feared place for anyone under eighteen with a less than perfect life. Getting in was easy; getting out was nigh on impossible and the object within was punishment and brainwashing. I would have preferred to have been taken back to my mother's where at least I knew I could soon escape again. This was the worst possible thing that could have happened to me.

Round Twenty

Highland Pea Green. An absolutely unique and easily identifiable sickly shade of yellow-green forever recorded in my memory, and never to be confused with moss, forest, asparagus or fern. The colour is only found in the peas served every three days for dinner and every other day for lunch in the Highland Hospital Cafeteria. It is such an unappetising shade of wasted pigmentation that if one has never been forced to become uncomfortably acquainted with it then one does not have the capacity to imagine how it might compel you to contemplate precisely how badly Man has distorted Nature. It was the colour and symbol for my new permanent residence: bars on the windows, code keys on every door, random room and body searches, Highland Pea Green

When I wasn't queuing up for my food I was marched from one therapy session to another. I immediately disabused the sports therapist of any notion he may have had that I took physical education seriously, saying I'd prefer another round at arts and crafts. He thought he could make me join in by repeatedly bouncing balls towards me that I silently and stilly let bounce by. I'd return the same steady gaze to him that I used on my Mother, the school counsellor, the interrogating police, Big Head and everyone who had come before him. This new life had been thrust upon me before I had time to understand what was even happening and it only reinforced my tendency to protest through inaction or a few sharp words.

It was nothing short of a prison to me, a prison my father's health insurance paid for. If I had come from a poorer family I would have been deposited in the rougher juvenile detention. For my entire childhood I had run mostly free, unchecked and expected to provide for myself, unless I was staying with my Grandparents. Since the move to St. Louis when I was ten I had been left completely to my own devices and I had just spent the better part of a year living wild and free with my boyfriend and friends. I'd even made an agreement with my parent to remain independent. After all that, to be locked in a sterile room was like caging a wild animal. I did often want to scream and batter the door, I fantasised about throwing a chair through my bedroom window and trying to jump out. But I saw how futile it was when my fellow inmates did those things. They were always wrestled to the ground by the ever present security, put into a straightjacket and locked away in solitary confinement. In my own way I was just as difficult. I went mute and used every authority figure in that place, from the physical therapy coach to the therapists and doctors as targets to practise my verbal acrobatics on, choosing to say nothing that did not relate to my immediate freedom. They wanted me to break down with a slew of emotional confessions to be used against me later on and I wasn't going to humour that desire. Sometimes I would view those workers as individuals rather than simply a cog in the machine I was trapped in; individuals working with everyone else's off casts, some because they clearly cared and others because they relished power over the helpless. But most of the time I despised them.

In the beginning the doctors asked for weekly supervised visits with my Mom. These were mediated by the doctors themselves, social workers, therapists and psychiatrists but they still managed to erupt into World War III. Our visits took place in a soundproof room with shatter proof windows. A square table was bolted down in the centre of the room and several chairs surrounded it. We were questioned relentlessly on family dynamics and particularly that final crucial day when I left home. More than once when our "discussions" got out of control she and I would fire words across the table at each other, each seeming to forget we were surrounded by professionals observing our every move, notes being scribbled around us. And so it was that every professional in that room heard me corner her into saying everything I knew she wanted to say, everything she had said to me my entire life. I pushed her. I pushed her back for every time I had been pushed up to that moment.

Insult after insult was lobbed at me while I sat back and smirked at her, driving her on.

I asked her to remember the stairs, what happened on them, to remember the lock on the door and the cockroaches in the basement. Why was I made to sleep in there when my bedroom was given to Elaine and her boyfriend? Was I ever pushed down, waking up the next day to find the door locked and a cockroach on my cheek? I asked her to tell everybody else in the room what should have happened to me when I was born. Every time she told me to shut up I asked her about another incident I could remember as I watched her face turn a familiar shade of rage red. When she finally snapped it happened so quickly, that I'm grateful life had made me dodge enough projectiles until I'd got good at it. She picked up an empty chair next to her and threw it across the table at my head. I ducked and it hit the shatterproof glass. I was shaken, almost gleefully delirious, terrified as I always was in the face of her temper, but triumphant. I knew I had intentionally goaded her but I'd been given the result I was hoping for, primarily to show every person in that room that what I had reported about living with her was true. She vindicated me in front of the only people who mattered then – the ones who would control when I was released and into whose custody. It was exactly what I'd hoped she'd do and it almost seemed too easy when it was done. When I caught my breath I remember laughing a little and saying "Tsk tsk Mom. You're not hiding the truth very well" as she was escorted away by security.

My psychiatrist admitted her to the adult section of Highland that day, but being an adult she could only be legally held for forty-eight hours without her consent, at which point she promptly checked herself out. I actually saw her checking out at the desk as I was marched past to another therapy session. After that she only came occasionally, when called in by the doctors. My father never came. She was assigned parenting counselling, though I could have told them that was absolutely pointless. The only counselling she truly craved was tutoring on how to build a time machine and not conceive me. Or go through the pregnancy just for the pleasure of finally drowning me at birth. She certainly hated me enough to. But in the face of every shred of evidence proclaiming otherwise, she was determined to hold to the fact that she had been the ideal mother. She even said to me that she had not once made a single mistake raising Elaine and I, which was such an outrageously bold statement it still leaves me at a loss. You cannot reason with someone who on one day can abuse you with a murderous glint in their eyes but the next day claim to have no memory of it. To even look at you as if you were insane, to say you were insane for hallucinating such atrocities when the bruises were there on flesh and decorations left smashed. I'd experienced her complete denials too many times to ever expect a confession or apology. If I had grown up in the same age of technology that I'm writing this in I could have recorded her violence. But it was left to her memory versus mine. Of course there were times when I wondered if I was the crazy one. But then I would recall something that left physical proof, something I knew I could prove if given the chance. And I learned to trust myself to tell the truth, even if I sometimes delivered it in an antagonistic manner. I know that at the time of her attack in Highland she was given a diagnosis of schizophrenia but that

154

came to nothing and I don't really know what's wrong with her. I can't put labels other than "dangerous" and "erratic" on Carol.

The time of my confinement that I enjoyed the most was when I was left alone unsupervised in my room. I did what I could to gain the trust of the workers on my ward, which to be honest wasn't that difficult after they had the privilege of meeting my mother several times. She so obviously hated the very air I breathed that it didn't take much convincing for them to see me as a young girl who had been driven to step outside the bounds of society. My situation was easier to feel sympathy for than that of most of my fellow inmates who were in for petty crime or drugs, though I'd hazard a guess that most of their families weren't so different from mine. The result of good behaviour was being left in relative peace in my room with my books when not obliged to attend a therapy session. Eventually I gained the right to have pen and paper which was like all of my Christmas' coming at once.

Troy and I weren't able to contact each other but somehow he got all of my bags delivered to the hospital for me, I believe via Eliza, so I had my clothes and my precious books. Of course there were many items in my bags that I wasn't allowed to have so those were put in lock up until my eventual release.

I lived in Troy's shirt and refused to let the staff wash it lest it lose the scent of him.

He'd given it to me one chilly summer's night. Troy had found it months before we met in the dumpsters behind the Lemay Salvation Army. We were often there, both to browse the shop floor and the dumpsters out back that often offered up treasures. For some reason this shirt had been thrown out despite being in its original packaging. It was the loveliest soft green flannel you could imagine. The night he gave it to me we were lying on the hood of his car talking and I began shivering with cold. He took his flannel off, wearing a t-shirt underneath it, and wrapped it around my body. It was comically huge on me but I loved it better than any other physical object. It was as if a magical spell was wrapped around us that night and the shirt was an essential ingredient. I didn't assume it was mine to keep so when we eventually returned to Troy's house I was dreading having to give it up. We walked up the stairs and into his bedroom hand in hand, neither of us wanting to speak and break the spell we were under. When we reached his room I reluctantly moved to take the shirt off but he stopped me with his hands and lips and told me to keep it for him.

Every day I asked when I would be released and every day I was told "Not until we know where you're going." Every day I argued that they could see for themselves that my parents didn't want me and with the exception of one damned bad night I had lived successfully on my own for almost a year. I begged again and again to make them hold to the contract my mother and I had drawn up – there were many legal precedents for children being emancipated from their parents and I pleaded that our contract be recognised as legally binding. All of my carefully framed arguments fell on deaf ears, eyes down, shaking heads. Nothing. I would be there until eventually.

Round Twenty One

Most other patients had to have their door open, a roommate and room checks as frequently as quarter-hourly so I was extremely lucky to have a private room which remained relatively undisturbed for up to three hours at a time. When possible I made good use of that time.

I found cigarettes hidden in some concealed pockets of some of the clothes that were delivered in my case and sent a silent thank you to whoever had been clever and kind enough to smuggle them in to me. However I had no lighter. There had been one in my case but it was one of the objects found and kept away from me. The lack of fire was a pretty serious impediment to smoking and it wasn't until I sat in a sterilised room with a useless pack of cigarettes that I felt I could possibly go insane from the deprivation of the freedoms I was used to. Many of the hours that I was left alone in my room, I did nothing but think of how to spark a flame.

I finally worked out that if I took a shower, if they heard the shower running, they wouldn't enter my room. There was a hair dryer chained to the wall. I ran the shower but stayed outside of it and turned the hair dryer on. I held the nozzle down flat to the ground until it over heated, so that finally it shorted out. When I lifted it up the bars underneath the front grill were bright burning orange. It worked just like a car cigarette lighter. I slid my cigarette between the grill bars and lit it, then stepped into the shower and blew the smoke up out of the air vent above it. I did this often, carefully rationing the cigarettes I had. Amazingly, I never got caught. I was known to often have long showers, and for some mysterious reason the maintenance man had to make regular trips to my room to mend the apparently malfunctioning hair dryer. If ever there was proof I grew up watching MacGyver, there it is, but in truth I had learned an enormous amount about survival and creativity from watching Troy. I've never stopped thinking like that; recently I was in a hotel and room service delivered me raw eggs. I poached them in the coffee machine in my room and silently thanked the universe for teaching me to have low expectations and know how to make do, a place from where the only way is up.

The heating element in that hair dryer was cold compared to the rage forming a tight ball of fire in my belly. It wasn't just the fact that I was a prisoner of the system as I had feared for so long. It was being kept away from Troy. It was knowing how very joyful Big Head would be with me locked away, knowing she would do everything she could to turn him against me. My deepest worst fears were playing out – that I would be out of sight and out of mind for too long and I would lose him. I believed he could do anything except possibly fight alone against the demons he needed to fight in order to retain the humanity we both needed him to have, the humanity he needed in order to be the man I loved. And he had so very much to fight against. I wanted to get out and get to him, assess the damage and start waging my campaign to undo it.

Memories of my time with Troy, so free and careless in the beautiful long St. Louis summer nights began to seem like fantastic hallucinations slipping further away from a cold new reality. So each day I replayed to myself every precious memory, to fix them in my mind forever. I tried to hold onto my original faith in us, faith that had been badly tested but remained. I knew he would likely be carrying on with his life much as he had before, only without me, and whatever thoughts he held on my absence he would be unlikely to discuss with anyone other than perhaps a word or two with Ralph. I knew very well how many drinking nights he would end up in bed with Big Head. I was never allowed to live under that much delusion regarding his moods and needs. I tried to hope we could pick up where we left off when I was released. It was an utterly stupid thing to hope for.

Unfortunately I realised quickly that the fastest route out of Highland was the appearance of total compliance, which went directly against my instinct to fight back against anything I perceived to be untrue or unjust. Since I believed to the core of my being that the very fact that I was being held in that building was a deep injustice I was never without a subject on which I had to hold my tongue. "Why was I locked up instead of my parents?" I asked over and over again. Hadn't it been wrong for my father to refuse me shelter the only night I needed it? Didn't Carol's tirades prove I was justified in leaving her home? They were the real criminals there, but they were over eighteen which clearly made all the difference. "The law" was the answer always given to me, to which I replied that "the law" was flawed and flying in the face of the logic of the situation. I was fighting a moral case, not a practical one.

My release required more than simply good behaviour. They wouldn't let me go until I had somewhere stable to live and that was proving to be the sticking point. Visits with my mother still had to be attended by security so it wasn't looking good on that front. My father told the doctors to leave him alone, that he was footing the bill and nothing more should be expected from him. However, strangely enough there was an offer from my father's sister, whom I had never met, to move to Colorado and live with her family. I was shocked that this person whom I had only ever regarded as a ridiculously wealthy stranger was offering me a home, and for a moment I liked the idea a little bit. But Colorado wasn't Lemay. At any rate I believe the offer was retracted. Then boarding school was suggested but both of my parents refused to pay for that. I felt like banging my head against the table as social worker after social worker came up with institution after institution that I wasn't going to be welcome in. The solution was obvious to me – just release me to myself and be done with all of this nonsense. I even asked if they would consider letting Troy become my legal guardian, though I still refused to say where I had been living before the morning I was taken into custody. I was gambling that he wouldn't say no if approached with the chance to take legal custody of me; as odd as that might sound it married up to the kind of relationship we had, which was one of necessity and a wish to remain together. But that suggestion was instantly dismissed, unsurprisingly.

Round Twenty Two

Other than the ever entertaining antics of my fellow residents, only one incident of note happened during my long incarceration. My primary psychiatrist was a dark skinned Muslim man. Every few days he and I sat across a desk in his distinguished office. It was another privilege I was given, most residents had their sessions in the lockdown room. He felt I was no danger and (correctly) thought that I might be more responsive speaking to him if he allowed me into his office, where I enjoyed browsing the books on the shelves. I liked him, but I tried to be careful not to show it. The whole source of my power against every law, parent and Highland employee controlling my fate was my well-honed passive resistance and ability to relentlessly communicate only the message I wanted to repeat.

This particular psychiatrist spoke to me as his intellectual equal, which was a powerful inducement to someone like me. I had known so few people who thought I was wonderful, or even worthy of anything other than abuse or neglect. I'd spent most of my life feeling like a piece of shit someone forgot to flush down the toilet. It was flattering to be spoken to as an intelligent individual, even offering me philosophical debates in which I was not scoffed at, by someone with so many degrees on the wall. He reminded me a little of Mr Wilson in the way he had of speaking, as if he understood everything I wasn't saying.

Over the course of several weeks I began to trust this particular psychiatrist quite a bit, and although an extremely formal atmosphere remained between us I felt at ease speaking with him and enjoyed the debates we had. But only as long as he didn't make any attempt to try to draw me out in a way that made me feel he was trying to trap me into personal confessions rather than intellectual meanderings. I had the sense that he was sometimes subtly trying to understand my heart rather than the part of my mind I was willing to share. When such moments came I went back to muteness and lost a little bit of respect for him because he refused to accept how futile that was. The only justification they needed to keep me in for a year or more was to prove that I was mentally unstable. Falling apart from having my emotions prodded was unacceptable.

Our moment of confrontation came when he pushed the button I'm sure he knew I had to react to. During one of our meetings he began talking about what he knew of Troy from the police report. This psychiatrist likely knew Troy was the key to me, and so he drew out his file and began reading off facts gathered from the police. I listened silently but felt the familiar rage building up within me.

He began pushing me about Troy, asking me if a known alcoholic with his lifestyle could really be worth my stubborn loyalty and future. He asked if I loved Troy. If I thought he loved me in return. I said nothing, but fought back tears, remembering a sweet moment Troy and I shared so painfully recently but now a world away. One of those quiet moments in the middle of the night in an expansive park, finally alone after dropping everyone else off. We were lying on the grass side by side holding hands, watching the stars and murmuring words of love. Of course I loved him. I knew and understood him in a personally unprecedented way. How cruel to ask me that while actively working to keep me away from him. He asked me what I thought Troy was doing just that moment; did I think he was being as loyal to me as I was being to him? Question after question came while I sat shaking, trying to form some response that would shut this down. I had a quick moment of clarity when I realised his brief was to "Decontaminate Girl from Boy". The fact that he couldn't see any deeper than that, not try to see that there might be more to Troy and I than those bare police reports, both disgusted me and indicated he lacked the insight I had credited him with. And so I struck back. Badly, below the belt and below myself, but I struck back.

For a moment I gazed sightlessly into the arm of the brown leather sofa that I sat on, not entirely sure what would come out of my mouth, only knowing it would be vicious. I scanned the certificates, books and paintings lining his walls while he waited for me to answer. Then I turned to face him and met his eyes with as much contempt as I could muster. I asked him if he understood how much I loved Troy. He said yes. I said that was a good thing that he knew that, because he could never hope to understand me if he didn't understand that. I paused and scanned him with my eyes, as rudely and intrusively as I had been peered at every single day of my hospital stay. Then I said, without the clarification I would have normally added, "He has 'SKIN' and 'NAZI' tattooed on the knuckles of his two hands."

I forced myself to look him in the eyes and smile as I allowed the clear implications of my statement drop like a bomb in the room. I was looking at a dark skinned man whom I knew very well Skinheads and Nazis would have liked to see strung up. He might have been the one person I had time for in that hospital, and I might not have meant what I said at all, but I could not allow him to think this part of me was open for one of our debates. Troy represented one of two lines in the sand that could not be crossed with me, the other being my resolute belief in my freedom and self-ownership.

Inwardly I felt myself shrinking into shame. I knew right away I should have used my own powers of argument rather than Troy's tattoos to strike back at this man. I hadn't just been racist, I'd been cowardly, the two so easily going hand in hand. I'd hid behind the very things that bore the man I loved down and betrayed every core belief of universal freedom I'd become so notorious fighting for. It was the first and last moment of blatant racism in my life and as much as I wish I had never done that, I own it because it was my error and my lesson to learn. I tried not to squirm or apologise, unable to see a way out of this without losing every shred of self-control.

His reaction was perfect, swift and put me in my place right where I needed to go. He was completely unruffled, and even looked intrigued. He cocked his chin in the air and looked down his nose at me, paused, and said, "And they, the Nazis and the Skinheads, they would have me killed, skinned alive even; my family and children too, just for being born. Is that correct?" I nodded, feeling sick. My eyes darted to the photos of his children on the desk. He continued, "Troy has those tattoos on his fingers, he may hold those beliefs and he may not. But I'm not interested in Troy. Is that what *you* believe should happen to me?" I shook my head no, choking on my own tongue, unable to utter a word. I felt I had deeply wronged everyone mentioned in the entire conversation. I wanted to try to form some kind of explanation, apology, and defence. But it wasn't the time for me to argue back. It was the time for me to absorb the guilt I was due. Our session ended at that stage of silence and I was escorted back to my room. I know why I did it. The ignorance of youth aside, I needed a weapon against this man who was getting dangerously close to forcing open every violent stored up

165

emotion I held tightly inside of me.

Soon after those reckless words left my mouth, I had a moment of greater understanding about Troy's tattoos, though I would never be able to think of them without feeling sick and broken hearted. He and I were strangely alike, both proud with a lot to prove. But we came from very different economic backgrounds. Despite the deprivations I suffered while living with my mother I at least had the health insurance provided by my father, something Troy never had. He had also suffered more severe abuse than I did growing up. Neither of us had been dealt a winning hand in life but his was worse than mine. So while my stupidity occurred in a psychiatrist's office with no witnesses, his happened in a drunken stupor in a tattoo parlour.

Round Twenty Three

I was in Highland for about ten weeks. Eventually I pretty much gave up arguing for anything but release on any terms. I was fully institutionalised and began to fear what would happen in the outside world when I was released. I'd learned the hospital ropes so well; how to get through the day trading pleasantries with the cafeteria ladies, adhering to the schedule set for me with cheerfulness and persistence and never becoming involved with the antics of my fellow patients. Sometimes it seemed safer and easier to stop fighting for release and instead stay in there as long as possible, but I never let that thought take hold. In fact every time it flitted across my mind I gave myself a mental slap in the face.

The last two weeks in Highland were spent solidly in that soundproofed room with its bolted down table, undergoing negotiations about where I would live upon my release. I suspect my Dad saw the mounting bill as the weeks turned into months and declared he would not pay for me to stay indefinitely. Thanks to her own financial incentive (the desire to avoid more bills herself) and the efforts of my hospital team, my mother finally agreed to allow me to come home. When I was told this, I felt one part relief that it was over and one part furious indignation that they were returning me to her, despite everything. There truly was no other way. I would have to accept her as my authority figure if I was ever going to leave the hospital. I honestly don't think that my medical team were happy to release me to her after all the confrontations they witnessed, but she was obliged by law to care for me - leverage used against her by the team in negotiations. I wasn't happy either but I correctly suspected that my mother was agreeing to this because she was just as backed into a corner as I was. I knew she didn't want me so I also correctly assumed that while I might be released into her care no one would know if I then left her house again. Of course I didn't tell my social workers this insight.

Round Twenty Four

Carol came to collect me on a beautiful early spring day. I remember her waiting while the staff on my ward bid me a fond and affectionate farewell. She snapped at me to hurry up. A few of the staff looked at me sympathetically as I walked out, blinking in the daylight.

The drive home was awkward, of course, because we were alone together for the first time in the better part of a year. It was very strange for me to see the sky, be in a moving car and feel the fresh air after being inside for so long. I believe she and I were both trying to think of how to get out of this new living arrangement that had been forced upon us. Without speaking we went into her house together. I began to carry my bags into my old bedroom, and she stood watching me, waiting for a reaction. When I opened my bedroom door every single thing I had left in it – every possession I had ever owned but those essentials that I took with me to Troy's, had been thrown away. Every picture, ornament, piece of furniture, item of clothing and record was gone, along with my stereo and even my bed. The room had been repainted. Standing in the doorway looking at an entirely empty room that had once held hundreds of my possessions, so many even paid for with my own hard earned money, I thought that might actually have been the most sadistic thing she had ever done to me. For a moment I wished the doctors who had just released me into her care could see what I was seeing. But I felt so defeated and exhausted I just squared my shoulders and walked in the room, closing the door behind me. I wasn't going to give her the satisfaction of an argument over it. I didn't bother unpacking my bags, the only way in which I temporarily "moved in" was by making a pallet on the floor with spare blankets. I reasoned that it was luxury compared to sleeping under the bridge.

The message sent loud and clear in that empty room was that I was only welcome there until I found somewhere else to go. Even if I had wanted one, there would be no reconciliation. We'd long gone past that point. I was bewildered and terrified and I avoided my mother like a toxic roommate, spending every minute in her house locked in my empty room. I had just turned sixteen and my ability to simply "move out" wasn't as straight-forward as all that. Although I'd had my first job at thirteen I had no income, car or indeed proof of ID at that point. The hill I saw ahead of me, waiting to be climbed, loomed like a giant's foot hovering over my head. I knew that she was still receiving thousands of dollars every month in child support for Elaine and I, neither of whom lived with her. That was the money that I felt entitled to in order to provide for my basic needs, so I asked her again when she'd start signing the cheques over to me. She looked at me as if I had lost my mind. Perhaps I had. She said if I wanted more money to ask my Dad myself. As if I would do that after the things he said to me that night I slept under the bridge! She knew all about that phone call. There was no point in arguing the hypocrisy of banning her children -- both of whose lives were falling apart -- from living in her house, while she blissfully went on weekly shopping sprees, spending court-ordered money intended for their care.

I had been away for almost three months. Ten weeks in Lemay time is roughly equivalent to three years Earth time. Lemay is the Land of the Surreal, no time line goes unmolested there, no coincidence unexploited, no straight line left untangled. Lemay was made for the John Waters movies that circulated amongst its residents like guidebooks. I was back in Carol's house, but not in school and with a very questionable place in my former group of friends. I had been allowed to speak to Eliza once towards the end of my stay in Highland. When I asked how Troy was she said she had hardly seen him and all she had heard was that he'd gone wild with drinking. It wasn't what I wanted to hear but I wasn't surprised. I was going to try to get back to where I had been with him, but secretly I wondered if he hadn't been celebrating his freedom while I was in Highland. I could only try not to be smothered under everything collapsing on top of me.

I saw Troy for the first time a week after my release. I had paged him on the day I came home, so our first meeting began with me feeling angry and resentful for being ignored for seven days. I didn't want to argue with him though; I just wanted to see how we would interact with each other, how different it would be from when we lived together and how much work I'd have to do to get us back there. I found him changed, but could get no concrete explanation as to why. I knew that so much could happen in a few months, so much had happened to me but I hadn't been living in Lemay time. He didn't meet my eyes very often. He seemed too nervous to do something as simple as touch my hand. His mood was more erratic, one moment laughing and teasing me, making me believe all was well only to become absolutely withdrawn the next moment. It was awful, like watching the threads of my life unravel through my fingers. The one single thing I knew how to love and trust was slipping away. I never asked him to explain his actions while I had been gone; I only wanted him to be the way he was before.

He still held me at times and kissed me, but with one excuse or another he never seemed to have the time for me he had before. He certainly made no offers for me to go back to living with him. Once or twice I asked him if he had stopped loving me and he said no. I asked if he had another girlfriend – not another Big Head but a real girlfriend. He said no. He said he'd fucked Big Head more than he used to while I'd been gone but she was as stupid as she'd ever been. Of course I wanted to scream when I heard that. But he was a puzzle and I couldn't stop trying to solve him. Everything about him seemed far more serious than he did before. His humour was one of the best things about him but every time I saw him after my release it was a struggle to get a small smile onto his face.

I didn't like the idea of fawning over Troy. One thing he had always loved about me is that I didn't cower under his gargantuan personality or try to flatter him the way many other people did. I didn't think it would make him love me any more if I suddenly began begging and making a fool of myself. I was still confident that he and I were *he and I*, so I decided to wait him out. I wanted him to see me glowing and on top of the world, as he had seen me before. I was sure if he saw me confident and carrying on without him he would see whatever it was that had first made him see me as the someone he didn't want to go without. So much greater than my fledging plan to entice him back was the unshakable faith I would not let go of that despite the issues we both lived with we would find our way back together. I literally couldn't comprehend how it could be any other way.

Only a few times as we sat on my mother's front step in the middle of the night did he drop his head into my lap as he had done so many times before. I stroked his hair and knew that he was still mine. But he would never say what he was thinking and I only needed to look at his face to know he was thinking deep and dangerous thoughts. Once or twice he promised me things would be like they used to be soon, he asked me to please be patient with him. I was able to give him patience, but he wasn't the only one with problems. Carol was getting increasingly aggressive as the days turned to weeks and I was unable to find a place to go to. The threat of social services still loomed large enough that she wouldn't kick me out again (yet), but it was clear the clock was ticking.

About a month after my release from Highland we were sitting together on my front step. Troy was in a buoyant mood, more like his old self, but he suddenly became quieter and surprised me by telling me that he'd made a couple of futile attempts to see me when I'd been in Highland. He said that several times he'd parked his car in the parking lot and scanned the windows, wondering which one I was in. He even said he had tried to think of a way to break me out but he was never able to come up with anything. Once he walked up to the front desk and asked to see me but he was turned away. Troy had me in stitches with laughter as he described the look of shock on the hospital receptionist's face when he sauntered in and casually asked to be taken to me; he was an excellent mimic. I was humbled and surprised, as well as grateful that during those long endless weeks he had been thinking of me at least a little, as I had thought of little else but him. I told him that any escape attempt would have been futile and only landed him in jail. I described how every single door had a key code lock on it, the security guards posted everywhere, and what it felt like to live without fresh air. That was something I vividly remember, what the fresh air felt like on my face when I walked out the day I was released. It was so sensual I marvelled that I had never in my whole life noticed or appreciated the way air cushioned and caressed your body.

After these shared confidences Troy told me he was sorry I had been taken in and sorry he hadn't been able to get me out earlier. I chided him and told him that he made me happier than he could ever know and he couldn't be blamed for my extended stay in the pea green machine, but he just shook his head. He couldn't understand how much it meant to me that he hadn't always been as far away from me as I had felt during my residence in Highland. I was beyond touched that he had done all of that, and equally sad to see him feel guilty for a result neither of us could have avoided.

Round Twenty Five

Although Highland was in the past, it battered our relationship. The present was all about traversing the wild landscape left from the storm. Troy and I carried on seeing each other on these new terms for almost the same length of time I'd spent in Highland. Each day life at home became tenser and I searched for a way to get back out of Carol's house. I was beginning to form tentative plans on how I might be able to live independently, without even Troy. But I still couldn't help but hope that one day soon Troy would find his way out of this trap he seemed to be in, drive up to my house, tell me to pack my bags and leave with him for the second time.

I was wrong.

The last time I'd seen Troy hadn't gone well. He'd left without saying goodbye, one second sitting by my side and the next walking away as I ran after him asking him why he was leaving. I was angry so I hadn't contacted him since then, feeling it was his turn

174

to try to reach out to me.

This nightmare day snuck up on me. Mid-morning I walked out of the bathroom having just had a shower. The phone was ringing and I hurried to answer it, holding the towel around my body and hiding behind a door so I couldn't be seen through the living room window. A comical pose. It was Lucy, at whose house I had first met Troy.

She was crying and she didn't say hello, she only said my name again and again like a plea or a question. I felt a chill go down my body. Lucy was known as a universally calm and cheerful soul; something very bad must have happened for her to sound like this. She kept crying and saying my name. I went very still as the weight of the moment began to push down on me. She asked me to please stay calm, to please not do anything bad. I listened to the words she spoke as they took a stranglehold around my breathing pipes. I tried to speak but my voice wouldn't come out clearly. I couldn't vocalise anything beyond a small choking sound. She kept repeating, "Erin I'm so sorry".

I stared ahead at the dust mites floating in the sunshine streaming in through the blinds as she finally began to say it all. To say to me, "He's dead. I'm so sorry Erin, Troy's dead. He's dead. He shot himself in the middle of the night, *in the stomach*. And he bled to death. His sister found him this morning. I'm so sorry, Erin, please don't do anything, please Erin," and she cried on.

My mind instantly rejected what I was hearing. This had to be one of the fantastic rumours that circulated around Troy, or a sick joke. He couldn't possibly be dead when I was still there breathing, bathed in sunshine.

My next thought was that I had to get to his house through any means at my disposal and take him to the hospital. Maybe he'd only been injured but mistaken for dead. I wasn't thinking rationally. I remember those thoughts so clearly - they were all about getting to him and confirming this was not true. Not true despite Lucy's sobbing. And then I heard myself as if listening to the radio, I was shouting at Lucy to shut up and stop saying he was dead when he wasn't, and she was crying even harder. Until I realised it was true. Nothing but total destruction would suffice for me and Troy, and it was finally here.

I felt the phone receiver slip out of my hands as I sunk flat to the floor. I could still hear her crying and I didn't want her to be a part of what I was feeling - something too vast and painful for words, even if I wrote from now to eternity. I found the strength to move just enough to replace the receiver, hanging up without saying goodbye. I was in an animalistic state of consciousness, beyond reach or communication.

I saw him where he was found that morning, lying next to the bed we'd shared with a hole in his stomach and I felt the blow myself as if I had taken the bullet with him. I wished I had. I couldn't breathe as I looked down at my own stomach, beholding its wholeness as if it were an impossibility, an abomination in the face of love and loyalty.

I'd dreamt of him the night before. In my dream he came knocking on my bedroom window as he usually did when he wanted to speak to me. I opened it and he climbed in, taking me in his arms and holding me, rubbing his hands up and down my back, kissing me, whispering nonsense words of love to me. I led him to my bed where I sat and he kneeled in front of me. I took his face in my hands and kissed him, eyes closed. When I pulled back from the kiss and looked at his face, he began to decompose between my hands as I watched in horror. Before he dissolved into a pile of dust he looked down at himself and then back up to my eyes. He looked so sad and he said "I'm sorry. I love you. Goodbye."

Despite every logical thought saying that dream was an impossibility, I did have it the night he shot himself. But in the face of the overwhelming, life smashing grief I experienced over his loss, the dream was nothing but an insignificant, momentary distraction. I was too devastated to be interested; it was something I noted and instantly rejected as too much and too pointless in the face of his absence on the planet. The dream was the whole reason I'd taken a shower that morning, to shake the images from my head. I remember thinking of it while I was in the shower and wondering if perhaps it was telling me to give in and call him, to abandon the idea of waiting for him lest I lose him for it. But it wasn't about that. It was a goodbye I can't explain.

The dream was surreal but irrelevant. The words "He's dead" rang in my head like the clanging of a thousand church bells tolling at once discordantly. The person I loved and adored beyond explanation was not only dead, but he'd killed himself. He chose to bleed to death rather than stay with me. I'd suffered much but I never knew a pain like that. The pain was physical and all-consuming and I wanted nothing more than to throw myself into the abyss of it until it killed me. When Troy and I first got together in a time that seemed so sweet, innocent and now far too long ago, he'd built a fortress around me that became a second skin. He took someone with nothing but half formed ideas and shaped her into a person who could withstand months of relentless questioning without once breaking. He taught me how to survive when everything was stacked against me and everyone hated my guts. And now he expected me to survive *this* without him? I couldn't do it. I wouldn't do it. I would refuse to do it. That was the one thing I couldn't give him. With him gone I had to be gone too, and that was all I clearly understood, one lucid thought mired under a disorder that drowned out everything else.

Surprisingly, I called my mother. It was a totally illogical thing to do and shows exactly how vacant my mind had become. I think I forgot everything else in that moment and I was nothing more than the five year old who used to crave her affection. I wanted her to make it all right again; I wanted her to suffer through it with me. I cried so hard my ribs ached as I told her Troy was dead. She listened until I stopped talking. She said she was very sorry but to try to think positively because these things happened sometimes and I would feel better soon. My god. It was a splash of freezing water, reminding me why and how I was living with her, and that I wasn't five years old. She didn't understand or care that I was literally going mad. I hung up the phone again, chastising myself angrily for speaking of something so sacred to someone who would never care or understand. I began to slap myself across the face, hating myself for even being able to function enough to make a phone call asking for help. I shouldn't be asking for help, I should be hurting.

I went into the bathroom and stood shaking looking into the mirror, staring into my own eyes as if I could kill myself through sheer force of will. Eyes opened but sightless, I saw only his death, seeing him brace the sawed off shotgun between his thighs and pull the trigger. Lying there bleeding, alone, with so much to think about while he waited to die. His beautiful face crying and draining of colour. Why? Why had he done it that way? Why didn't he at least blow his brains out and make it quicker? Why did he leave me to know he was dying alone for so many hours? What if he was murdered, and the police were too relieved by his death to ever investigate?

How could he do that, how could someone who was almost universally adored think no one would love him enough to do whatever it took to save him? I would have done whatever it took to save him. He was the most essential person I knew but it was obvious now he never felt that way about himself. Had it all been for this?

I mentally unravelled under the weight of so much emotion. I refocused my eyes in the mirror and ran my fingers over the bones of my face. I could feel the vibrant life coursing underneath my skin and it was an affront to nature, to Troy and my love for him. I saw him lying in a pool of blood on that wooden floor with so many gaps between the floorboards and wondered if his blood dripped through to the floor below. I went rigid and screamed, one long primal scream aimed at the me in the mirror. I don't know for how long I screamed but when I finally stopped I thought that if it had been enough to express how I felt the mirror would have shattered. I wanted everything to shatter. I wanted to pick up the pieces of broken glass and carve the very guts out of my body. I wanted to slash my face to shreds. I looked at the mirror like an enemy and without a second thought turned on my heels and ran naked into the basement.

My mind began to splinter off into thousands of tiny rivulets washing out into a vast and deep ocean where all things were possible and I was drowning in it. I dropped to my knees in front of Carol's tool box and opened it, scattering one discarded item after another on the floor until I found what I was seeking. Working on the instinct that anything that could put holes in wood could put holes in me, I found an unopened box of large blades made to fit on a small handsaw. I chose the biggest, most jagged looking one of the bunch. Gripping it hard in my palm, satisfied with the sting as it met my flesh, I returned to the bathroom to have it out once more with the monster in the mirror. I shouted at myself, swore, screamed.

I sliced my left arm in methodical rows, maintaining eye contact with myself in the mirror and echoing out loud "He is dead, he is dead, he is dead." I cut and if it didn't bleed enough I cut deeper and then ripped the edges of my broken skin apart with my fingers. I cut until I bled so much the bathroom looked like a murder scene.

Eventually I finally stopped slashing at myself and dropped to the floor. The adrenaline was gone and I was beginning to come to something resembling sanity again. I realised I would have to clean all the blood away and hide this from Carol, who would have loved nothing more than to send me back to Highland. I registered guilt for not having killed myself, but was too tired to contemplate trying again then, making a mental note to think about it later. Mechanically I stood up and got to work first bandaging myself and then cleaning the tiles, bath and walls. By the time I was finished I was so exhausted I could barely stand. I was still naked so I put Troy's shirt on, so huge on me it went past my knees, the sleeves dangling six inches past my hands. A little blood seeped through the bandages and stained the shirt, stains I still look at sometimes, remembering the day they were made. I didn't leave my make-shift bed for the next two days, not taking calls from Eliza, Lucy or Ralph. The only thing that finally stirred me was when I realised his funeral must be coming and I had to be there. I'd do that and then shut myself away again.

Round Twenty Six

It was as if all the colours the universe offered were drained into a million shades of grey. All substance and worth was gone. Up to that moment I had fought with every fibre of my being to not only exist as the world seemed to expect from me, but to live well. That was all over now. Every breath I took felt like a betrayal, the thought of seeking out a fulfilling life was nothing short of blasphemy. I tried daily to understand how the most vibrant, strong body and mind I had known could simply no longer exist. It was as if overnight the world had flipped from valid, to invalid. I couldn't even understand logistically how only one bullet in the stomach could destroy such a powerful body. How that person could have taken his own life, when he had to have known how loved he was, was incomprehensible to me. I'd never known anyone who was as charismatic as Troy. Everyone who met him loved him no matter what their preconceived opinions of him might have been. I loved him for those reasons, of course. But I never loved him more than when we were alone together, sharing confessions, ideas and affection. He was my very best friend and the man I'd hoped to be with forever. He killed himself but he could have been posthumously accused of homicide for taking me with him.

When Troy died it hadn't been that long since Kurt Cobain's suicide. Suicide seemed to suddenly dominate my life. It made me think differently about life and death. As I gradually came out of my stupor over the next few months, I emerged totally numb with nihilistic beliefs firmly cemented in my mind. I realised the same freedom of self I had fought for so long now included the freedom to choose whether to continue to live. I was no longer at the mercy of an unknown death. At any moment I could decide to end my life, which was an incredibly comforting thought. It was good to know I had ultimate control of myself; it gave me the ability to live through one day at a time safe in the knowledge that I had an exit route if life became untenable.

I could write for pages about the many thoughts I've had about Troy's death. Bitterness, resentment, grief, guilt. None of it would be enough. I spent my days alternating between cutting myself more, smashing random items or sobbing uncontrollably. I spent hours doing nothing but breathing in the lingering scent of him on his clothes, stroking items he had given me as if I could touch his fingers still through them. Other days I'd lie in bed all day replaying every second I had ever spent with him. I'd hear his side of the conversation in my head and reply to him out loud,

183

even laughing when he made a joke. I was trapped in hell and it was all I could do to keep breathing while the survivor in me tried to climb out.

It was my great tragedy that Troy never allowed me to know him better, that he held so much back from me. It left me with more questions than answers that would eat away at me for decades. I wondered if he thought of me as he was dying. Did he at least know then that I loved him? Did it comfort him in any way or make it worse? I wanted to cradle his head again and bring it back to life with the tears falling from my eyes. I should have been at his side as I had always been before. I should have handled our reunion differently.

Round Twenty Seven

I went to Troy's wake with Eliza and Lucy, frightened and reluctant but determined to lay eyes on him one last time. I had hardly seen most of his friends since my release from Highland. In fact the last time I had seen any of them Troy had been kissing me goodbye in my doorway while they shot us hostile glances from his car. That was almost two weeks before he died. They'd never wanted me in his life and I had no doubt they wouldn't want me at his funeral either. I won't lie; several of them frightened me a great deal, mainly Big Head and some of the more violent men of Troy's acquaintance, most of which supported her. As I walked into the funeral home surrounded by dozens of them I was acutely aware that Troy was no longer there to protect me. For months afterwards I would live in fear of a revenge attack, always nervously checking over my shoulder when in public, but first I'd have to get through his funeral. I was right to be worried about how I'd be received. No one spoke to me, not his family who knew me as the girl who lived in Troy's bedroom nor any of his friends beyond the few we shared.

I had to walk up the long aisle leading to his casket. I felt so many eyes on me, heard so many whispers. I tried to concentrate solely on him, keeping my eyes fixed straight ahead. At last, I was there, and looking down at his beloved face. His skin was oddly orange and the undertakers had made a futile attempt to cover his tattoos with make-up. For a second I thought of how indignant he'd be to know that all of that was on his face. But his bones were as beautifully etched as ever, long eye lashes resting on his cheeks as I had seen so many times before when he slept. I tried to touch him without being seen but I couldn't quite reach his face. I stood looking at him for as long as I felt I could, and then a little bit longer. I didn't want to leave him, I wanted to crawl in and lie beside him. I didn't want to stop seeing him for the very last time ever. If I'd been left to my own devices I might have stayed there for days, but eventually Lucy or Eliza came and whispered in my ear that I had to move on. I turned around and walked back down the aisle, feeling as if I was pulling hard against an invisible cord drawing me back to him, feeling as if I shouldn't resist the pull, that I shouldn't care everyone was watching I should go throw myself over his body. But I walked on, sightlessly, seeing only his face orange and beautiful, trying to comprehend a new vision or reality superimposed upon a familiar sight.

I was aware of Big Head staring at me from the side of the room. I smiled as I thought that finally she'd be able to do whatever she wanted to me. I knew she'd do something but I couldn't imagine what, I only knew it was coming. I went to the back of the room to wait while Eliza and Lucy paid respects at Troy's coffin. Looking to my right, I saw Big Head and the person who first told me about Troy's infidelity on that porch so long ago. They were heading directly to me. I knew I could try to leave, that they wouldn't make a scene if I threatened to. But I wanted to hear what they had to say, and felt there was no point in prolonging the inevitable. I waited patiently, trying to calm my heartbeat.

I waited for them to speak first. She said only a few words. "It's your fault you know. Troy was fine before you came along." Personally I felt Troy would have been better off without their influence, but regardless of that the words were nothing new to me. I'd been saying them to myself hourly since his death. Perhaps because the thought wasn't at all novel to me I didn't react how they wanted me to. I glanced towards Troy's coffin for one long last moment while they both stood there, waiting for my reply. In my head I said a sincere apology to him for everything I hadn't been able to do. I told him how much I loved him and I swore I would never forget everything he taught me. I swore I wouldn't break and I swore he wouldn't be forgotten, just another nameless delinquent dead under the weight of a crumbling society that allowed for no deviations and offered no sympathy or forgiveness. I said that to him silently while being stared at by two people who had just blamed me for his death. I looked back to them and scanned their faces, as if I was trying to see in their eyes what made them so evil. Then I turned and walked out of the room. I wasn't going to give them the satisfaction of seeing me fall apart. I did that plenty in private.

As I entered the funeral parlour's hallway my eyes began to blink with unshed tears. I was waiting for Eliza and Lucy to come out before I could leave altogether. I saw a sign with the details of his imminent burial and headed towards it. I assumed it would be in the cemetery attached to the funeral home, it was in the heart of Lemay and only a few blocks from his house. I didn't want to go to the burial because of the crowd I knew would be gathered there. But I did want to know where his grave was going to be so I could go to it alone the next day and every day possible after that.

Those plans were dashed as I read the notice. I felt stupefied, and kept blinking and looking again, thinking I must have misread it. The sign clearly announced that Troy was going to be buried in a tiny rural Missouri town that almost no one had heard of – that is, unless they had family living there. Just as I did. It was the same little farming town, with its one small cemetery that I'd spent every summer of my childhood in. It was the home of my Great-Grandmother, the woman who I'd been named after. My Grandmother's family owned a large family plot in that cemetery; I had attended a funeral there several years before when my Great Grandma Summers was buried.

I felt light headed as I took in the manifold points of coincidence before me. In so many thousands of conversations I couldn't remember either Troy or I mentioning this town of only a few hundred residents. But it seemed both of our families, at least in the generation of our Grandparents, had lived there long enough to invest in family plots. But then the trajectory of his family and mine went in very different ways, his ending up in Lemay and mine scattered between the wealthy University City, rural Missouri and middle class Afton. Somehow he and I found each other, but never knew exactly how close our origins were. Most potent of all, I marvelled that Troy would be buried only a matter of several dozen paces away from my own decomposing Great Grandmother, our shared name engraved on her headstone. It was almost as if Troy and I were being buried together, as much as that was possible while I was still breathing.

I was still reeling from the general mind fuck of this new development when Eliza and Lucy joined me in the hall. They took my dazed silence as nothing more than the mourning expected of me, but I was beginning to see a larger pattern playing out in my life. I wasn't sure if I was an active participant in this play or just being dragged through the scenes; with an unseen stage manage controlling it all.

Round Twenty Eight

Things had irreversibly changed. It was as if suddenly I woke up and I was sixteen with a slashed up arm, a dead boyfriend buried with my Great Grandma, nearly three months in a mental hospital under my belt, no school, an absent militant father, and a dangerous mother asking me daily when I would be moving out. I was spinning in place. It was all set against the hopelessly romantic childhood spent with my Grandparents, reading National Geographic magazines and day dreaming on the banks of the Mississippi. I was a decidedly odd individual. The oddness seemed painted on my face for everyone to see and I couldn't open my mouth without confirming it.

Living with Carol was a delicate task, like being a lizard who hops from one foot to the other to stop any of its feet from being burnt by the hot sand. Every opportunity I had, I spent the night elsewhere. Shortly after Troy's death Carol bought herself a house, finally free of the endless cycle of renting. While I'd been living with Troy she'd been house shopping. If I hadn't been caught by the police she would have moved and I wouldn't even have known where to. This only added to my slow boil of rage that I had been taken from Troy based on the label "runaway", arrested and caged up away from him when my own parents didn't even want me. But Carol was in her new house, happy and proud of her success. No doubt years of unnecessary child support payments paved the way for her deposit and new furnishings. She managed to get Elaine out by seventeen and me at fifteen, still claiming that child support with no child in question being present to care for. That was without taking into account everything that Elaine and I went without while we were still living under her roof. My father's culpability was that he knew very well none of his money was filtering down to his children. The only thing that he cared about was staying on the right side of the law by making regular payments.

Carol declared that if I wanted to live in that new (uncontaminated) house with her I would be expected to pay three hundred dollars a month in rent, as well as paying for my own food. Her audacity left me breathless, knowing that the payments for Elaine and I were still rolling in each month. I was still underage and legally entitled to the support of my parents, but that meant nothing to either of them.

A large part of me blamed Troy's death on everyone who had contributed to my stay in Highland. That would namely be my sister, mother and father in no particular order, and to a lesser extent, the institution of Highland itself. After all the protection and loyalty I had given my sister despite what I suffered because of her I felt deeply betrayed that she had given the location of my whereabouts to the police without even checking the facts with me first. She knew better than anyone else I had justification for choosing to live outside the bounds of our family and she should have dealt with me directly before handing me over to the authorities. It might have been justified as an action taken out of concern for me but knowing her as I do I know it was more of an opportunity for her to flex her muscles at my expense. Our whole lives she'd alternated between bullying me and choosing me as her ally – usually when she needed me in a campaign against Carol or as a caretaker for her baby when she wanted to live like a teenager. Power trips were her speciality and I'd been through plenty of them but that time she crossed a line. I don't think I need to explain how my parents were partly culpable for my night under the bridge and subsequent incarceration.

I drifted away from Eliza and Lucy soon after Troy died. I felt too different from them, both living at home and going to school. It also felt like we might have been through too much confusing pain together to move past it. The two of them became closer and I felt pushed out, alienated for the air of grief that clung to me like a heavy fog. Through chance I soon made new friends who were very different from my first friends. It was a group of three girls who had gone to my former high school but were several years older than me. One day several weeks after Troy's death they showed up at my house to offer sympathy.

They were called Becky, Rhiannon and Brenda. All but Becky were born and raised in Lemay and so like everyone else knew of Troy and I. They were a little morbidly fascinated by me after his suicide, a fact I registered but didn't care about. I liked them for some of the very reasons other people disliked them. They didn't listen to the old punk music I'd been indoctrinated in by Troy, preferring the same kind of music I did before I'd met him, as well as introducing me to all types of techno. They were unquestionably snobs, rudely snubbing anyone they felt was inferior to them and their coolness. They were all beautiful and to one degree or another, utterly heartless. I felt I could learn a lot from them and they loved the lustre "The Widow" (*their* nickname for me) added to their group. They were shameless social climbers, and my life over the previous two years had given me an interesting reputation. When I was still involved with Troy I wouldn't have had time for them but without him, without anything, I was going along for the ride.

Our friendship began with them coming to my house daily, forcing me to dress and put on make-up, loading me into Becky's car and taking me out to roam the social hot spots of the city all day and night. I was genuinely uninterested in almost everything, and would have happily stayed in bed until I starved to death. So perhaps their appearance in my life was more fortuitous than simply opportunistic. As we drove around the city I was generally very quiet until one or the other of them snapped me out of my reverie and insisted I join in the conversation.

Brenda, who was as beautiful on the outside as she was cruel and self-centred on the inside, was the one who most often pulled me up for any signs of grief. And while it might have had some useful results, I knew that with her there was an element of spite behind her prodding. It was well known that she'd tried and failed to snag Troy as her own boyfriend before he and I met and she wasn't one to take rejection well. She even once pinched me and said that she would have loved to have been "The Widow", that she would have made more of the moment of notoriety than I had ever bothered to. I never liked Brenda much and I don't think she liked me either but our other two friends liked us both very much. We generally tried to stay out of each other's way.

Round Twenty Nine

Gradually I began to fill up with energy again. For a very long time I was nothing but a walking, responding robot. But after a several months being dragged from one St. Louis hot spot to the next, I started to feel a sense of fight and vigour again. This time, those energies were directed into entirely self-destructive channels. My grief remained as potent as ever, and not an hour went by in which I didn't wish for it all to be undone and to have him back. But I learned to hide it better, to keep it private and locked up inside myself; something to draw out and pore over every moment I was left alone. My old personality began to emerge, matured and sharpened slightly and certainly very different but still containing the essential elements that made me who I was.

I wanted to rebuild my life on a foundation of ice, living to no one's desires but my own, and exploring every aspect of life I could find. I vowed never to be dominated by emotions again and I was going to learn to practise every nihilistic word I preached. I viewed myself and every other form of life as nothing more than a lucky biological combination of flesh, neural signals and chemical reactions. It was easier to handle my emotions when I felt they weren't essentially there. If ever the tide of insanity began to overtake me again I could calm myself back from the ledge by reminding myself that I wasn't actually hurting. I was only experiencing chemical reactions induced by the stimuli affecting me and therefore entirely under my control.

I reread Candide by Voltaire, a book I'd first read several years before. This time as I read it I saw the chaos of my life reflected in the chaos of the story. During my childhood I'd gone to Bible study with my Grandma. In Eliza's closet I'd read the Satanic Bible by Anton LeVey. In Highland I'd been able to study Islam and Buddhism. But none of those things spoke to me as did the revolutionary words of Voltaire. I identified strongly with his beliefs regarding freedom and the sins of society.

Helpless against life in all its gore, Candide learns to ride the wave of events that carry him into a peaceful understanding of his purpose in life. No miracle promises, no saviour to save him or me.

Round Thirty

The girls and I quickly became regulars in the club and rave scene of St. Louis, so a whole new world was opened up to me. I did well in it, very well in fact. I was very pretty but that wasn't the real source of my popularity in that fickle scene. It was my ability to intimidate people with a steady gaze and acerbic wit, and to seem to remain totally unruffled. My power was in saying the words that no one else was saying, whether they were jokes or scathing arguments. Aloof was In and it was the one thing that came naturally to me. Although we enjoyed some aspects of friendship and comradery I was never under any illusion that my new girlfriends were so devoted to parading me around just for the pleasure of my company. I was a curiosity, and I did well in taking that pebble and turning it into a reputation as powerful and ominous as a great wall, protecting and concealing myself. In truth and with hindsight, what ultimately began to pull me out of my stupor was a fury building up deep inside my belly like a heap of coals. The fury was universal, aimed at Troy, my family, my fake friends and more than anything else, the society I was living in that created it all.

The first thing I wanted to do with all of that anger and heat was lose my pernicious virginity that Troy had so fruitlessly guarded over. My new friends were happy to help, thinking it was an embarrassment to me and by extension them that at sixteen I still hadn't ticked the box of having sex. I began to feel like Troy had played a sick joke on me, living his life fucking someone he claimed to care less for than me under the promise that one day, *one day*, he and I would be together properly. Only for him to kill himself and leave me alone before *one day* ever came. He left me intact, but so empty it felt like the Grand Canyon could fit in the hole inside my chest. I despaired of ever being touched by love again as I case my eyes around and saw no one even close to being worthy enough to take his place.

Wanting to lose my virginity with the person I loved seemed like a ridiculously naïve notion after Troy died. It didn't even marry up with my newly devout belief in Nihilism. I didn't feel any need to have sex with someone I loved, nor did I particularly need a boyfriend. I just wanted to be rid of my virginity and see first-hand what all the fuss was about. I didn't want to be part child, part sex object, entirely an object of pity and ridicule. Sex was nothing more than a transaction which both parties should expect to profit from. It was no more intimate than the act of brushing my teeth. One object inserted into a hole in my body to accomplish a desired purpose; namely pleasure (hopefully), experience and social climbing. When I thought about my virginity I pictured a dirty old rag that had promised to magically turn into Cinderella's dress but remained unchanged, drab and unwanted.

Virginity had blighted the last year and a half of my life. It represented both the barrier that had driven Troy and I apart as well as his betrayal of me. I was stupid to think sex had anything to do with affection. Sometimes I took a spiteful glee knowing how badly Troy would hate my plans, and I'd fantasise about saying to him that I was doing nothing more than he'd done with Big Head – keep sex and intimacy categorically segregated. Other times I felt shame and hoped my Nihilism was correct and he couldn't see what I was doing with myself. Troy had expected extraordinary things from me. I was meant to be the pure one, the one with thoughts higher than the muck that circulated in Lemay. But after his death I lost my motivation to remain pure. There was no longer an end goal in sight that I could patiently wait for; a circumstance that I've never been very good at coping with, generally preferring to rush in and achieve any result over endless waiting.

I met someone named Vince at a rave. He was attractive enough without making my heart patter. He clearly wanted me. His main selling point to me was that he was twenty one years old, the same age Troy would eternally be to me. It seemed as good an indication as any other that Vince would do fine. I went home with him, stayed the night, and we had sex. It really wasn't at all pleasurable for me beyond the satisfaction of knowing I had achieved what I'd set out to do. I intentionally withheld the information that I was a virgin for fear he wouldn't go through with the act if he knew, but I needn't have worried. I assumed it had been painful and not at all pleasurable because I didn't know the right way to do it, so after we finished, I confessed by way of apology that he'd been my first. He said he had already assumed as much and it had become obvious to him during the act. I was ignorant enough of the inner workings of my own body that I wasn't sure what might have given me away.

Despite my lacklustre appreciation of the event, Vince seemed jovial and unconcerned, and therefore so was I. I assumed from his reaction that I had at least acquitted myself adequately despite my own lack of pleasure. We parted company in a friendly way, neither of us expecting or wanting a one night stand to develop into anything more. I saw him again various times throughout the next few years and while we always greeted each other as friends we were never together again. The important thing as far as I was concerned was that I had undone Troy's work. He had negated our contract and so would I.

Round Thirty One

My former dewy eyed faith in some elusive magic representing love, faith and stability was buried with Troy and Great Grandma Summers. He was my last great stand after a short life during which I had turned the other cheek more times than Pollyanna could count. He was my last futile push at something greater than mere survival, but my god I had meant every minute of him. It's difficult to explain how love that strong could sometimes turn into a fierce desire to wound him back in the wake of his death. One moment I would be lost in thought, reminiscing over our time together. The next I'd be crying and the next after that throwing everything I could get my hands on at the walls and cursing Troy with every ounce of power I had. I still had a hard time accepting the finality of his death, even as I was giving my body to someone else. I still scrambled in my mind to try to light upon a way to rewind time and have my chance to change what happened. The expectations I had of myself during that time were so outrageously high that I vividly remember loathing myself for being too stupid to know how to bend time backwards. Some part of my mind was so sure that if only I concentrated hard enough I'd find time to be as unpredictable as everything else and end up back in Troy's bedroom holding him tight. If I was clever enough I should be able to harness time like wind.

I couldn't bring myself to believe in spirits generally, but as if he was obliged to mind fuck me forever I felt Troy everywhere. All of my logic told me that Troy was nothing more than a rotting corpse now, irrespective of what he had once been. But my senses reported differently. They smelled him like a cloud surrounding me, saw him walking around corners just out of reach, felt his chest breathing up and down under my head as I lay on my pillow. His ghost clung to me so tightly that there were times I felt as close to him dead as I had when we'd drifted off to sleep in each other's arms. Our relationship never effectively ended, it merely carried on in secret, maintained with as much fervour as ever. I tried to compartmentalise my life into the living world, which I shared with a hundred useless acquaintances and false friends, and my private world, where I could retreat to him.

It wasn't only when I was alone that I could become lost in my communication with Troy. Sometimes I felt him looming fierce and furious behind me as I casually flirted with some nameless man at a club. It felt like a chill coming over me, a shiver I'd say was due to cold, and I'd carry on flirting while inwardly fantasising about Troy throttling the man in front of me. Sometimes I went too far both in my actions and in my internal dialogue, doing and saying things to hurt Troy which I would immediately regret. In private I often dropped to my knees and cried, asking him to forgive me for everything I had become. Every time I would feel his arms wrapping around me, rocking me and loving me despite it all.

My love for Troy refused to die, no matter how much poison I poured on it. I couldn't deny it was something rather more than a mere chemical imbalance but I was vibrantly awake to the fact that it would never again fulfil my life. And my life, if I was pressed to put it into words, was worth no more than a pile of shit filled mud, only a different configuration of molecules and materials. I felt none of the moral qualms that many other people experienced, because I was fully aware that nothing mattered enough to get worked up about. Who cared what happened to mud?

I sincerely didn't care what anyone thought about pretty much anything, and I was determined that nobody would ever be able to stand in my way again. I was nobody's child, just a creature on the planet surviving until it inevitably ceased to do so, nothing precious. Life itself was one horrific bout of diarrhoea, one great round of childbirth and death, one orgasm waiting to be welcomed into existence by pushing the right button, one bullet waiting to tear a body apart. I got the idea from a certain movie to practise my self-control by making small cuts into my flesh under a table while maintaining an engaging conversation with whomever I was sitting with. To cut myself while I participated in conversation flying faster than lightning without showing any signs of pain, or letting anyone know what I was doing under the table was the ultimate expression of the iron grip I held on myself. And therein lies the paradox of self-harming; that the pain is self-inflicted for the direct purpose of warding off every other type of misery. I was simultaneously a masochist and a hedonist; a combination that goes remarkably well together. As soon as I concluded that there was no point in attempting to live a saintly life for an eternal reward I made the logical jump to living only for practicality and pleasure. I didn't want to hurt anyone else, but I was fair game. I'd been raised to be fair game.

Round Thirty Two

Despite the fact that I had a constantly weeping arm that certainly should have had stitches, I had to get a job. If I was to continue living with Carol I needed to stump up

201

three hundred almighty dollars a month for the privilege, but I was setting my sights higher than being her indentured servant. I began to form a very hazy plan of revenge against my family and the society that threw people like Troy and I into the gutter. I knew I would have to first get myself to a place of education and stability and somehow, when I was ready I would strike back. It took longer than I'd anticipated but it remained the driving force that propelled me to where I am today. I didn't want to merely prove to my parents and society that they were wrong to treat me like nothing more than a shit stain. I wanted to rub it back in their faces.

Baby step after baby step I began this process by making myself as independent as possible. First I had to get legal ID and then I went in search of a job. I went looking in the only place I knew inside out, as well as one of the few places with low enough standards to employ someone like me. It was the Lemay Steak 'n Shake. Everyone in Lemay was poor as shit and mostly deranged with liquor so standards were helpfully low. Despite the fact that I had to avert my eyes from the payphone in the corner of the parking lot each time I walked in, I knew I had a chance of being accepted there. Rhiannon was working there as a waitress and recommended me to the manager.

There was still a large hurdle to cross, and that was my shredded arm. Nobody would want to hire someone meant to serve food if they looked like they survived a zombie attack; it gives a body indigestion. I needed the job all the same.

Self-harming scars are a hard thing to bear but the still bleeding cuts are even more awkward. It's as good as a brand that labels you off your rocker, no matter what circumstance might hide behind the blood. People will use it against you as leverage; proof that you are inherently incapable of coping with life, that you are a failure. Twenty years later I still occasionally experience complete strangers grabbing my arm to examine my scars and ask me what was wrong with me. Those people are unlikely to meet anything but a hostile reaction. My scars are not conversation starters and I loathe those people who are arrogant enough to touch them as if they make my body public property.

I've learned to wear long sleeves to every doctor's appointment. I could see a doctor for an ear ache and if they catch sight of my arm they'll begin quizzing me on my mental state. This has happened so frequently and in so many wildly inappropriate ways that I have a stock phrase to march out for those occasions. I say "You are a doctor so unless you're blind or incompetent you should be able to see that these scars are ancient and of no medical relevance to this appointment. I am not obliged to answer purely voyeuristic questions that have nothing whatsoever to do with an ear ache. Please continue with the relevant examination or I will seek out a doctor with a more professional bedside manner." It doesn't necessarily make me popular with all of them, but surprisingly some doctors have reacted well to this speech, conceding they had asked out of curiosity rather than medical necessity. Before I found the confidence to deal with rude intrusions regarding my arm I avoided doctors like the plague, terrified one would make an arbitrary and unnecessary decision to commit me to another institution such as Highland. Part of living with the aftermath of self-harm is learning how to live with it without shame or fear. A complete stranger once grabbed my left arm and held it close to his face for inspection. He saw my right arm, free from any scars and joked "Do you seriously hate your left arm?" I was annoyed enough to jerk my arm away, but also a tiny bit amused, as this was one of the funniest ways I'd ever been asked about my scars. So I replied "Not at all, I'm just right handed to a fault".

Which neatly brings me back to where I was, about to interview for a job that was my ticket to freedom, but with a tattered arm.

I had to borrow a long sleeved top because I only owned a few items of clothing. As it happened the shirt was pure white and thin as gauze. I sat at a table in the restaurant, ready to be interviewed by the manager. As I waited for her to join me, I glanced down and saw that my cuts were once again bleeding through the bandages I had to change several times a day, right through to the white sleeve. I began to covertly smuggle napkins under the table in an attempt to stop the bleeding from spreading all the way across my arm.

Sally, the manager, appeared and began the interview. I tried to focus and reply with everything I had rehearsed, using all the good manners that had been drilled into me as a child. However the increasing amount of blood spilling under the table was a serious distraction. I saw Sally look in the direction of my arm which was held conspicuously low. She carried on telling me about the duties of the job and asking me questions, valiantly pretending nothing bizarre was going on. It was a disastrous job interview, even by Lemay standards, and I assumed I'd be turned down.

She looked kind and slightly exasperated when she finally stopped trying to pretend to take an interest in telling me about the job. Right when I expected her to politely send me packing, she said "Look dear, I'll give you the job, but before we go any further why don't we go in the bathroom and I'll help you clean up your arm with the first aid kit." She'd quickly and accurately pegged me as a motherless waif, and so I found another safe port in the storm. Even a kind woman who allowed me to cry on her shoulder at the end of a job interview, without expecting me to confess my every pain. It was so good to have a home base in Lemay again.

Round Thirty Three

The Lemay Steak 'n Shake is a small restaurant with an almost entirely local clientéle, so it wasn't long before I knew the diner back to front. My regular customers became accustomed to seeing my bandaged arm without questioning me about it (the mandatory uniform being a short sleeved shirt). The worst thing was when I worked the grill and grease leapt onto the cuts, burning them. Sally went through a lot of First Aid kits in my first months there.

Sally shared management of the restaurant with a man named Bob. He was a sweet man and a born comedian. He and I became awfully fond of each other, in a pseudo father/daughter role. He made my work shifts feel less like work and more like mucking about with mates and every time I walked through the door he made me smile by declaring that NOW the day could begin. We often got caught up in an endless cycle of revenge practical jokes. Work was my favourite place to be.

Working at Steak 'n Shake was a lot like being a part of a daily pantomime, with the diners the audience and the staff players. One of my co-workers was named Phil. He had a voice made for radio and it was his pride and joy. He had ambitions to be the next big movie voiceover man, a voice every American would immediately recognise. He lived to be discovered so he insisted on only ever operating the drive-thru window with its accompanying microphone, treating every customer or potential agent to a sampling of his baritone accents. His hair was almost white blond and styled like that of a young man from the 1950s. His uniform was always immaculately pressed, bleached and starched. He was the quintessential American diner boy, right down to the clip on red bow-tie and artificially white teeth. But because he wasn't a young boy, he was a man in his late thirties and it was the 1990's, something about his overly polished demeanour rang very false. The final effect of all his affectations failed miserably in generating nostalgia, but rather seemed slightly creepy.

Phil made me a serious and persistent standing offer of five hundred dollars to have sex with him. And he wasn't in the slightest bit joking. I said no countless times but he never gave up. Everyone knew I was constantly short of money, most of my pay cheque then going straight to Carol to maintain the roof over my head. He'd argue that I needed the money and he wanted me, so it was the perfect transaction. He'd argue that five hundred dollars could buy me a car and I'd wonder what had happened to Troy's Catalina, and whether I might be able to find it for sale somewhere. But the Catalina was totally idle speculation; I never once gave the thought of having sex for money serious thought.

Part of me thought that perhaps that wasn't very sensible of me, that I would do well making money off the body so many men seemed to love. Wouldn't it be so much easier to simply lie on my back for half an hour and then collect a whole week's worth of wages? And wasn't it slightly hypocritical of me to insist sex meant nothing to me, but clearly it meant enough I didn't want to sell it? It was all very interesting but my answer remained a firm "no". I wanted to make it out but I didn't plan on doing so by being a fuck tool for random men. So I said "no" several times every week as he persisted in trying to persuade me.

It wasn't long before Rhiannon wasn't my only friend who I worked with. I met a boy a couple of years older than me, named Perry. He was gay and therefore we could safely be friends without me having to fear being leapt on. I loved him, he was one of the first people I became genuinely attached to after Troy. He was a musical genius, I've still never met anyone who had his aptitude for consuming and understanding music most people didn't know existed. His record collection was like the Bodleian Library of vinyl. He had a gift for collecting rare and exceptional pieces of music, and he was an extremely talented DJ. I spent hours in his room, chain smoking and watching him spin one genre into another with effortless grace.

On the whole, I thanked my lucky stars that Troy's death hadn't run me out of Lemay, the place I'd come to think of as my only home.

Round Thirty Four

One day after work I was sitting at the counter, leisurely eating my daily lunch of choice: a double steakburger with cheese and bacon, plenty of mayo and 1000 Island dressing with Steak 'n Shake's classic skinny fries on the side. (Top it off with an iced tea and some coffee and I lived off that meal for days like a camel.)

I was reading something while I ate. A young man walked in, I glanced up, my eyes sweeping up and down for a quick assessment and, once he was properly categorised, I returned to my book. He looked to be in his early to mid-twenties and was wearing black motorcycle gear. His face and hair looked a bit like Trent Reznor's – if Trent Reznor had been beaten to a pulp in a boxing ring. He was shorter than average but built like a warrior troll and carried a great deal of physical presence. Despite the quick summary I made of him I really wasn't interested in men or him generally at that point, beyond observing him as an interesting specimen. He sat on my left, two stools away from my own.

He was blatantly staring at me, eyes wondering between my arm, my book and my face. I was finding it difficult to concentrate on my reading under the obvious scrutiny. I was not well known for being overly friendly to men who seemed "interested" in me at this stage of my life; I was unable to feel that beautiful swooning associated with feelings of desire for the opposite sex. That feeling was so entirely gone from me that anyone who presumed to try to rouse it almost instantly roused instead a feeling of contempt for their sheer stupidity in mistaking honest disinterest for playing hard to get. I wasn't open for offers, paid or otherwise.

This particular man was off to an especially bad start for interrupting me while I read and staring rudely. Finally, I stopped trying to ignore his blatant attention because it was becoming ridiculous and he looked dangerously close to laughing out loud. Closing my book reluctantly I turned on my stool and said "Yes?" without any attempt made to hide my irritation with his provoking behaviour.

Ignoring my tone he remarked on what obviously held great interest for him, my arm. He said "Those cuts are quite something for a little girl like you," causing me to wonder if in his world prizes were awarded for the most mangled body in the land. I raised my eyebrow and asked if I was supposed to thank him for noticing. He laughed, and when I saw him laugh his face lit up, making him suddenly feel familiar to me, like a friend. I decided to give him a break and be nice. He asked me why I did it – the cuts - and I sat for a moment, feelings warring inside. One campaign telling me to tell him to go to hell for asking a total stranger such a personal question, the other telling me to allow him more time than I did most people.

I briefly contemplated telling him one of my random and outrageous lies to account for the cuts, lies I knew no one believed. I didn't say them to try to make people believe them, I said them to lighten the mood and make people laugh despite the awkward situation. I'd say things like, "I tripped over a hose pipe and landed on a bumblebee. It stung me in the ass at which point I rebounded and flew into a window sideways, thankfully managing to fall through it only on my left arm and thus sparing my neck." And so on. But something about him made me tell the truth, something I had never done previously when asked about my arm.

I shrugged and said "My boyfriend shot himself a couple of months ago. I went mental when I was told." Suddenly I felt hot and near to tears so I turned away from him and took a sip of my iced tea.

During this brief conversation he'd been removing his motorcycle gloves, smirking back at my smirk, probably anticipating the lie I was contemplating. But when I answered with the truth his hands and face became quite still. When I had gathered myself enough to look at him again he was staring into my eyes with a feverish look in his. He looked at the name tag on my uniform, and then back to my face. He asked me who my boyfriend was, his voice cutting through the air, demanding information from me, as if his question was the most important thing in the world. Again, I thought of lying, but mechanically I said Troy's name as if the stranger's questions weren't rapidly derailing my otherwise average day.

My interrogator sucked in his breath when I said Troy's name. I should have known him if he was from Lemay and a friend of Troy's but I didn't. Nevertheless it was evident from his reaction that he knew Troy. I felt a moment of fear, feeling something like… having my cover blown. I'd been hiding in Lemay in plain sight and I'd managed to avoid everyone in Troy's life up to then. I was tired of the constant questions; I wanted to be left alone. I decided the best thing would be for me to retreat to the staff room where he couldn't follow. I began to gather my belongings when he stopped me, shaking himself out of his own reverie and smiling at me kindly.

He introduced himself as Reilly, and suddenly it all made perfect sense. No, I'd never met him. But I'd heard Troy talk more about him than about anyone else. He and Troy had grown up together in Lemay and then left it together for life in California several years before we met. Troy returned to Lemay after only a year in California but Reilly had stayed behind. Troy had often told me how upset Reilly had been when Troy chose to move back to Lemay, but Troy felt that was where he truly belonged. Troy spoke of him as a brother, with genuine love and affection, and I knew he had trusted Reilly implicitly. Knowing this allowed me to trust him too.

I'd heard countless stories of their antics together. I always felt slightly intimidated by the shadow of this unknown man Troy said he would take a thousand bullets for. I wondered if he would be like so many of Troy's friends and make the simple assumption that the girlfriend was to blame for the death. Happily, that was a burden Reilly had no intention of placing on my shoulders; he was genuinely happy to meet me.

Reilly scooted to the stool next to me, asking if we could talk. I said yes. It was irresistible to speak about Troy with someone who knew him so well. There was no one in my life I could do that with, no one to share memories with. Reilly told me he was visiting St. Louis for a few weeks and he'd only come because he wanted to find out more about Troy's death. He wanted to see Lemay again, Troy's Lemay. He'd ridden his motorcycle all the way from California, his first port of call Steak 'n Shake to refuel before he set out looking for Troy's friends. It was pure coincidence that the first person he saw was "The Widow". The coincidence of our meeting made both of us feel slightly uncomfortable, like we were fighting the urge to look over our shoulders expecting to see Troy operating us like marionettes.

I was surprised to hear that Reilly had heard of me too. As soon as our identities were established we could barely take our eyes off each other, but that was never because we were attracted to each other in our own right. We were both searching for a glimpse of the man we loved in the face of the other; hopeful we might catch a clue to the real reasons behind his sudden death. I reflected as I looked at him that if this man before me did hold me at all accountable for his best friend's death I would have good reason to fear him. In fact it was emerging that he felt a responsibility towards me that I didn't expect. He was there to see what business of Troy's might need tying up and apparently, I was a part of that.

We rapidly finished our meals which were far less interesting than our conversation, going straight to the issue of Troy and his death. Reilly quizzed me about anything I knew, which was sadly very little. I told him about the night under the bridge, Highland, and how I found Troy changed when I came out. He listened intently, nodding me along or closing his eyes in pain. He told me about the final communications he had with Troy, over the phone and via letters sent in the post. Together we tried to form a clearer picture of why Troy had killed himself but we never knew anything beyond various educated guesses. Suicide didn't seem like something Troy, who was such a fighter, would do. We both knew of his struggles with drink and depression but what was so confusing was that those things were nothing new, and Troy had always regained his balance before. It felt like something extra had tipped him over the edge, but what that something was would remain a mystery. I'm still not even sure it was suicide.

I knew that since Reilly was planning on asking all of Troy's friends these same questions it was highly likely that someone, or several someones, would point the finger at me. Some said I'd interfered too much in Troy's life, making him too soft. Others said I hadn't interfered enough, calling me negligent for not saving him from a fate I had no idea was coming. I wanted Reilly to hear those accusations from my own lips, so I told him what was said about me and by whom. He listened gravely and I could almost see him mentally file away every bit of information I offered. He looked into the distance while I talked, and then turned back to me with a pained and tight smile. In a friendly way he patted my knee and told me that everyone saying those things was wrong and that he'd do what he could to make them leave me alone.

As soon as we came to this understanding, Reilly stood up from his stool. He extended a hand to me and asked me if I'd like to come with him. I liked the idea very much. I liked him very much already from our short acquaintance, but what I loved more was someone who could give me so many details from Troy's life. He offered me a spare motorcycle helmet, and we drove off.

I'd never been on a motorcycle before and I was terrified of them, with good reason. The only significant fact about motorcycles I knew was that my Uncle on my mother's side had managed to get through the entire Vietnam War unscathed, but three weeks after his return home from active duty he crashed his motorbike and had to have his leg amputated. It was replaced with a wooden prosthetic that made me feel slightly sick every time I watched him detach it and lay it against the sofa. As a child it was something I didn't understand. Most ranchers take their shoes off after a long day managing the property. My Uncle took his leg off. What did I conclude from that experience? That motorcycles were possibly more dangerous than the Viet Cong.

Reilly did nothing to disabuse me from this prejudice. He drove ridiculously fast and took corners at almost horizontal angles, despite insisting that he was taking it easy for my benefit. "Don't worry!" he said, "You're safe with me." Despite his words of reassurance I didn't relax, knowing well enough that anyone who'd been Troy's lifelong accomplice probably had a vastly different concept of "safe" than I did. I could only cling on to his back and pray we made it to our destination in one piece.

I wasn't sure where we were heading and I was so busy concentrating on clinging on that I wasn't able to follow our route with my eyes. After a few long minutes we pulled up outside a house that I vaguely recognised. Reilly helped me off the bike, my legs shaking. He told me this was his house, or rather his family's house and where he lived when he was in Lemay. Bypassing the front door and walking around to the back, I was amused to find I'd actually been inside it before, when its occupant had been in California. Troy and I had broken into it once; going through a window that he had worked open. There was something in the house Troy needed; he told me the house belonged to his best friend who wouldn't mind the intrusion. Fast forward a year later and my fingers ran down the window pane we climbed through while Reilly opened the back door with a key.

We made some drinks and quickly headed downstairs to Reilly's bedroom. I told him I'd actually been in there once before, with Troy, and Reilly laughed and called him a canny bastard.   Suddenly it felt slightly awkward to be there alone in a bedroom with Reilly, but this was just the Lemay way, everyone socialised in everyone's bedrooms, so I made myself comfortable and settled in for a long and winding conversation.

It was lovely talking to Reilly about Troy. We remembered him the same way, as an affectionate good man who had many problems and burdens on his shoulders. Both of us loved Troy for the force of nature that he was, something greater than the sum of his confusing parts. This commonality was enough to allow both of us to relax in each other's company in a way I did not with other people. It felt very much like Troy was there; working as a bridge between two people in the world who loved him so much. Understanding the same basic truths about each other, Troy, and life smoothed over any nerves we might have had into an immediate easy connection.   Reilly was as heartbroken as I was over Troy's death, though it wasn't scored into his skin like a brand. He mourned Troy without any of the posturing that there would have been with so many of the others that surrounded him.

Our companionable talk was interrupted by an annoying, interfering knock on the window. Reilly crossed the room to push the curtain aside and I did not even bother trying to suppress a groan of misery and laughter when I saw Big Head peering in at us with a furious screwed up expression on her ugly orange face. Reilly opened the window a crack and said a few curt words to her, telling her to go away and saying he'd speak to her later. She replied angrily with something indiscernible to me, her eyes darting back and forth from me to him, in response to which he slammed the window closed and pulled the curtains across again. Reilly turned back to me, and he had enough good grace to look slightly ashamed. He'd already known from Troy, and then me, the terms in which Big Head and I had lived parallel to each other for so long, and he knew that she had directly blamed me for Troy's death. I was slouched on the bed with my head in my hands, shaking with laughter and tears of despair. I never seemed able to escape the odds of any unlikely situation bound to cause me grief.

I asked him if he had been amongst almost every young man I knew in Lemay who had screwed her. He shrugged, rolled his eyes and said he'd done it on occasion but it was no good. I wondered idly if he was trying to make it seem as if he'd unwittingly fallen onto her by accident with an erection aimed in the right place and I said as much, finally tired of accepting this sort of behaviour from them. He asked me not to be hurt about Troy being with her, he said everyone used her like that and Troy had good reasons for making me wait. I asked Reilly if he and Troy talked about me the way they did her. Reilly hugged me and said "No, sweetheart. Troy wouldn't even fuck you!" A clear attempt at comfort that failed badly, I burst into tears.

These words weren't exactly the comfort you might think they'd be. I was disgusted by this group of male friends, all sharing one girl but happy to treat her like a piece of shit.

I loved Troy but I couldn't help but think he was wrong to do that. I didn't want to think badly of him, in fact I would have preferred to blame myself and keep him on his pedestal. I could forgive many things the rest of society couldn't, but that behaviour was too much. For a moment I felt an exceptionally tiny grain of sympathy for Big Head, never even honoured with a name. But I knew that in fact if she suddenly lost all the male attention that she wielded for status she would have been the very first and loudest one kicking and screaming in protest. I'm not saying I don't think she would have preferred to be Troy's real girlfriend, but when she had been five years before she'd cheated on him regularly until he broke up with her. I didn't like the way Troy or Reilly used her but at least it could never be said they led her on with sweet words.

More concerning to me than her wellbeing was the worry that the smudge on one woman's character might tarnish my own. I didn't want to ever be anybody's Big Head. I could never live with being used and discarded like that. They fucked her and then hated her for it. I didn't blame her for having sex; I blamed her for the terms she did it on. In my life I would pick and choose who I had sex with and I would be happy to walk away each time, finding it absolutely repugnant the way she hung on them begging for scraps of dick.

Reilly had his arm around me as I cried, cried over everything. He began kissing me cautiously and I was torn between a feeling of disloyalty to the ghost between us and an intense wish to bury all my pain in the sensations he was arousing in me. He was an extremely good kisser and although there was little finesse in the very thorough sex we began to have, there was a vast amount of pleasure and emotion in it. I suppose you could call it my second one night stand despite that this time I was doing it in the middle of the day. But it was completely different to my first time. Namely in that I felt physical pleasure and that there was an emotional connection between he and I, if not a romantic one.

The entire experience ended almost as suddenly as it had begun, but it was pleasurable enough to have caught my sincere attention. I was left quite stunned and breathless, but more than anything else, confused. Was I attracted to Reilly for his own merits, and he attracted to me, or was it only because we each reflected Troy's so marvellously? It wasn't right that I should become filled with lust, even for an hour, for the substitute. I think Reilly felt the same way and neither of us was eager to look the other in the eye afterwards. It was so obviously a one-off, and it felt like we were both cheating on Troy. Wordlessly we began getting ready to leave, for him to take me home. We couldn't talk to each other after that. What we did was something that happened quickly and naturally in the wake of shared grief. It was meant to be done and then forgotten. I was full of paranoia that we were under the constant spell of Troy's conducting hands and I wondered if perhaps I had failed a test laid out for me.

Right before we left his house, when we were both beginning to regain our composure, Reilly gave me a battered old copy of a collection of plays by Moliere, the main one being The Misanthrope. He told me that he and Troy used to read it aloud to each other, taking turns playing different parts in the play. I couldn't believe it at first, picturing these two beastly looking, fire bombing, Big Head fucking men reading poetic plays to each other. Rather arrogantly, I was so sure Reilly was making a joke at my expense that I even tested him with a few passages, all of which he knew perfectly. I felt like I knew Troy much better for knowing this new side of his life, and I looked forward to thumbing through the same pages he had. I thanked Reilly profusely for giving me the book.

I saw Reilly once more about a week later at Steak 'n Shake. He stopped in to say goodbye to me before he left to return to California. He hadn't discovered anything very enlightening about Troy's death, though he did have one piece of interesting information. The police said in the official report that no suicide note was left, something that in my more paranoid moments made me wonder if Troy had in fact been murdered. But Reilly heard a rumour that he passed onto me, that in fact a short note was found that the family didn't want made public. Rumour had it the note read only "I don't think you love me anymore." It was never confirmed by any reliable source but it would become yet another unanswered question I lived with. Did the note even exist? If it did, did it say what it was claimed it said, and if so who was it directed to? It could have been many people. It didn't really help.

Reilly asked me if I wanted to go to California with him. Not because any great love affair had blossomed between us but because he felt responsible for what Troy had been responsible for, and he knew my current living situation with Carol was heading to another end. I was sad he wasn't staying a little longer. I wanted to know him better, but I didn't want to move to California with him. I was attached to Lemay and happier with what I was familiar with, and I also doubted how long he would be able or willing to take care of me, just as it had been with Troy. If I was going to be alone I'd prefer to be alone in a city I knew inside out with a wide circle of acquaintances. I said "thank you, but no" and wished him well, knowing it was unlikely we'd ever see each other again. He nodded, wished me well in return and left. That was all. There was nothing dramatic about any of it; it just was.

Round Thirty Five

Everything 'just was' then, everything lacked strong feelings, vitality and life. I simply coasted along like a dying swan on a freezing lake looking neither left nor right. I wiped the counter, drank my coffee, worked my hours and listened to my music. I wrote. I wrote about Troy, I wrote to Troy. I wrote about every day we'd spent together, every argument I wanted to have out with him and everything I wished I was doing with him. Sometimes I'd count the days since his death and then a sudden, choking panic would come over me. It filled me with a desperate urge to run on foot to that Small Town, MO cemetery, tear through the earth to the lid of his coffin, throw it open and fill him with air. I would have lain myself down on him, I wanted to go to sleep with him in the earth and never wake up again. Troy might have left me, but I'd secretly slid my hand in his at the last moment, walking by his side into hell.

One day shortly after Reilly returned to California I went to the Lemay Salvation Army with Becky, Brenda and Rhiannon. The place was full of memories of Troy. We had spent countless quiet hours thumbing through the stacks of vinyl and searching through the racks for gems of clothing. I was rifling through a rack of clothes when Billy Joel's "She's Always a Woman" began playing over the store radio.

I became immobile, time and space closing around me forming a bubble in which all life seemed to hold still and I was only aware of every subtle note of the song. Outside it was a beautiful, sunny St. Louis day. Inside it was air conditioned and everything was just as it should be in a Lemay store, shabby but tidy with minimal graffiti and sceptical sales clerks looking out for thieves. Brenda was in the corner looking at shoes; I became distantly aware that I would be accused of having a Widow Moment if she turned and saw me standing so still. I shoved the thought out like an intruding foot in a door.

My hands were resting on the cool metal rack with bumpy hangers beneath my fingers. My heart felt suspended in time mid-beat. But my head slid back to a morning the previous summer, when Troy and I were alone in his bedroom. We were having a beautifully lazy day just the two of us. I was lying on his bed reading and he was playing records. He spent several minutes searching for one particular record while I watched him lovingly, my heart full of gratitude that he was mine. He finally found what he'd been seeking, a Billy Joel record with "She's Always a Woman" on it. He put it on the record player and carefully placed the needle down. Then he turned to me watching him from the bed and said "This song is about you" as he came to lay himself on top of me, always so careful to never put his weight on me, and we kissed. I was so carried away in the kiss that I barely heard the words in the song. I hoped they were happy as I became lost in the closeness between us, abandoning thought. Of course I'd played the song again later on, and I was a little mystified on how the woman sung about in it might remind Troy of me. I often felt that he knew me better than myself sometimes, and since the song was essentially one of admiration and love I was content enough that he called it mine.

I remained frozen in memory in the Salvation Army. I heard the song as if it were a deceptively simple masterpiece; I felt every note as if my body were the instrument being played. Finally it came to an end and I felt as if I were being jerked back from

Troy's bed to the overly bright store. Hot tears welled in my stinging eyes. I looked down to hide my face and pretend interest in the clothes beneath my hands. I saw what my hands had been resting on. It was a Cure t-shirt from the Kiss Me Kiss Me Kiss Me tour for $2.50. I bought it and wore it almost threadbare until a little more than a decade later when it somewhat curiously became my baby son's essential comfort item. Then it no longer belonged to me, it was his precious and sentient friend christened simply "T-Shirt".

There was a dichotomy that formed about me in the months following Troy's death, somewhere between my weeping arm, chain wallet, leopard print coat, and my translucent skin, watery green eyes, soft voice and tendency towards pacifism. I had the ability to appear beautiful and feminine, but I covered myself in gore and spikes. I certainly didn't carry the intimidation factor that Troy did, but I was hardly the wholesome image of a teenage girl. I spoke clearly and softly and walked gracefully, but I dressed myself up like a goth-punk sex doll. This friction in my presentation made me either extremely attractive to people or made them very wary of me. I was extremely uncomfortable with both reactions. None of what I wore defined me, and the signals people thought I was sending out were often nothing of the kind. Some were deliberate misdirection, others were simply choices I made as my personal style evolved. I was lonely because nobody could reach me, but I was incapable of making myself more like everyone else. Everyone else didn't live as I did, I was in a uniquely nowhere place.

While I proceeded with the mechanical routine of working in a restaurant, I had an endless, whispered internal dialogue that stretched out from a point within me to the rest of eternity and back again, asking what accident of birth led to the monstrosity that was carrying out the tasks my hands were performing. I saw patterns wherever I turned and I wanted to know why they were there, why life wasn't as random as it should have been. I thought it would have been best if I had never existed, there being no place for me in the world.

If only there was an exit off the path, if only there was a path at all! I was scrambling through the brambles and getting ripped to shreds on the journey. I didn't want to be so unusual; I didn't want to be so complex. I just kept wiping the counter and pouring the coffee, randomly cutting inch by inch of myself, learning to put the cuts in places on my body that wouldn't be visible while I was dressed. I thought of Marie Antoinette, one of my great heroes who said towards the end of the revolution and her life, "I have seen all, I have heard all, and I have forgotten all."

If I refused to acknowledge any pain and faced each second one at a time, I reasoned I could survive almost anything but a bullet through the head. I did not refrain from testing that theory. What damage this way of thinking did to my psyche and body in the long term I'll likely never know. It was how I tried to cope. This forced detachment from my own reality was created in a desperate bid to protect myself. However it evolved into the means by which I would nearly kill myself.

Round Thirty Six

Becky, Brenda, Rhiannon and I went to every club, every show, and saw every band that came through St. Louis. We lived and breathed music and all the promoters knew us and appreciated our loyalty to the music scene. In fact, we were indomitable. We had the kind of confidence that comes from being young, gorgeous and knowing you are absolutely wanted in any room. We were often invited backstage to meet the performing bands.

I became seriously ill for several weeks, during which time I was unable to work, and therefore pay Carol's rent. The time I was sick was spent at Becky's house and when I got better and was ready to return to work Becky and her mother invited me to live with them. I happily agreed. The atmosphere at Becky's house was far less hostile than mine. In fact, her Mother and I got along so well that she made enquires about legally adopting me.

Carol had spent years telling my grandparents everything she could to convince them that their darling was a monster. That was probably the most painful part of the whole family rift. I loved my Grandparents more than anything, and although I knew they would struggle to understand what I was going through and how it was manifesting itself I still wanted them to love me. Sometimes I'd pop a pile of quarters into a payphone and call them just to say "I love you". They'd express sorrow that my mother was going through a rift with both me and Elaine. I never tried to convince them that I was right in what I was doing; I didn't think it was right to bring them into the middle of it. They were showing increasing signs of age both physically and mentally, and I preferred to think of them living in the country with few pressing cares. When our conversations came -- all too soon -- to an end, I'd wipe the tears from my eyes and carry on with my reality, far from Amish land and my beginnings.

Round Thirty Seven

I saw Nine Inch Nails at the Fox Theatre more than once during their endless Downward Spiral tours. The second show at the Fox was several months after Troy's death. I was confronted with painful memories, and it was a sad night for me, despite the fun and music. During Marilyn Manson's act I wormed my way out of the mosh pit into the abandoned foyer to have a cigarette in peace. The Jim Rose Circus Sideshow had just performed.

I was very different from the person I had been during the previous show, inside and out. To the casual observer, the most obvious changes in me were my looks. When I'd been with Troy I dressed not very differently from the way he did, wearing combat shorts, a t-shirt and boots. I wore my hair very simply and hardly any make-up. Becky, Rhiannon and Brenda gave me a sultry make-over as soon as they took me on as a project. Now my hair hung down in beautiful black ringlets and my skin was alabaster with carefully applied make-up. I'd developed very early as a pre-teen and despite being rail thin I had a quite generous chest size that I soon learned made men drool when it wasn't hidden behind a baggy t-shirt. Frankly, I exuded hormones and was a walking invitation to lust. On that particular night I was wearing a divine little black silky piece of babydoll lingerie as my dress, with fishnets underneath and a leopard print coat on top.

As I paced the floor smoking, I tried to picture the foyer full of bodies as it had been the night Troy had collected me from The Fox but all I could see was an empty room. I tried to conjure the feeling of flying I had when I'd spotted him across the room, but feelings of flight were weighed down with the boulder inside of me. I believe I'd been staring into space and I wasn't fully aware of my actual physical surroundings. I'd thought I was alone in the foyer but a man startled me by tapping me on the shoulder. I turned to see him, feeling the familiar prickle of unease and wariness I felt every time a man approached me.

He was in his late twenties and waving a backstage pass hanging around his neck. He introduced himself as Chris, Jim Rose's best friend, there to keep him company on tour. He seemed to think this announcement would make me fall at his feet and he looked slightly disappointed for a moment by my underwhelmed reaction. He invited me to go back stage with him after the show, as his guest. I'd been backstage at several smaller shows before but going backstage for a NIN show was nothing to be sniffed at. In fact it would probably have been considered the pinnacle of local social success, and here it was falling in my lap. I made the correct assumption that Chris was inviting me back as his guest because he wanted something from me, namely sex. I wasn't at all attracted to him and had no intention of giving him what he wanted but I was happy to give him a chance as a friend and enjoy going backstage with him. I quickly calculated the amount of hassle it would be when the inevitable moment came when he'd expect me to put out, and decided I could handle it and it was worth the greater experience. So I said thank you, and yes.

Partly out of a slight concern for my safety and partly out of loyalty to Jamie, the girl I'd gone to the show with I said I'd only be able to go to the after-show party if I could have a second pass for my friend. He quickly agreed, no doubt thinking why have only one girl when you had the potential to have two? He told me to meet him at the side of the stage after the show and we parted ways. I returned to my friends in the pit feeling a little as if I'd just inhaled copious amounts of helium. I spent the rest of the show wondering if I'd got myself into something very good or very bad. My friends were thrilled.

At the end of the show Jamie and I nervously allowed the crowd to file out while we remained in the empty auditorium. I took a moment to admire the beautiful architecture of the theatre that my Great-Grandpa had helped build as a carpenter. It was the very reason Trent Reznor insisted on playing there when he played St. Louis even though he could have sold out larger venues; it was well known he was a lover of The Fox. After a few minutes of anxious waiting, wondering if the whole thing was a trick, I saw Chris duly appear, smiling warmly to escort us back. We went through a maze of rooms and hallways before finally entering a large room filled with people. A party was in full swing; everywhere I looked I saw fantastic scenes. Cocaine being snorted off a woman's belly, alcohol being passed from hand to hand, couples making out in corners. It was a little overwhelming even though I'd seen and done so much by then.

I was the youngest person there by around a decade, with the exception of Jamie, only two years older than me. Chris handed me a drink and began taking us around the room, making introductions. It was all a blur and I had to focus very hard to acquit myself decently when I was spoken to. Chris took me by the arm and began to steer me to the other side of the room. I saw who he was taking me to; it was The Enigma also known as "the puzzle piece man". He was known as a star of the Jim Rose show, but to me he was a link to Troy. I was positive he'd have forgotten me in the year or so since we'd met, and I had no intention of reminding him that we'd met before.

To my frustration, his eyes lit up with recognition as Chris introduced us. He said to me "Aren't you the girlfriend of the man I met here last time?" I saw him search his mind for a moment and then he said "Troy, wasn't it? Yeah I liked him a lot, how's he doing? Is he here?"

For possibly the three hundred seventy-fourth time I was obliged to tell someone asking me about Troy that he'd killed himself. I hated having to say that every time someone asked me how he was. I could see them wondering what had driven Troy over the edge, I could feel the silent implications from so many people that as his girlfriend I was directly involved in his death. It was a shadow I couldn't escape; I already carried enough grief and guilt to fill the Mississippi river, I didn't need to see it reflected in a hundred strangers eyes. The questions were always the same. They'd ask how he did it and I'd say he shot himself. I'd hear an exclamation and they'd inevitably whisper, "In the head?" at which point I'd have to say, "No, the stomach" and watch a familiar confusion pass over their face. Then they'd ask if he left me a note, to which I had to say no, swallowing the pain of being reminded that I hadn't been worth a few words of goodbye to him. I'd watched person after person connecting nonsensical dots as the words fell out of my mouth.

The Enigma didn't respond in the way I was preparing myself for; he looked at me with compassion and genuine sympathy. He didn't ask me any questions, he just said the world had lost a unique and special person; he was extremely sorry to hear it, and extremely sorry for me. Suddenly I felt a wave of shame. I wasn't standing before him as the beaming girlfriend of a great man. I was standing there looking like I was trying to be a groupie. I felt the urge to try to justify myself, to say how broken Troy had left me and that this was all I had left, keeping myself frenetically busy to avoid being left alone with his ghost. I didn't say any of those things. I just said that I missed Troy more than I could say and he would have been happy to know that Enigma had remembered him so well, and that Troy had liked him very much too.

While we were exchanging these few words Chris looked on, shocked that I already knew someone backstage and slightly annoyed that he was being ignored. Enigma stood up and deliberately took my arm from Chris's, telling him he'd have to borrow me for a moment. We wondered off together and left a grumbling Chris behind, likely looking up "poaching" in the roadie's handbook.

As we walked through the crowd Enigma told me he had liked Troy a great deal, and he knew Troy and I had loved each other very much. A lump formed in my throat and I nodded. He carried on, explaining that he felt obliged to look after me on Troy's behalf while I was there. As if he'd known us well (and he didn't) he correctly said that he didn't think Troy would like to see me there. I was beginning to feel a little bit like a child being scolded by my elders, within and without the grave. But I liked Enigma, his understanding and company well enough that I didn't mind too much.

Enigma told me that earlier in the night he'd heard Chris boasting that he had a hot young piece of ass he was bringing backstage after the show to fuck. Now that it was clear that I was that piece of ass, Enigma strongly advised me to stay away from Chris and not get involved in the antics of the party. I nodded, it was sensible enough. I glanced across the room and saw Chris leaning over my friend and made a mental note to keep her with me too. She and I spent the rest of the evening either with Enigma or on the fringes of the crowd and I disabused Chris quickly of any notions that he'd be screwing either of us. He was clearly disappointed, to which I could only shrug in apology. I expected him to completely leave me alone after my rejection but he surprised me by giving me his address and asking if I would keep in touch with him. I took it out of politeness but never wrote. It wasn't snobbery or anything like that, I just felt he was a little creepy and I wasn't at all attracted to him. In the wee hours of the morning my friend and I staggered home. I screwed up the address and tossed it in the bin as I collapsed into bed.

When I reflected on the night the next morning, I thought that it seemed Troy was still managing my life. I wasn't sure if I was happy about that or not.

Round Thirty Eight

Becky, whose house I was then living at, decided she wanted freedom from her Mother. Personally, I thought she was crazy. Her Mom was lovely, generous and enforced no rules such as curfews or restrictions on music or dress. She was happy to provide for Becky as long as Becky wanted. It wasn't even as if the two of them argued. Becky just wanted to be independent.

I wasn't at all enamoured of the idea. I'd spent just a couple of months living in a home with my own proper bedroom and all the money I earned at Steak 'n Shake mine to do with as I wanted. No longer obliged to turn every penny over for rent I was finally able to buy things like clothes and records. But none of that mattered to Becky. Her mom actually told me I was welcome to stay and take Becky's room, but that made Becky furious. She said if I did that she'd never speak to me again. It was an impossible position to be in. Every friend I had then, every social activity and sense of security was tied up with the group of friends that Becky and I were in together. If she dropped me I'd likely lose everything again. It was also much more complicated than

235

that. For one, I wasn't very confident that Becky's Mom would be willing to be entirely responsible for me until I was able to stand on my own two feet, which I projected would be several years from then. No promises had been made to me, but even if they had been, I'd learned to look for the holes in plans for my future. I highly doubted that Becky's mother would choose me over her own daughter, and Becky was giving me an ultimatum. I was very sceptical. In addition, at that time the only way I was able to attend work each day was by paying Becky gas money every month to drive me to work. Her mom was not able to take over that role, so it would have been even harder for me to gain independence. I didn't know how I'd even be able to keep an income without Becky's cooperation.

So I agreed to move out with her, though I made a lot of unhappy noises about it. I hoped that with a roommate I would at least have stability, even if it meant I'd have no spare money again. We began looking for apartments, but that was soon unnecessary. Becky was a waitress at an Italian restaurant and her boss's 35 year old son Stephen had a huge newly built house in the middle of nowhere. It was twenty minutes outside St. Louis near a small town called Herculaneum, later made famous for a discovery that its entire water supply had been poisoned for years. When Stephen heard we were looking for a place to live he offered to rent each of us one of the five bedrooms in his house, with the agreement that we'd share the house's ample communal space.

The house itself was light years more luxurious than any apartment we could have afforded, which blinded Becky to any other option. But I was very unhappy about living so far in the country and outside of St. Louis. The isolation of the house felt ominous in the dark. I pointed out that once we were ensconced in that house there would be nothing to stop Stephen from raping Becky and I til kingdom come. I'd only met him once, and my first impression was that he was slimy and dodgy. My misgivings went unheard, as soon as Becky saw the luxury house absolutely nothing else would do for her. To be honest, she called most of the shots during the duration of our "friendship", which was something I resented her for at times. For the umpteenth time I crossed my fingers and put my faith in humanity, praying to the earth rotting below me that Herculaneum wasn't the home of a nefarious sex trafficking ring. Becky and I moved in.

As I write this I realise how much I went along with that I didn't like. But I was in a never-ending struggle to keep a roof over my head, and many times the way in which I did that was by doing things I would have preferred not to do, and spending time with people I would have preferred to avoid. It didn't matter how many hours I worked at the restaurant. Nobody would give a sixteen year old girl an apartment or car of her own. I did what I felt I had to do to keep myself going and put one foot in front of the other. I tried to be a good friend even when I was aware that my friends were using me and didn't care much about how I felt about anything, so long as I continued to be a

237

social success.

Becky and I soon discovered that Stephen had severe OCD and couldn't bear to have even one spoon left in the sink for as much as twenty minutes. Nor could he tolerate a remote control set casually down on the coffee table; it had to be in perfect alignment with the magazines that we were forbidden to move. The living room's one redeeming feature was the giant screened TV that was connected to a huge satellite dish mounted in the back yard. It directed every single porn channel then in existence into the TV. Thus my obsession, curiosity and fascination with the mysterious depths of sex was vicariously satisfied. I'd had sex only a couple of times, and never had I experienced anything other than missionary penetration. Although I'd enjoyed my time with Reilly more than my first encounter I still struggled to see what all the fuss was about. Porn was certainly eye opening, though with hindsight I know that what I saw bore little resemblance to real sex. Nevertheless, a porn channel was left playing on the TV almost twenty-four hours a day. I'd watch it sleepily while eating my breakfast porridge, trying to behave as if this was all perfectly normal to me, and hear the sounds of it as I closed the door to my room at the end of the night.

One weekend, two months into our new and uncomfortable arrangement, I was woken by the bass of Cypress Hill's "Insane in the Brain" pumping out on Stephen's enormous speakers downstairs. I could hear many male voices in the house -- more than twenty

238

by my estimation. I heard them shouting back and forth, their footsteps going up and down the stairs. I locked my bedroom door while I threw on some clothes, unsure if I should barricade myself in or go downstairs and play hostess. Grandma and I had never covered the etiquette for this situation. I barely knew Stephen and I'd never met any of his friends. I also didn't listen to Cypress Hill, and I judged these unexpected guests shadier and less trustworthy than if they had been listening to something a bit less macho, such as The Cure. That, I could have coped with: I couldn't imagine a load of Robert Smith wannabes causing significant damage to anything other than their make-up. My bedroom was one of four rooms whose doors opened into a gallery, overlooking the cavernous living room below. I crept out, and as I did the full and heady smell of pot wafted up to me. I took that as a good sign, hoping that they'd be too mellow to be aggressive.

As I tiptoed across the gallery towards Becky's bedroom, I peeked downstairs and could not believe my eyes. Every surface on the ground floor below me, every table, chair and even the sacred coffee table was covered in shiny black guns; automatics, semi-automatics, shotguns, handguns, guns of every size and piles of boxes of bullets to go along. All around the house were swarming men, playing with their toys, cleaning them, lining up the sights in the air. They were smoking pot but they were drinking heavily too. I also saw a line of cocaine laid out on the coffee table, with the obligatory porn still playing on the TV. That seemed the most alarming indication of

239

how they would treat me and Becky. I quickly turned the other way, and crawling across the floor so as not to be seen by anyone below, made it to Becky's door and let myself in. I woke her with some frantic shaking of the shoulders and a hand over her mouth.

It wasn't hard to convey to her the precarious situation we were in. We were at least a decade younger than everyone else there and half the size of all of them. All of them were fully armed. I whispered at her angrily, asking if she'd known Stephen was a gun fanatic. For fairly obvious reasons I had a deep dread of guns and an even deeper distrust of dozens of strange men toting them in my house. My hand was still over her mouth, so she just shook her head no. I told her to not make a sound and pulled back, letting her sit up. I told Becky that if we went down in the middle of that we'd be nothing but waiting victims. I'd had more than my fair share of life with lawless males when I was with Troy and I knew the combination of things going on downstairs would lead to nowhere good fast. I wanted to be out of the house immediately, without offending any of the intoxicated men I wanted to escape.

Becky seemed dazed by it all. I was used to her calling the shots in our friendship – where we went, where we lived. But it was me who was used to getting out of awkward situations while she'd lived a ridiculously spoiled life. I could see she was panicking, so I summoned my most commanding voice and told her to get dressed. As

I waited for her to finish, I tried to think of a way to get from the second floor of the house to the driveway outside without being seen. Suddenly, we both jumped as shot after shot began to ring through the house. They were shooting from the deck outside the living room. Where we were, no one else would ever hear us scream. I tried to reason with myself that they were unlikely to harm us but I'd had one too many unwanted sexual advances from men just like them for me to feel comfortable being in the house under those circumstances.

I crept back across the hall again to my room and stuffed my trusty backpack with all the belongings I always grabbed when I had to leave somewhere quickly. Troy's shirt, gifts he'd given me, notebooks, music and a change of clothes. I left the rest of my belongings and wondered if they'd be intact when I eventually returned. I crossed back to Becky's room and together we crept along the edge of the wall and down the stairs. Almost all of the men were now facing the land beyond the deck, only a few were lingering in the living room to reload. The house was big enough that we were able to keep to the wall until we reached the front door. We rushed into Becky's car and tore onto the main road.

Shaken from the experience, we didn't speak for most of the ride back to St. Louis. We headed to a Denny's for breakfast and finally began to discuss the ramifications of the morning. We agreed that going back now was going to be awkward to say the least.

We also decided we would have to find somewhere else to live immediately. Living with Stephen had already been a slightly unpleasant experience, but we felt that morning had crossed a line. Thankfully we were able to return to Becky's mother's house while we decided what to do.

Becky and Stephen had an argument at their work that evening, so we didn't return to his house to collect the rest of our belongings for several days. I was very happy to return to St. Louis, and I didn't miss the porn one bit.

Round Thirty Nine

While still living in Herculaneum, I was gaining more and more entries into the backstage world, thanks to the interest taken in me by a man called Lawrence. This was ironic because that is my father's name, but in this case it also happened to be the name of the manager and promoter of St. Louis's coolest club and venue, Galaxy. We met at a show and he decided I was the ideal advertisement for his raves. He invited me to be his co-host and work with him, spreading details and hype about the many events he hosted. On the nights themselves we would work together circulating the room and working with the DJ. This didn't earn me any money, but it was very fun and I enjoyed the challenge.

I led him on a long and frustrating dance that was mutually enjoyed. One night, after a particularly successful rave, he took me back to his loft apartment. It was on one of the top floors of a high rise downtown and had panoramic views of the city displayed through floor to ceiling windows. I remember gazing at all the lights of the high-rises around me. I've always had a strong love of heights and I loved the feeling of having sex while feeling as if I were in the middle of the starry sky. The sex wasn't as romantic as my love of the heights was, but we got on well enough.

My relationship with Lawrence was in fact entirely non-romantic. Neither of us wished to be a part of a couple, but we admired each other for what we'd both achieved. He enjoyed having a beautiful, popular girl on his arm and I enjoyed a permanent backstage pass to the Galaxy. We did like each other as people, but in a rather distant way. Neither of us were hypocritical enough to pretend we meant more to each other than we did, which was part of the reason we dealt with each other so efficiently.

Occasionally we'd have sex but most of the time we just enjoyed each other as friends and working in the club together. I still worked at Steak 'n Shake and I didn't officially work at the club but I was usually there before and after it opened and would end up getting involved in setting up the stage with the roadies or passing out flyers. It was a fun thing for me to do and I met a lot of fascinating people. He once led me to the side of the stage of Mississippi Nights while KMFDM were playing a set and we had sex

243

right there, the steps leading up to the stage jutting into my back and live amps inches away from my face, deafening me. For once I felt truly irresistible. It was intoxicating to be wanted somewhere so inappropriate, so urgently. I was just as satisfied with it as he was and I never felt a moment's shame. I felt like an equal.

Round Forty

Within a year of Troy's death I'd had sex with three men, but none of those fleeting encounters approached the level of intimacy I had shared with Troy. So many months spent pleasure seeking and frenetically trying to run away from everything everyone had ever expected of me had given me a harder edge. Towards the end of my seventeenth year I hit a heavy low, when no amount of club hopping could lift me out of my depression. I'd been my former vital self for a precious, fun few months, but I sank back into being little more than a puppet Becky and the others dragged around.

I have had many regrets in my life, and few more than one incident that took place during this time of renewed depression. I now recognise that none of what happened that night was my fault, but this realisation was a very long time coming. It was shortly before my seventeenth birthday, and I was at a club with a large group. Becky had a new boyfriend, and he and all of his friends were with us there. I didn't know any of them. I had my usual drink: an amaretto sour. I can't so much as smell amaretto now without being sick. I don't remember anything past ordering my drink at the bar and chatting to one of these new friends of Becky's. His name was Mark, and he was thirty-one. I remember thinking I had to talk to him to be polite, but I wished I could escape the conversation and head to Lawrence and my friends.

The next morning I woke up naked with a quite disgusting and similarly naked but still sleeping Mark. I looked around a room I'd never seen before. There was evidence that we'd had sex and the floor was smeared in blood. I looked down at myself, trying to understand what had happened. To my horror I saw that the blood was coming from me, from what he'd done to me while I slept. I'd had sex before but I'd never been brutalised like that, it had always been a mutually beneficial act. I instantly threw up all over the floor I was lying on, covering myself in not only cum and blood but also vomit for good measure. It was the worst morning of my life and I couldn't quite believe I was living in it. Never before had I loathed myself so much, never before had I ached so badly for the life I'd lost with Troy; a life of instability to be sure but at least one of love and safety from all this.

I firmly believe from what I later learned of Mark that he slipped something into my drink, in fact when I came to know him better he often joked about how he'd done that with other girls. I'd been drunk plenty of times before but I'd never blacked out like that after one drink. I also knew that I would never have willingly had sex with Mark.

245

I'd only been speaking to him to be polite. I was too depressed to want sex anyway but if I had I'd have gone to Lawrence for it. Nothing about what happened was right.

I did hate him for what he'd done to me, but I felt culpable in it. There simply weren't many girls like me, living amongst people so much older and without the usual obligations such as school and parents. I'd tried to be sexually liberated after Troy's death, and now I was paying for having that reputation. I have different feelings on the issue now, but that was how I felt when I was still sixteen. My previous sexual partners had been carefully chosen so that I felt in control at all times. This was the polar opposite to that. I felt like common trash for perhaps the first time in my life. That was when I came closest to being broken. In my initial shock I felt it was too late, I had already been so thoroughly ruined that I couldn't be salvaged.

I loathed Mark from the moment I woke up and found myself beside him. He made me feel dirty where I had managed to feel clean against every odd stacked up high against me. He greedily took handfuls of what I carefully measured out. He was utter filth. He was the kind of man I'd tried so hard to avoid, one who would take a girl half his age and torture her for his own amusement, smothering her in his own infestation.

While I was gingerly trying to clean myself up and locate my clothes he woke up, laughing at my tears and embarrassment. He asked me if I wanted to go to the methadone clinic with him to collect his daily dose and I asked him what methadone was. He continued laughing at me; he said he was going to have so much fun with me. No one I knew was at that house; I didn't know where Becky had gone. I didn't know the area of St. Louis I was in and I had no idea how to make my way home. But more important than any of these little things, I was utterly broken from heart ache as well as in a great deal of physical pain. I couldn't cope anymore. I couldn't cope with what had happened to me that night. I couldn't cope with the fact that I'd lost every shred of my pride, the one thing that had kept me alive through everything that had gone before. I couldn't cope with the fact that an existence where this could happen to me was the daily life I was expected to survive and flourish in. It felt like I'd accidently mis-stepped and ended up in a place so dirty and evil that I'd never be clean again, never be worth fighting for again. It was one trauma too many.

Mark had no redeeming features. He wasn't clever, attractive, talented or kind. In fact he showed clear intent to harm me from the beginning. But I'd run out of clever solutions to get myself out of sticky situations. I didn't know what to do anymore. I was at such a loss - Words so easy to write and read that it's equally easy to underestimate the truth behind them. I was spun by questions. What was I to do? Where else could I go? Who would take me? There was nothing and nobody, no exit off this path. I was really Nobody's child. The imprint of love left on me from my Grandparents seemed more and more like memories of another life belonging to another human. I was fit for purpose nowhere.

I felt hypnotised by despair that morning, and without the will to choose my own course, I walked where Mark led me. Or, in this case, I rode, in his car, to the methadone clinic. I watched him queue up outside and exchange jokes with the other addicts in the early morning cold, blowing hands and rocking back and forth to keep warm. The others looked at me as if they could see through my clothes to my bloody undergarments, like they could see on my face that I was a broken shell of a wasted girl. I was a barely concealed laughing stock amongst men happy to trade jokes with Mark at my expense. I wanted to get home and have a shower. I hated Mark beyond any description of words. So many times I wondered what sort of world I was living in when a piece of shit like him was alive and breathing in his thirties when my Troy was buried in the earth at twenty-two. If I could have swapped them and condemned Mark to a life buried alive I would have without a moment's hesitation. Despite this I didn't immediately remove myself from his company.

Part of me felt like it was time I finally gave up and gave myself over to a slow death. Most of me felt so ruined that I was unfit for anything else. A small part of me thought that if only I could learn to care for him a little it would somehow undo the terrible actions of that night, make them okay. It doesn't make any sense, I know that. But nor did life and the choices I had to make on a daily basis. After he defiled me so badly I wanted to die more than ever in my life, and he was looking a lot like a means to that end.

My instincts were right, he was bent on bringing me to his level, and the first onslaught in that battle was the constant pressure to allow him to inject me with heroin. To some extent I'm actually surprised he allowed me to say no, there were plenty of other occasions where my wishes regarding what happened to my body were blithely ignored. I think he believed he'd eventually wear me down and he wanted me to say yes. But his body and every aspect of it made me physically sick. The idea of sharing a needle with someone as repulsive as him made me want to vomit. Heroin itself was also repulsive to me because it was symbolised entirely by him. If I had had the misfortune to have been raped by a more intelligent or attractive heroin addict perhaps I would have been done for, but ultimately I was easily the stronger willed of the two of us, and I overcame him.

Still, for a while, he got the better of me. I lost all of my self-respect, and all the pride I normally carried around with me vanished. I no longer felt beautiful, clever, or special in any way. I was Big Head. I was worse than Big Head, because I had started out better and sunk so low, whereas she had never known any differently. Even worse than the fact that I felt actual nausea in his presence, I began to fear and cower before him; something I had never done before for anyone. My self-hatred was compounded reflection after reflection.

To make matters worse, I lost my home with Becky and her mother, as predicted. Becky became jealous of the close relationship her mother and I had formed together and threw an almighty tantrum. It was agreed that it would be best for all three of us if I took myself elsewhere. I began the old familiar juggle of seeking out a new bed or sofa to sleep on each night, carrying all of my belongings with me everywhere I went. I was still working but I also had to find a way to and from work each day, now that Becky was no longer driving me. I was completely falling apart inside and it just happened to be the perfect moment in my life for a monster to step in and take advantage.

It was during this time that I began collapsing from extreme and unexplained pain. It happened a few times in private and I never mentioned it to anyone because I didn't know how to explain it. When the waves of pain came over me in public and people noticed my face turn white and drawn back tightly in pain I said things like "I'm not feeling great, that's all.", "I've got a pain in my side." or "I've got a pain in my temple." No one ever guessed what a superhuman effort I was expending to maintain my self-control. The levels of pain I could be in while still up and moving was extraordinary. I'd carry on until I couldn't anymore and then take myself off to another room to vomit or curl up into a little ball, praying for oblivion. It was becoming normal for me to be at work and suddenly announce that I needed to go to the back room and disappear. I'd lie down on the floor and jerk and shake until it stopped, then lie there quietly for a quarter of an hour or so. Then I'd pull myself up and drag myself back to work.

Somehow I knew when the worst was coming and almost always managed to get to a private place in time. Then I'd have a full body shaking seizure and pass out. When I came to, my memory of it all was so imprecise that any time I tried to explain it to someone else I ended up feeling silly and confused. The pain seemed to come in my head and abdomen together and make me unable to speak, hear or respond normally. But I continued hiding it as much as possible. Another hindrance to understanding what was wrong with me was that there was no way I could see a doctor any more. I was technically still covered by my parent's insurance, but I needed one of their signatures for each claim, and there were still co-payments to be paid that I couldn't afford. Without either parents or money, my insurance was essentially worthless.

Only my very closest friends had any idea that there was something wrong with me. Then, one day, I collapsed in the back room of Vintage Vinyl. I remember the pain coming onto me, and clenching onto the side of a table full of records. All the voices around me were making my head swim, and my vision was going to black from the outside corners inwards. At least a dozen people saw me go into the seizure and then lose consciousness. One of my best friends, Vianne (soon to be introduced to you) was

251

the only one among our group who noticed my struggle, but by the time she got to my side it was too late; I had already hit the floor.

The next thing I was aware of was being inside an ambulance with an oxygen mask on my face. Vianne was holding my hand and they were asking her if I was on drugs, they were stressing the importance that she tell the truth. She angrily insisted that I was not, which was correct. I didn't do any drugs at all then, nor did I drink. "Is she pregnant?" She said she didn't think so. "Is she epileptic?" No, she didn't think so. I couldn't speak.

Even after several tests at the hospital my seizures remained largely unexplained, though the doctors had several theories. They did also confirm I had several ulcers in my belly -- which went on to plague me for many years and caused me a great deal of pain. From my hospital records the staff obtained my Mother's phone number and she was called to the emergency room very much against my vociferous will. Vianne tried furiously to defend me, as my mother arrived like a battering ram, shouting at my half-conscious body that I'd interrupted her favourite TV show when the hospital called her. It took all my strength to reply that I didn't want her there any more than she wanted to be there. I said the hospital had called her against my will and because they were suffering under the illusion that she had a shred of natural maternal feelings. I hadn't seen Carol for over six months and I sincerely wished I wasn't seeing her then.

252

Vianne, like a loyal guard dog, refused to move from her place between my bed and my mother. Carol viewed Vianne's obvious protectiveness of me as a direct insult to her; not comprehending that coming into the emergency room screaming at me for interrupting her TV shows might suggest to a concerned third party that she wasn't going to be exactly comforting to someone in the condition I was in. She ordered Vianne to leave the room and Vianne refused. They began arguing and I was struggling to make myself heard from the hospital bed, barely able to move or speak and with an oxygen mask on my face. As their voices grew increasingly raised I was afraid security would be called and Vianne would be taken away from me; minors always seem to come off the worst in these situations no matter how justified they may be. I managed to convey to Vianne to go ahead and leave my room for a moment. She said she'd stand outside the door in case I needed her.

When she left the room Carol bluntly asked me what was wrong with me. I said I didn't know. We argued for a few minutes until it became difficult for me to speak and breathe. She told me she expected me to repay her for paying the insurance co-payment – all of twenty dollars. I turned my face to the wall and stopped responding to her. Even when I was in a frightening physical condition all she cared about was money and hurting me. I remained silent as she ticked off several more jibes and insults. After several minutes of that, she turned around and stomped out of the room, slamming the door behind her. Vianne came back in and held me while a few tears trickled down my cheeks. Several hours later I was discharged. The emergency room doctors recommended I get a series of tests through my family doctor. I listened to their advice politely, knowing I would never be able to follow through with it.

One good thing came from my rapidly declining health. Somehow, the sicker I got the stronger I became mentally. For too long I'd walked through life in a self-destructive daze. I'd totally lost sight of the ideals I had had when I began this journey. I'd lost my pride and my right to pride by remaining in the company of Mark for a few months beyond that first fateful day with him. I'd lost the strength to stand up for myself and I'd been so overwhelmed with shame from being with him in the first place that I didn't feel I deserved any better.

But sometime while I sat in that hospital bed – maybe even as I argued with Carol again, using all the battle tactics I'd long forgotten, I came to the clear understanding that I needed to rebuild myself, piece by painful piece. And the first step in that process would be to rid my life of that putrid piece of human bile.

I'd turned seventeen since I'd met him and he'd turned thirty-two. I made arrangements to meet him at Denny's as soon as I was released from the hospital. I sat across the table from him and calmly explained that if I ever heard so much as his voice again, if I ever saw him again, I would report him for raping a minor and every other crime I'd witnessed him commit in the several months of our sick acquaintance. He was shocked, and clearly frightened. I never saw or heard from him again.

Round Forty One

It wasn't just Mark I cut out of my life. I hadn't lived with Becky for some months at this point. I'd been sleeping in random places on a night to night basis, but I was beginning to spend much of my time at Vianne's house. I cut ties with Becky, Rhiannon, Brenda and the club/rave scene they represented. No more bitchy widow envy, no more snorting lines in the backseat before circling the clubs. I'd enjoyed reading *Story of O*, their collective favourite book, but it wasn't going to be my life. Let it be theirs.

There was an element of innocence, fun and spontaneity in me that had been buried with Troy, but I slowly began trying to put myself back again, trying to salvage some sense of self-respect after the Mark debacle. I no longer wanted to feel obliged to tread the line between life and death; I wanted to live and live well but I had few tools to build a life with. I was a husk; I wasn't even fully human anymore. Living according to the doctrine of Nihilism had nearly been the end of me. It was simply too easy to hurt myself and allow myself to be hurt if I believed I was nothing more than a piece of meat. I had to try to get back to where I was before Troy's death, where I could believe in some magic and love in the world again and hope it would touch me. I tried to hear the birds singing once again, grab back a bit of that purity I had left so far behind but had been so proud of. In my lower moments I wondered if I had ever been pure, remembering what happened with my neighbour at Marlborough Trails. I wondered if even as a child I had "To Be Used" stamped on my forehead. I really wasn't sure if I was worth the effort of trying to save myself, but I was filled with a fresh determination to find out. I wanted a purpose in life, and the purpose that filled my mind night and day was to become a healthy, stable, productive, active member of society. To firstly prove to my parents and myself that I was worth life, and secondly to put right the many wrongs I'd experienced. I wasn't entirely sure how I would pull off an act of justice and revenge on the scale I required, but I was beginning to regularly brainstorm on the subject; the solution I came to should be fairly obvious by now.

Shortly after I broke up with Mark I was taken to my Dad and Karen's for dinner. During the first full year after leaving Carol's house I didn't see them at all but when I began to try to rebuild myself after the collapse leading to my hospitalisation I felt compelled to make contact with them. It went without saying that they never called me, since I had no phone number and they likely never thought of me anyway. So I called, and I invited myself to dinner. I don't think my appearance was very welcome, but it was something they felt obligated to tolerate after such a long time without contact.

Their house was exactly the same as it always had been. I sat perched on the beautifully carved antique dining room chair, reminding myself of my childhood lessons in etiquette and holding my cutlery as I should. I'd sat through many agonising dinners at that table as a child. Their house was a world apart from the life I had become accustomed to. I was increasingly in awe of the wealth of my Father's house compared to the life I was living, sleeping on anyone's floor that was willing, never knowing from one day to the next how I would feed myself and always depending on my wits to get me through each twenty-four hour period. Being in his vicinity again, in his daily space left me almost speechless. I was in his neighbourhood, with gates on every entrance built to keep the likes of me out.

The conversation was stilted and awkward. None of the truly relevant issues between us would ever be discussed. I didn't mention the last time I'd spoken to my Dad - the night I asked to sleep at his house and ended up under the bridge. They asked me where I was living then and I answered honestly, saying "wherever I could". They showed no concern, alarm or guilt for the fact that I was homeless while they had three empty bedrooms upstairs.

As if he were a normal father, my Dad jovially asked me over the dinner table if there were any "special boys" in my life. I paused before replying, drawing on all the diplomatic powers at my disposal to provide an answer that wouldn't make the very walls turn red from mortification. The last "special boy" in my life was Mark and I had declared myself celibate since him in an attempt to fix what was broken.

After a moment's contemplation, fork suspended in mid-air, I finally said "No. I had a boyfriend, I broke up with him."

My Dad's eyebrow rose, "Oh, why was that?"

This sort of in depth level of personal questioning was almost unprecedented, and took me off my guard. My face remained impassive as I briefly reminisced on Mark's proclivities and mutely thought how to answer Lawrence's question. I noticed Karen's expectant face; clearly it was taking me too long to answer. Having learned early in life that when truth is your constant objective, omission is where safety lies, I simply said "He hit me." It was honest, if not a whit of the full truth.

My Dad paused eating for a moment, sat back and looked at me – directly in the eyes, an act that he usually noticeably avoided. I tried not to squirm, I don't think I'd ever had his full attention one other time in my entire life, nor had he ever looked directly at me. Then he spoke and said, "You tell him you have a Father who hasn't killed anyone in thirty years and he actually kind of misses it. Tell him to keep his hands off of you."

I was stunned by his sudden emotive outburst, and momentarily thrown off balance by it; such a show of affection! I blushed, flustered. How do you respond to that sort of declaration of protection from someone you'd only ever exchanged pained pleasantries with, but have wanted so much more from? For a moment I felt like I had stepped into the life I'd been born into, the one I'd been entitled to but had been taken away from me by my parents' actions. The delusion passed quickly as I remembered the one and only time I had ever asked my father for anything. This declaration of protection was nothing more than the same macho posturing I'd seen Troy's friends play out, just a wealthier version.

The interesting thing was, the tables had turned somewhat. It used to be that he didn't want me and I pined for him. But as I looked at him across that table the animosity became fairly mutual. I anticipated the day that would eventually come, far in the future when he'd be an old man and I'd have my revenge for myself, and Troy. Our ruined lives would lie at his, Karen's and my mother's feet equally if it was the last thing I ever did. Are they ready to hear more, do you think, as *they* read?

I'd been caught off guard when Lawrence made that first and only statement implying that he would participate in my welfare. But as the feeling of longing to belong faded away I almost laughed out loud at the absurdity of it all. I mumbled the necessary words of appreciation to my father sitting at the head of the table, even as I knew he was speaking utter bullshit. Not only had I been thrust in the way of Mark because both my parents were negligent but I'd managed to despatch him just fine on my own. And had I ever actually called my heroic father and asked him for help when I was under Mark's thumb I have no doubt he would have turned me away once again. It was all a joke at my expense, intended to maintain his self-esteem.

Of course Lawrence didn't actually *want* some other man pushing me about, but the idea of him actually making an appearance to stop it was laughable. In fact, his behaviour ensured that he would never witness any such events in my life, and he trained me well to ensure I would never turn to him for anything. He had all the power and ability to keep me safe from anyone he chose but none of it would materialise because my proximity to him was offensive.

Later that evening Karen stroked the raw (still) healing scars on my arm and said "Oh Erin, what did you do to your beautiful skin?" She floated away as soon as the words left her mouth so I was not expected to reply. This was fortunate because if I'd been pushed into an answer I would have exploded with every iota of fury bottled up inside of me and blistered their ears with a litany of grievances against them. Parenting was a job none of my three legal parents ever felt obliged to perform. They behaved as if I came into existence of my own free and malicious will purely to spite their own terribly important lives.

Round Forty Two

Lest this book begin to read like a list of sexual misadventures I think here is the perfect point to properly introduce the only stabilising parts of my life at this time; my few close friends. I was blessed with several steady and worthwhile friends who enriched my days no matter how bad everything was. When I was with the right people, had a full belly and no monsters lurking over my shoulders I could be as happy as the next seventeen year old girl. When I played DJ all night I had people who humoured me and acted audience, or sometimes shouted at me and threw things, depending on the repetition of what was played. When I wrote I had someone to read my words and say I had a lovely way with them. My friends filled the gaps of family and even housing.

When I was sixteen years old and still driving from one club to the next with Becky, Rhiannon and Brenda, I was lucky enough that I had these few other, true friends to speak to from time to time. But due to geographical distances and time constraints, it wasn't until I was seventeen that I began to see my other friends more regularly.

My best friend was Leah and I'd known her the longest. We met shortly after Troy died, when she was seventeen and approaching her high school graduation. I had stayed overnight at a mutual friend's house and the following morning Leah dropped in. I was a little nervous and edgy to meet someone new, I didn't know what to expect and I assumed she'd dislike me. It was so soon after Troy's death that I was still extremely raw and defensive. Leah walked in looking relaxed, blasé and best of all, friendly! She had dazzling clear blue eyes and beautiful long red hair. She was the first person since Troy to make a deep impression on me, to make me think, "Now here is someone I can really deal with on a level."

Leah looked a bit like a Gibson Girl. Except she was obsessed with Fugazi, wanted to get her tongue pierced, and followed no obvious tribe or trend except her own taste, which was excellent and often excitingly different to mine. It wasn't just all of that; she exuded kindness and knowledge. I had to play pretend with almost everyone else in my life. With Leah I didn't have to try to please her to remain in her good graces or build a wall of protection around myself. We got along so well being nothing more or less than what we honestly were that life with her was a true pleasure. She made space for my grief when it came but could still let me be goofy and fun when I was able. The morning we met we exchanged phone numbers and the next afternoon she phoned me to ask if I'd like to go to the Loop with her. And really, from that day on, we spent as much time together as possible.

The Loop was the perfect place for us to get to know each other better. It's an area in St. Louis known for its provocative, diverse and cultural feel, so called "The Loop" because the formation of its main road. It's a rather large area and financially diverse as well as culturally. Like bookends, on one end the Loop is cosseted by the wealthiest part of St. Louis, University City, on the other it is pure ghetto. The Loop was mainly of interest to me because it happens to be home to one of the most amazing record stores I've ever seen, Vintage Vinyl, a place I spent so much time at that it was the unfortunate scene of my collapse. At the opposite end of the Loop to Vintage is the Tivoli Theatre, which shows old, independent and foreign films on screens that are pleasantly smaller than the ones we're accustomed to seeing in modern cinemas, creating an intimate atmosphere. The chairs are still covered in red velvet plush. A curtain rises in front of the screen at the beginning of a showing and the manager steps onto a small stage to announce the show. But the most notable aspect of the Tivoli Theatre is its sign. It's a giant, upside down neon pink penis, pointing downwards with balls either side at the top. When lit up, glowing proudly, it positively dares you to see anything else. Marking the halfway point between Vintage and the Tivoli is Blueberry Hill, the restaurant and famous music venue Chuck Berry owns and performs at. Between these three giants the Loop is chock full of smaller independent shops and the sun seems to always shine on the St. Louis Star Walk of Fame. A trip to the Loop any day is utterly welcome. Going with Leah – well springtime in Paris would have to jog to keep up.

Leah's family was stable, well rounded and loving; she had a Mom, a Dad, and a younger brother and sister to boot, and despite typical little squabbles all in all they actually liked each other quite a lot. The only drawback to Leah becoming the undisputed conqueror of the position of my Very Best Friend was that she was just about to leave St. Louis to attend the University of Michigan. I had just met the girl of my dreams and after one precious summer together she was going away to college. It was cruel but we'd have to make the best of it; and we did. I couldn't find anything in her that I didn't admire and all my time with her was intensely pleasurable, even if our activities were totally boring. Being with Leah was easy in a way that being with other people never was for me. She understood me perfectly without any struggles of explanation.

Leah and I shared a sense of sang-froid that came from, I believe, a strong sense that our entitlement was equal to our obligations. Leah and I once sat eating blueberries on the great empty stone stage at Jefferson Barracks Memorial park sometime around midnight. We talked, joked and larked around, enjoying having the stage all to ourselves. It overlooked an expanse of green that filters down to the great Mississippi, that long water road back to Hannibal. In the midst of our harmless amusement, the light of flashlights shone upon us. Behind them were two police officers patrolling the cemetery, surrounding barracks and parkland.

Of course they were initially prepared to think the worst of us, being teenagers existing in public in the middle of the night. But we simply smiled and openly and honestly answered their questions; they could see for themselves we had nothing illegal on us. Leah said, with the sweetest smile, holding the punnet of blueberries out, "Would you like to have some too, Sir?" There was a pause while they weighed their own dignity against the pleasure of sharing fruit with strangers in moonlight, and then held out their hands for what was offered them. For several minutes we four sat and chatted about the river and the park just like any normal, slightly wary, friendly strangers would do. And then they left us to our business, despite the fact that they could have made things difficult for us if they had chosen to. We were underage and out after curfew. But as Leah said, you can get away with a lot when you're polite.

As far as police went I held the opinion that was first and best vocalised to me by Leah, although unconsciously understood by me before. She reminded me that the slogan of the police was to "protect *and serve* the community". I never forgot that my much loved Uncle, Grandma and Grandpa's only son, was a police officer, and I knew him to be a good and honourable man. Therefore I never bought wholesale into the "us v. the pigs" mentality held by many of my peers. However I had experienced several unpleasant experiences with the police when I was with Troy, both in their refusal to

265

come out to distress calls in the worst neighbourhoods and in the physical violence I witnessed during arrests. I felt (and feel) happily obliged to give police my respect because they endanger their lives daily to offer protection to society as a whole. But I expect that respect back to come back to me and every other citizen. If we as citizens are not worth being protected from the police, then there's little point in allowing the police the role of protecting us from each other.

Over the following years Leah was away in Michigan annoyingly often, except for summers and the spring and Christmas breaks. During the first several years we were friends we went on many road trips together between St. Louis and Ann Arbor (colloquially known as A2). Later when I was older and earning more money it slowly dawned on me that air travel had been invented some time before my birth and it was possible to buy a plane ticket from St. Louis to Ann Arbor for less than sixty dollars. So I went as often as possible to stay with her in the very fun student house she lived in. In between times we wrote letters back and forth (Leah being the far more regular correspondent) and our friendship never suffered from the distance.

When her family toured around Europe she sent me postcards chatting to me as if I were sitting with her, and then brought the most perfect presents home for me, ones that no one else would have thought of even if there *was* anyone else who would think to give me a gift. I would have walked across hot coals for her. In short, ours was the

266

unassailable friendship.

I remember once I was crying, and talking to her about being raped, and the guilt I lived with daily. She shocked me out of tears by saying something so radical I'd never heard it before. "You should be able to walk down the street naked and still be safe from being raped. It's not your fault. The man who does it is to blame." She seemed so wise and calm compared to me.

We went through a period of exploring drugs together, and my particular love was Ecstasy. E and I got on like a house on fire. My capacity to feel deeply and my conviction that gratifying the senses was as close to having a purpose in life I was ever going to reach made me think that I was onto a Very Good Thing when ripples of orgasmic like feelings shivered under every inch of my skin at the slightest touch or breath.

Leah included me on some lovely hazy weekends when she and her boyfriend went to stay at his Uncle's cabin somewhere in Michigan. I blissfully remember little from that cabin but for the fun we had and the lovely old sofas I slept on each night. It was getting away from my life in St. Louis, it was a holiday! My friends all had family vacations to go on, school holidays, days off work and school. Nothing ever ended for me, my toil never stopped. There was no variation, let up or relief of the pressure I was

267

under. Every day I had to find a place to sleep, a way to get to work and back and enough money to buy food, never mind luxuries such as clothes or books. It was a ceaseless merry-go-round that I was strapped onto, but I had Ann Arbor and that cabin for escape every now and then.

My trips to Michigan were a beloved feature of my life. I even brought along my friends Cora and Perry; a Lemay contingent in A2. Perry (of Steak 'n Shake) and Cora were some sort of strange gothic combination of asexual lovers. Their bond was at times frustratingly impenetrable for outsiders, but individually I was very close to both of them. I'd known Perry since my first days of working at Steak 'n Shake and he'd soon after introduced me to Cora. For many years the three of us simply socialised, but eventually we'd become far more entangled with each other.

Last, but by no means least, was Vianne. Slightly loose in the head, but utterly dazzling, like a rocky diamond set in a bent crown. Explaining Vee was never easy; our friendship was as temperamental and fluid as it was loyal and influential. We loved each other deeply but had none of the stability that Leah and I shared. The intensity of our feelings for each other meant that our relationship was often a very fluid place, affected by too many turbulent emotions. But even when we'd hurt each other the love always remained unchanged. She and I also met shortly after Troy's death.

To explain how Vianne and I met, I must go back to a terrifying day some years earlier. I was twelve, and I was at middle school. It was lunchtime, and I was standing next to my locker. Suddenly, with no warning at all, my right leg shin bone snapped in two. It was excruciatingly, agonisingly painful. It hurt so badly I fainted for several minutes. The school called an ambulance and I was rushed into emergency surgery. An undiscovered bone deformity caused my right leg to be unable to support any weight for a significant amount of time. Essentially, I had been born with a ticking time bomb, and at some point it was going to go off. Over the next two years, my leg spontaneously broke several times, and I had operation after operation to rebuild it. I had arthritis in both legs before I was twenty.

Troy used to lightly stroke the skin around the scars on my leg; he was very protective of it, always aware I couldn't run fast like the others in the many times we saw police and had to head the opposite direction. He was always there to help me over a fence or carry me when I began to hurt and lag behind. Leah was the same. I used to love climbing and sitting up on top of the brick walls at the Loop. She was great at remembering what I forgot each time; that I could get up but not down as my leg couldn't take the impact of a jump. She was always there holding out her arms to help me lower myself down.

Immediately after Troy's death, while still living with Carol, I had the final operation on my leg. It was during the time when I was feeling so reclusive, before Becky and her friends adopted me. I was still too taboo for anyone to socialise with, Troy's suicide lingering over me like an accusation. My leg was in a large cast. Rather than accept the ugly hospital issue crutches that were offered to me I bought an amazing collapsible black cane with a wooden handle and trained myself to use that instead. It just extended with a flick of the wrist. Then for a lark I took to sometimes wearing a top hat, because it seemed the next sensible step to having a collapsible cane.

I met Vianne the first evening of an after-care group my mother and I were required to attend for a certain number of weeks after my release from Highland. I didn't want to go. Fuming, I swathed myself in black, wielded cane and top hat, and limped my way through the doors, prepared for a miserable night. But across the room was a small girl with purple hair wearing a Samhain t-shirt and a spiked collar, comfortingly familiar gear. Looking at her worked for me like a psychic anchor. She told me later that she saw me as soon as I walked in and knew immediately she wanted me to be her best friend because she'd never seen anyone as striking looking as me. And I was amazed that someone so beautiful was standing in the same admiration I stood in for her. She was mysterious, beautiful, cool, and complex. Her hair was like the Horse of Many Colours in the Land of Oz, never precisely the same shade two weeks in a row. It was impossible to pin down her eye colour with a neat word. We fell in a sort of love. I became a regular fixture at her house; her Mom was quite happy for me to stay as often as I wanted.

And Vianne's house, well it was nothing but jaw droppingly amazing. It actually had a small turret and they employed full time house help. In the very beginning of our friendship I brought Eliza with me to stay the night and Vianne and I, being too lazy to walk her to the bathroom from the TV room drew a little map instead. It seemed expedient at the time but later at 4am when the three of us had the giggles it had us in hysterics, imagining doing that with a Lemay house "turn left at the doorknob and mind the hole in the floor".

Vianne's Mom, Christina, was extremely warm and welcoming to me, treating me like an interesting person in my own right whom she would very much like to know. That in itself was quite amazing because she was the single most sophisticated woman I had ever known. She often told me how strong I was, to live as I did. She was the only adult who seemed to notice the strain I was under. When she asked my opinion on any trivial thing I felt it as a shocking compliment. I admired her greatly and was very grateful to the shelter, food and rest she gave me.

Round Forty Three

Vianne's house was, by another of those bizarre coincidences, just around the corner

271

and down the road a little from my dad's, in another gated neighbourhood full of beautiful brick houses. Both were in the University City district of St. Louis, the wealthy area adjacent to the loop. Sometimes while I slept at Vianne's I thought of how near I was to my Dad, no longer on the other side of the city in Lemay but right there in his own neighbourhood. I could walk to him if I wanted. But that was just trivia. Actually knocking on his door uninvited would have been perceived by him as an act of hostility.

The closest I came to demanding my father's time and attention was a creeping, meek little telephone call, every six to eight months. I called him when I either became overcome with rage regarding his neglect, or had a moment of weakness and hoped that maybe the next visit would be the one when he would finally, truly see me. It was always futile. Usually, he invited me out to dinner. The few times I recall trying to move our dinner visits from twice yearly to quarterly, I was blatantly asked what was the purpose of my call - hadn't we talked three months ago? He'd tell me to give it a few months and then try him again, and I'd hang up and try as hard as I could not to cry. That humiliation repeated over and over until I finally grew out of the habit of instigating it.

If the time was right and he did wish to see me, than my Dad and Karen would pick me up from wherever I happened to be at that time and we'd go back to their house for pre-dinner coffees. I'd admire their pedigreed cats, stroke the beautifully polished piano and look at the awe inspiring wall full of framed old family photos. Some were as old as the first attempts at photography and they ranged in style from black and whites, to colour, slightly tinted from the 1970's and 80's, and a few more current photos. Every so often Karen would breeze by in the midst of her coffee making, and point to one person or another in the pictures and say, "That's my Great Aunt Mable", or "That's your Great-Great Grandmother Regina" or "That's your cousin Anna, she's twelve – She's one of your Dad's sister's daughters."

I marvelled at the hundreds of framed photos of our expansive family, yet not in one single place was I ever found amongst them. My father had no pictures of me at all. In his house, his life, it was as if I had never been born. Time and time again, visit after visit, I scanned that wall to see if any changes had been made and if I had, perhaps, finally been included. But it never happened. I was handed a china cup full of freshly brewed coffee and suddenly remembered to be on my best behaviour. But those pictures remained, taunting my stupid aspirations to belong, as I sat there perched on the edge of a finely upholstered Chippendale sofa. The wall of pictures stood like an army against an invader, like the god damn Kennedys, partaking of sports and tea parties on the lawn, posing for professional photographers. They would never let me in; I stood against them, flesh pale and perfect but for the dozen scars on my arm, testifying to my own existence and condemning them for cutting me out of theirs so

273

easily. The wall of smilingly smug faces would remain, whereas I would soon be escorted out of the hallowed dwelling. The insult was astonishing.

After coffee we'd go out to dinner somewhere nice. Places with dress codes, causing my father to scold me for not being more suitably attired. He seemed to miss the irony that this would be the first full meal I'd have likely had in a week or more. I wanted to tell him that if I'd known fancy clothes were expected from me I'd have checked the dumpster behind Salvation Army, but I always bit my tongue. After a couple of hours Lawrence's fingers began to tap, long sighs escaped him and he stared at the clock. Then he'd make a brave attempt at a smile that would come out like a grimace and say, "Well kiddo it's getting to my bedtime. Where do you want to be dropped off?" Time up for another six months.

On several occasions I was collected or dropped off at Vianne's house. When that happened my Dad looked pleased with where I was; such a lovely house, such a good address, all so elegant and polished. In those moments, he smiled at me as if I'd finally done well after so many failures. He even said to me the first time he saw me at that house that I'd *finally* done well for myself. Every time he smiled at that house and at me like that, I wanted to [assault] him. And I wanted to scream. How dare he pass comment on anywhere I slept? Who was he to scorn some of the places I found to give me shelter, and be so pleased with this one, when his own house was just down the road, he had legal custody of me, and he never invited me to sleep there? And how dare he think I was friends with Vianne because she was rich, or to impress him! I was friends with her because she was crazy like me, with a selfish father like mine. I longed to tell him how grossly he had forfeited the right to size up my accommodation, when he adamantly refused to help me.

Despite the fact that my childish choking shyness was very slowly morphing into adult choking rage, I was still always docile and polite to my father, regardless of the choke. As I grew older the desire to be friendly to him despite everything was thankfully lost.

Round Forty Four

Vianne and I shared an appreciation for sleep. I was forever trying to catch up on it, and she was just plain fond. We used to spend an indeterminate amount of time tangled in her downy duvet, happy in a haze between sleeping and talking. We were hypnotised by the hum of the window air conditioner unit that kept her massive cube shaped bedroom feeling like a cool cave when the heat outside was unbearable. When we gradually became bored doing our best impersonations of sloths we'd emerge from bed to play with make-up and clothes while listening to music. Vianne favoured the punk rock that I'd come to associate with Troy; it was oddly comforting despite the fact it wasn't my most favourite music to listen to. When we decided we were ready to leave the house we'd be driven to the Loop for some shopping and socialising by her housekeeper. It was not a hard life. During the time that I had indefinite leave to remain at her house, my burden was greatly eased.

Vianne and I bared our souls to each other in a way that only two girls can do. We loved each other; we could sense each other's moods like a scent on the wind. Vee and I were very different from each other in both style and personality, and we would never bend to imitate the other. That sounds like a fairly straight-forward and unimportant distinction to point out, but in a scene where everyone tried to be exactly like the ones at the top of the pile it was extremely refreshing to be together but very different. It was the same with Leah, whereas Perry and Cora preferred conformity in their "non-conformity", wanting only to be with those who were precisely like themselves.

For the first few months of our friendship, we spent a great deal of time together at the "recovery support group" where we met. It was an atmosphere heavily geared towards positivity, confessional living, and being held accountable for all of our actions. We were both emotionally troubled. She had a boy in her past who was a little parallel to my Troy and her father had not only committed crimes against her family but was also totally absent. Where our problems differed was that I had no parents or home, whereas she had a loving mother and total security. However she had a severe eating disorder that I did not suffer from; my extreme skinniness was due to hunger and lack of funds, not intent. I ate like a camel whenever I had the opportunity.

Vee and I dealt with our enforced counselling in different ways. I was indifferent and said only what I knew the counsellors wanted to hear in order to deem me finished with the program. But Vee, when she went clean from drugs and drink and vowed to become healthier, went to an extreme - as she almost always did. She was downright hostile to anyone still committing the sins she'd so recently sworn off, whereas I tended to think that everyone would get to that place at their own pace, if they were ever to get there. Sometimes she was exceptionally cruel to people who weren't as "straight-edged" as she became. For such a long time I observed that tendency in her and sometimes even tried to persuade her to be slightly more moderate in her condemnation, but I wasn't ever on the receiving end of her tirades. But for everything that hasn't happened yet there exists a first time, and mine came right out of the blue.

One evening I went out with her family to eat, and at one point during the meal I went to the bathroom, for obvious reasons (or at least, obvious to me). When I came out my eyes were watering and my nose was slightly red because I had a cold coming on, which unfortunately I hadn't previously mentioned to Vee. She was adamant that my watering eyes and nose were proof that I'd made myself vomit in the bathroom and while I protested that I most certainly had not she became so frenzied that she threw a plate in the middle of the restaurant and her mother had to restrain her. It was bewildering, I truly hadn't made myself vomit and actually she knew that I'd never suffered from an eating disorder. I tried, but there was literally no reasoning with her in the rage she was in. I was in tears, pleading with her to calm down and listen to me. It was very hurtful and confusing for me. She ordered her mother to drop me off at a Denny's with all my belongings, as I had been living with them for around six weeks at that point. Her mother told her she was behaving badly, but dropped me off anyway. I was immediately returned to the daily search for someone who would let me sleep on their floor. It was two weeks before Vianne came apologising to me and asking me to come back to her house. It was a sharp lesson but one I would have to learn again.

I had a humbling realisation, the day I returned to her house. I had a roof over my head with her again, but only so long as she was happy with me. It was demoralising to know that even with one of my very best and closest friends, someone who knew how much I hurt and how much strain I was under, everything was still entirely conditional. I was no more than a charity case that could be indulged or cast out at will. After that I found it harder to be quite as comfortable and relaxed when I stayed at her house, which for a short time I'd been silly enough to take it for granted as a new real home.

Round Forty Five

Over time, in lieu of a permanent residence my home base became a small privately owned diner called Eat-Rite. No matter who I was staying with, or who I was friends with you could usually track me down through Eat-Rite somehow. Their slogan was "Eat-Rite or don't eat at all!" and for me this was often true. The family who owned it also owned several other diners scattered throughout St. Louis and the surrounding area, but this one was the best, hands down. The second best was another Eat-Rite, but that was little more than a long wraparound coffee bar with a collection of men sitting on stools, bellies hanging out of badly buttoned shirts and a hostile waitress resentfully serving.

My Eat-Rite could have been lifted out of any small town in Missouri. Plastic tables, textured wallpaper, dark faux Tiffany lampshades and pine detailing made the atmosphere warm and welcoming without any pretensions to grandeur. The restaurant was L shaped, and my preferred table was in the back corner of the long end. Behind my chair and on the wall opposite it at the other long end of the room were large mirrors, so I had a complete view of the door and counter around the corner without sacrificing the feeling of comfort that being huddled in a corner gives. I subtly infiltrated the land of Eat-Rite and then crowned myself its queen; that chair was my throne. They had a jukebox that played Elvis, Nirvana, Sinatra, Depeche Mode, Tori Amos, Don McLean and so on. It was regularly updated with new tracks, the selection of which was at the discretion of the head waitress – and she came to me to ask what "the kids" liked. I loved that!

The other wonderful thing about Eat-Rite was that for $1.00 you bought a bottomless pot of coffee and after that you were free to sit there all day. And I did. Many times I sat there for more than one day in a trot but I was never charged more than $1.00 for my coffee, no matter how many refills I had. I more or less outgrew the desire to drink alcohol or dabble in drugs but I was wired to the moon and back on caffeine, which I credited with keeping me alive and active enough to live life at the pace I had to live it. In fact, the waitresses taught me how to use the coffee machine so I could fetch my own refills, and in addition to helping myself I sometimes helped serve if they had a particular rush. Some days the coffee was brisk and full but on a bad day it was a strong shade of forest green and would leave you with cramps and a bout of the runs. It was thrilling, the chances you took each time you poured yourself a cup, the excitement building as you sat hour after hour gradually watching the quality of the brew decrease until you realised you were actually becoming quite ill.

There was an understanding between us regulars and the waitresses that we had to take turns buying food at regular intervals so the absent owners wouldn't think the waitresses were simply letting us squat for coffee and tips (an entirely correct assumption). My favourite waitress, Tammy, knew I rarely had much money, so when I duly bought my obligatory plate of fries she'd often make the cook add a cheeseburger and a slice of cake to go with it. The waitresses were good friends to all of us and as long as you respected them and left them a tip they didn't mind "constant" visitors, and would often sit down for a chat if they had the time. I think I spent more money on tips than I ever did on fries and coffee combined.

Tammy was the timeless welcoming bar wench incarnate. She was rosy cheeked with tight curly hair and a round figure modestly wrapped up in a white shirt with blue skirt and apron, polished off with a sturdy pair of shoes and pantyhose. She was just old enough to be my mother and she was rather maternal towards me. She was kind and industrious. I liked the way she got on with things without becoming bitter over life's struggles. She simply chugged along making ends meet and was pretty cheerful about it too. I admired that. Her entire (large) family lived in a homely trailer that I was honoured to be a guest in on occasion. It was cramped but neat as a pin. Tammy was just what you wanted from a diner waitress, so we were very lucky to have had her during that time when we were all intellectualising life over coffee. Someone less tolerant would have driven all of us away. She was much more like the country Missouri people my Grandparent's would have known than the city people from St. Louis.

Round Forty Six

I was seventeen, and was living with Vianne again, when her mom took me along with

281

them on a spontaneous trip to Chicago. It was lovely; she treated me equal to her own two children and even gave me some spending money. I had so much fun, it was an unimaginable luxury to be taken care of like a child and stay in a hotel with bellhops and butlers. Sadly it was as fleeting as it was lovely. They had another family holiday shortly after, but I wasn't welcome on that one. I understood, I wasn't actually a family member. I never expected them to treat me to things like holidays, it was just that I was so easily disposable without a thought to my welfare. Vee "forgot" to inform me of their impending holiday until they were due to leave in two days so I had a very short amount of time to try to find alternative accommodation. Silently, I felt that after I had been with them for so long, and even held a key to their house, it would have been kinder of them to allow me to stay there while they were gone. But they had a housekeeper to house-sit and in truth it was a gentle reminder that I was only a temporary guest, and really, my accommodation was not their problem. I won't deny that it hurt. It was another little wake-up call. I'd become too comfortable living with them and it was making me soft. The only conclusion to draw from that, from every person who turned me out at their convenience, was that ultimately they didn't care if I had somewhere to sleep or not unless they happened to desire my company. I was "Somebody Else's Problem", namely, my own. I made my graceful exit on cue to avoid any awkward moments. They promised I could come back when they returned and I tried to be grateful for that and happy for them that they were going to enjoy such a lovely holiday.

They were going to be gone for three weeks, during which time I was going to try to rotate my hosts so that I wasn't too much of a burden to any one person. Leah was in Michigan and at that time Perry and Cora were living in Texas for a year. I tried to maintain a self-assured and optimistic outlook as I came against brick wall after brick wall looking for a place to temporarily live, even to spend one night, but inside all was not as calm as I appeared. I was deeply shaken by being suddenly thrust back into this routine after having a steady place to live for a couple of months. I knew I was only a few more rejections away from returning to the bridge in Lemay.

I managed to secure two nights at Josh's house, Vianne's boyfriend. But his parents were very conservative and we had to come up with an elaborate lie that would allow me to sleep in their guest room. During the two very, very hostile nights and days I frantically scrambled to find someone to take me in next. I dared not show my face from outside the guestroom door until his parents left the house. Outside the room I heard them argue over me. Josh wanted his parents to give me more time, they said absolutely not. A normal seventeen year old girl might have taken to her bed and slept and cried for days on end when faced with such a crisis of emotion and stress, but I had no bed to do that in. I'm sure Josh's parents would have called either paramedics or police if they began to hear hysterics emanating from their prim and proper guest room.

Suddenly the whole familiar process of taking out my little red phone book and going down the list from A-Z, calculating my options in order of preference and the least amount of hassle I would cause to those I was hoping would host me, seemed like an impossible mountain to climb. I lost the energy for it after the first few "no's". I cast my mind about and it came up blank. I'd made a point in the previous year of narrowing down my acquaintances by deliberately leaving the club scene and everything associated with it. I had fewer, but closer friends now, but none of them were available. I knew some people who would take me in but I also knew those people were dangerous for me. I was caught in a trap, and my mind could do nothing but run round in circles.

The worst part was that I was still in that place, of no fixed address and living at the mercy and whim of everyone in my life. It was too exhausting and stressful to live that way when I'd also been through so much else. I think I felt something like genuine physical and mental shock and I duly began to shut down. I just wanted a bedroom. It was such a deceptively simple desire that suddenly I was flattened by the fact that it was the single most unattainable thing for me. Since I was freshly fifteen I'd summoned the energy to be the eternal guest: making small talk, passing out cutlery or hiding in a corner trying not to be noticed. I tried to remember the last time I had felt at home somewhere, felt comfortable, at ease and in no danger at all - somewhere I felt entitled to be. And I realised it had been when I was with my Grandparents in

Hannibal, aged ten and under. I didn't know how to finally accept that I was homeless, that it wasn't going to imminently end when I found someone who would finally love me enough to help save me.

I wondered if I was even fully human. No one took it for granted that I deserved so much as a roof over my head, a bed to sleep in or food in my mouth. So many people around me had money, house and family, and they all knew I had none of those things. Still, nothing was designated as mine. I was alone. Always, in the end, eternally alone. During the uncomfortable stay in Josh's spare room I sincerely wished that Carol had drowned me at birth. I knew I'd been driven out of her house but I felt covered in shame that my life was such an aberration from society. So many nights I'd slept on piss soaked floors that my father wouldn't have allowed his beloved dog to sleep on, all for nothing, no progress. During the whole journey I'd survived those degradations by believing that one day I would overcome them and make good on it all. But I hadn't managed it and after rubbing a very thin layer of gloss off me it was clear that I was still only fit to sleep under a bridge.

The second and final day at Josh's was the worst for me. I hadn't found anywhere to go, which meant I was going to have to go back to the bridge. I knew it, and I cowered from it. I'd been through so much in the two years since I spent the night there. I knew better than I did before just how much there is to fear in this world. I wasn't brave enough to let Josh drop me off there and prepare to live there for three weeks. I was never more a broken child than I was that day, crying the quietest tears I could manage while the reality of being homeless paralysed me.

Like a dog who returns to the master who kicks him, I actually phoned my Mother and asked if I could go to her house for lunch. It was an action so utterly insane and desperate that it perfectly exemplifies how fully broken I was. I hadn't seen or spoken to her in a year. She said I could come over but added "Only for lunch, don't expect to stay." I hadn't told her of my housing dilemma, she just has a remarkable talent for saying the most hurtful thing I can hear in any given conversation. I replied smartly that I didn't want or need anything more from her and I was just calling out of curiosity. I didn't want her to know how badly off I was. I don't even honestly know why I called her. I knew she wouldn't let me stay with her, I didn't want to stay there anyway and I knew she was the worst possible person for me to be around when I wasn't feeling strong. I think it was a moment of weakness during which I wanted a mother and home so badly that I lost touch with reality. It can take children a remarkably long time to fully come to terms with the fact that they aren't wanted by their parents and that their parents are dangerous to them beyond repair.

Josh dropped me off at her house. I wasn't welcome to stay at his house anymore, but he was going to collect me again when I called him and then drop me off wherever I wished to go. I was hoping that sometime during the hours I'd be at Carol's I'd be struck with some sort of inspiration.

The lunch was an exercise in torture. As soon as I entered her door I knew it was a mistake. She was gloating that I'd contacted her and asked to come over as though it was admission of guilt on my part for everything she blamed me for. We began arguing almost instantly because despite how deeply low I felt, I bristled at her many taunts. There wasn't a subject she didn't touch upon: my continued homelessness, my persistent ill health, my lack of gratitude towards her. What I was meant to be grateful for I don't know, but she certainly mentioned it a great deal.

I wasn't really in top fighting form, which was the only way I'd learned to survive the company of my mother since my early teens. She could see that I was absorbing the insults more than I was defending myself against them. It was clear I was at a point of crisis in my life even if I didn't give her the details of it. She loved seeing me weak, sitting quietly with a vice around my throat, listening to the poisoned stream of words rushing over me, choking my soul. It was a far cry from the way our encounters usually went, when I'd come back spitting and fighting like a wild cat, using logic and her own words against her so well.

She was sitting opposite me on the sofa and talking incessantly on my many failures as a human being, from my inconvenient premature birth that spelled the end of her marriage to that day. She even threw in a spiteful comment about Troy, his death featuring on my list of failures. The things she said no loving mother would say, but I'd heard them so many times before it was old news to me. Eventually I became lost in my own thoughts as her voice faded into background noise. I looked around her living room, full of clutter and shopping bags and mused on how the child support checks from my Dad were being spent. After a while I realised she was waiting for me to answer a question. I snapped my attention back to her and asked her to repeat herself. She asked me if I was truly happy with myself, if I actually thought I was any good or if I had ever succeeded at anything. She spat the questions out like the words tasted disgusting and it was obvious from her tone what her answers to each of those questions were. They were exactly the same questions I'd been asking myself over the previous 72 hours. What they boiled down to was, am I actually worth anything?

I thought for a long time, during which there was complete silence. I considered fighting back like I generally did. I thought about lying and saying I loved my life. But eventually, as if by accident, I said the truth. I said that no, I wasn't happy at all. And no, I didn't think I had accomplished my dreams, yes they still all seemed completely out of reach. I said I didn't feel good about my life at all and I often wondered if there was any purpose to my existence.

It seemed to be the answer she'd been hoping for but not daring to expect. She looked almost jubilant. Her eyes were bright and gleaming; she leaned forward towards me and said "Why do you bother then? If you're so miserable, why don't you just kill yourself?"

My head snapped up. We held eye contact for a long minute. My own mother was encouraging me to kill myself. She really did mean it when she said she should have drowned me at birth. I started to think, coldly and calmly, about whether or not I should indeed commit suicide. She sat back as if her job was done and picked up a magazine, dismissing me to consider her words, the conversation clearly at an end.

I looked around her living room, out the window at the traffic outside and thought, "Yes, it must seem as if I should shit or get off the pot, and yes, it does seem as if it's no good for me to try to live anymore… I don't belong anywhere. I shouldn't have been born. I must address the issue, redress the balance." I saw everything in perfect clarity, I heard every bird's whistle as if it were the very first nature had ever sung and I still enjoyed the hum of traffic beyond it. My senses were alive as I'd only experienced a couple of times before. I finally felt firmly in control of my own life. I usually felt like I was being swept downriver on a vicious current. This alert calm seemed like a peace that came to confirm my thoughts. I wondered if that was how Troy had felt a few years back when he decided to end his own rootless existence. I felt a pang of regret for what we could have been together. If only he'd given us more time, time for me to grow and for him to heal, perhaps he and I could have made something out of the nothing that faced me that day and him several years before. That had always been our intention, whenever we slowed down enough to discuss the future.

Finding meaning and safety in life was something that it seemed I couldn't do alone. I had no lighthouse, no northern star. I made a decision in that moment, but I didn't want my Mother to notice a change in me. So I blinked, and the moment of clarity passed, leaving the truth it exposed in its place. Recollecting something of my usual composure, I faced her with the most enigmatic smile that I could muster, insisted on a change of subject and refused to speak of my potential suicide again. She huffed with annoyance that the argument was over and carried on flicking through her magazine.

I waited for what I felt was a decent amount of time for the subject to be forgotten. Then I announced I was going into her basement to do a load of laundry. I mentioned casually that I'd be looking through some of my old boxes in the basement, so she wasn't to expect me back upstairs for a while. She barely looked up from her magazine. I walked down the stairs and closed the door behind me. Mechanically, I put the laundry in to wash, simply so the sounds would be authentic.

I was her mess to clean up. That was my reasoning. It wouldn't have been fair if I'd let some poor innocent bystander be the one to find my body. But I still wanted to clear my head and make sure I was doing the right thing before I acted. I sat down at an old plastic kitchen table and drew out the paper and pen I carried in my backpack. I drew a line down the middle of the paper. One side said "PROs" the other "CONs", and then I paused, sitting back for a moment to think. I was going to settle this ongoing issue of whether I should be alive or not once and for all.

Round Forty Seven

On the CONs side of committing suicide, I wrote down: "my friends", "it would upset everyone", "love". (By "love" I meant either that of a family or romantic love – love strong enough to be unconditional and help me through life.) Rather lamely I added "Books", "music" and "things may still get better" which concluded the CONs half of my list. I looked at the PROs column, the one in which I was meant to write down all the reasons I and the world would be better off if I was dead. It loomed in front of my eyes like a widening abyss. There was too much to say. I gazed at the PROs column and realised I could have written in it from then until Kingdom Come and even then I could not have given my reasons full justice. The only people I'd ever had true mutual love with were either absent beyond reach or dead, and it would only ever be love that could tether me firmly to the earth. In the absence of love there had been so much abuse, pain and devastation. I'd lived through so many days of mind blowing grief, mortification and struggle that there were times when I was alone when I would fall apart mentally and claw the skin on my face, rocking back and forth in whatever bed I'd been given and theorise that I was being tortured in some sort of nefarious experiment by an evil god.

It was the very fact that I knew that no matter how long I sat at that table writing my PROs list I wouldn't reach the end that made up my mind. It was a no-brainer really. I wanted to die *because* I had to write a list to ask myself if my life was of any value. I couldn't see any future for myself, at least no good one. I'd never been anything more than a bit of detritus pushed about on a rock circling the sun, where I'd dared to dream of freedom, love and equality. I wasn't *eager* to kill myself, as such. I felt about it much the same as you might feel about having a tooth pulled. It would be painful and unpleasant but for the greater good, so I'd just have to get on with it with as little fuss as possible. I wanted off the merry-go-round and to be with Troy again. I prayed to a nameless, vague god that I'd be reunited with him and granted a swift death. It was the only relief I could imagine.

Yes, I felt sorry for the people who I loved and who loved me. I knew better than anybody the desolation a suicide leaves in its wake. I knew they'd be distraught if I killed myself. But I also knew their lives would go on without me, just as they always had, until one day I'd become just a sad memory. I was loved by a couple of people, but it wasn't enough to justify an existence like that.

Having decided once and for all that I needed to commit suicide I only wished for my sake it would be quick and as painless as possible. I didn't have the same tolerance for pain I had cultivated a couple of years before when I was still self-harming, and before my health got so much worse. I didn't have Troy's balls, literally or metaphorically, nor did I have his guns which would have made it much quicker for me. If I had had a gun I wouldn't have shot myself in the stomach as he did, I would have blown my brains out all over Carol's walls. I had no desire to reflect on my error while I waited to die in agonising pain.

Several times I sat down to try to write a note to the few people who mattered to me. Leah, Vianne, Perry and Cora and my Grandparents, now so old and hours away in the country. They were the ones I worried about the most. I hadn't seen them as much since I'd lived in St. Louis but I talked to them any chance I had. They kept faith in me despite all the terrible things Carol said to them about me. I knew I was precious to at least those two distant saints, and I was terrified the news of my death might cause one of them to have a heart attack. It was ultimately very selfish of me that I knew they'd suffer that much but I was willing to carry on with my plan. But the point that I kept coming back to was that no one else was required to live my life but me. If they were in my shoes they'd know why I was doing this. More than anything else, it wasn't fair to hold me hostage in a life like mine just so others could carry on in their better lives without guilt or sadness.

I couldn't write the notes. Every time I tried to say goodbye and explain why I had to die, every time I told them I loved them, I became weaker and weaker in my determination to carry out the suicide. Writing the notes was holding me back, so finally I decided that just as I'd had to survive without a note from Troy, they would have to survive without a note from me. I couldn't put myself in their shoes and imagine their pain without feeling obliged to back out of my rationally made decision.

I headed once again to my mother's handy tool box, and pulled out the same pack of saw blades that I'd used previously. Time seemed to slow down a little as I took it over to the cleanest part of the floor I could find. I sat down, back against the wall, and stared at the blade pressed against my left wrist for several minutes before attempting to cut. Cautiously, I ran the razor over my skin. A thin line of blood appeared and I exhaled, relief flooding over me that the pain wasn't too bad. But I also knew it wasn't enough to kill me. So I cut again, deeper this time and gritting my teeth against the pain. I tried to remember how I'd done it so easily before because this time I felt every single millimetre of tearing skin. I took a deep breath and summoned the PROs and CONs list in my mind, and cut again, this time as quickly and deeply as possible, without thinking about it beforehand. Finally I had a satisfyingly deep cut. I stared at it in wonder as the blood began to pour freely, amazed that in a matter of only a few hours I would be a thing of the past. I pried the skin on both sides of the cut apart to encourage more bleeding.

Suddenly I remembered something I'd heard before; that if you want to slit your wrists you're supposed to do it somewhere like a bathtub, because the water worked to stop the blood clotting and encouraged a heavier flow. I didn't want all this to be for nothing so with my left arm now useless and dripping blood I pulled myself up from the floor. I was dizzy but focused. I went to the other side of the basement and found a bucket, which I took to the sink to fill up. I leaned over the sink, letting my blood wash down the drain while I waited for the bucket to fill. When it was done I lugged it back to my original seat with my right arm. I cut my left wrist once again for good measure and then stuck it in the bucket sitting on the floor next to me. Unable to withstand facing death with a sore bottom, I also grabbed a cushion and set it on the concrete floor next to the bucket, and sat down again.

I watched as the water turned from pink to red and for a while that alone held my interest. But then I became bored, wondering if I hadn't done it properly and how much longer it was going to take. There was a pile of magazines I could just about reach with my right hand, so I grabbed the one nearest me. I believe it was an issue of McCall's. For around twenty minutes perhaps, I sat there, flicking through the pages of the magazine with my right hand, and my left draining blood into the bucket. The minutes seemed to tick by slowly. Occasionally I glanced up from my page to check that the water in the bucket was continuing to become a deeper red, and although it was, I still felt quite well for the most part. I wondered if I needed to do the right wrist as well.

I can't really explain what changed. I had been so calm through the entire process, excepting the few tears that escaped me as I tried to write my notes. But the last time I glanced into the bucket the room began swimming before my eyes and I felt a wave of nausea. The change occurred in half a second. I went from sitting calmly and waiting to die with an issue of McCall's on my lap to being full of adrenaline. I felt disgusted with myself for sitting passively on the floor waiting to bleed to death. Instead I suddenly felt full of strength and power; I would have loved to have been thrown in a boxing ring to beat the shit out of everyone and everything that drove me to that point.

I leapt up; heedless of the water and blood my arm splashed and sprayed everywhere. Every iota of passive calm I'd felt since that moment by Carol's living room window vanished utterly. I felt a new kind of energetic calm, a focus undivided on the purpose of reclaiming myself. I needed to take care of my wounds, get myself mentally back in fighting form, tell my mother to go to hell and lastly, be Erin again. Someone who would survive, succeed and have a right to pride. The vow I'd repeated so many times came ringing in my ears; to make good on what happened to me, all of it, and Troy's death. I hadn't done that yet and I'd be damned if I'd take the easy way out until I'd heard my two cents echo all over the world.

I found a towel in my mother's laundry, wrapped it securely around my left wrist and slowly began climbing up the basement stairs. Blood was beginning to show through the towel. I felt dizzy each time I thought of it so I blocked it out of my mind, focusing on putting one foot in front of the other and preparing myself for the battle to come.

Round Forty Eight

Carol was still sitting on the sofa flicking through the pages of a magazine when I entered the living room. I didn't say anything because I didn't have time to argue with her, so I headed directly to her phone. It was time I called Josh to come and collect me, perhaps an hour or so later than I should have. As I was speaking to him Carol clocked the towel around my wrist and began shrieking like a banshee – any excuse for fireworks. I had a plan and I wasn't distressed at all. Josh and I would go to Walgreens where we'd buy everything necessary to bandage my arm. I'd bandaged and nursed countless cuts before and I fancied I had something like natural nursing talent. Then I'd find somewhere to sleep – I would, even if it meant I had to stay in Eat-Rite for a few days first. I'd carry on working as I always had and I'd get through this. It was just a blip on the radar caused by being in the wrong place, with the wrong person at the wrong time.

Carol didn't see it that way. When I hung up the phone with Josh she was screaming that she was going to call the police. I pointed out that I'd hurt myself, not her, so no crime had been committed. I painstakingly reminded her that I'd been taking care of myself totally independently since I was fifteen and she'd willingly and eagerly given up any right to call herself my mother. She had no right to step in now, no more so than if I was a stranger who would be free to leave her house unmolested. I said that if she wasn't happy for me to wait for my ride on her property I would go for a walk and wait for Josh outside. Nothing stopped her incessant screaming.

No one who hasn't had the singular experience of living with my mother can quite understand how strange she is. Many people might reasonably assume that she was screaming due to distress that her child had slit her wrist. But I'm sorry, that simply wasn't the case. She was screaming because she thrived off any chance to make herself feel and appear to be a victim, no matter what the situation.

Whatever was precisely wrong with her, she displayed behaviour consistent with Munchausen Syndrome by Proxy throughout my childhood. When I was in elementary school she convinced the school nurse that I was diabetic, despite the fact that I'm not.

I was pulled out of class every hour to drink a glass of orange juice to "maintain my blood sugar". That is only one incident of many. The more subtle side to this was far more damaging: she abused us relentlessly, all the while complaining to anyone who'd give her the time of day that she was a martyred, hard done-by single mother at the mercy of two evil girls. The role of martyr was the most important in her life, and we were the convenient means of achieving it. I sincerely believe that although she ordered Elaine and then me to vacate her house, she missed us after we were gone, because she lost the only two resources she could shamelessly use for attention seeking and temper venting.

Just a couple of hours before she'd listed to me all the reasons why I should die, and now she was pretending to faint on the sofa. Growing up with Carol has made me immune to hysterics. I waited patiently and tried to speak over her shrieks, telling her to pull herself together and that it was fairly obvious by that point that my wound wasn't going to kill me. I explained as if I was speaking to a child that she had no more reason to be upset than she had been when I cut my arm after Troy's death, and she'd barely noticed that. It was a pointless and frustrating endeavour to try to speak to her in a calm and sensible way. All she did was writhe and scream on the sofa.

Finally I gave up and said I was sorry to have inconvenienced her but that I wouldn't make the mistake of inviting myself over again. I said that since she couldn't pull herself together I was going to wait for Josh outside, that her shrieks were giving me a headache. Before I was half-way out the door she rapidly recovered from her faux-faint and jumped to grab the phone. She was calling the police on me. I gave her one last look full of loathing and contempt, and stepped outside. Forever, all she had done was grind me down and then punish me for being ground. She never gave a fuck about me unless she spotted an opportunity to punish and destroy. That seemed to be the only concept of parenting that she could grasp and easily the only kind she ever dealt out.

I stepped out into the sunshine outside and took a quick peek at my wrist under the towel. "It was clotting nicely, and based on my experience with my never-healing arm I thought I'd actually got away easily with the whole thing, so I remained unconcerned. I knew the police would be coming but I didn't feel I had done anything wrong; I'd never even raised my voice at Carol once during the entire visit. Yes, I'd hurt myself, but I was ignorant of the fact that that was a crime. I wasn't sure what I should do, but hope that Josh arrived before the police did. While I waited for something to happen either way, I wandered up and down the residential street Carol lives on.

When I saw two police cars and an ambulance pull up, a long sigh of defeat escaped me. I wasn't looking forward to dealing with the confrontation coming. To be honest, I felt remarkably fine and just wanted to move on past this trauma as I had every other. I began walking back to Carol's front yard where everyone was gathered. She was

300

putting on a marvellous show of hysterics, leaning against a police officer and asking for oxygen from the paramedics. She was loudly weeping and reminded me exactly of a conspicuously grieving widow at her mysteriously dead husband's funeral in an episode of Columbo. As I approached I heard her describing me as a wild animal that should be locked up. Another sigh escaped me.

To many people, some potentially intuitive police included, many of the things she was saying would have scanned like blinding red lights. She was screaming and sobbing that I was a flaw of nature and was also freely admitting that she'd made me leave home two years earlier because I was so unnatural and unlovable that the sight of me made her ill. I heard all of that and watched the policeman she was leaning on dutifully taking notes. For some reason, repeating many of the emotionally abusive things she'd always said to me as well as admitting that she'd thrown a minor onto the streets aged fifteen didn't raise any suspicions that perhaps her side of the story wasn't the only one, and maybe, just maybe, there was a direct connection to how she treated me and my actions of that day.

I heard it all, and decided to hold my head high and answer any questions honestly and calmly. I hoped that my calm compared to her hysteria might make a stronger impression than my bleeding wrist. I was stupid to hope any of that. This was the Afton/Lemay police department I was dealing with, famous for police brutality and

301

raping women pulled over for speeding. They were the good old boys who beat up black men, teenagers that looked different, and viewed women as fair game. The police force was notorious locally for corruption, abuse and a total lack of compassion for those they were meant to protect.

When the other characters in this charade noticed my quiet appearance pandemonium broke out. Carol broke into high pitched shrieks, as if I was wielding a chain saw at her. The paramedics made a bee-line for me, as did the police officer taking Carol's statement. I stood still and let them come to me to show I meant no harm. I even waved and said hello as they reached me. The medics began unravelling the towel around my wrist as the policeman began to shout at me for putting my poor mother through such an ordeal. I was slightly dazed by his aggressive introduction, shocked that he didn't even think it necessary to ask me what happened, even in the face of the outrageous display she was putting on and the things she was saying.

After he ranted at me for several minutes on the proper respect to show your parents, he finally demanded I answer him. So I said, "Don't you even want to hear what happened from me? Do I not even get a chance to speak before you assume everything she's saying is true? Did she tell you about the broken nose I got from her as a child? Did she mention kicking me down the stairs and locking me in the basement? Did she tell you that she fucking suggested I kill myself right before I tried it?" I said most of it very evenly but my voice began to rise at the end. I genuinely think I never had a chance to get through to him no matter what I could have said or done, but I convicted myself in his eyes the second I said "fucking". As soon as the word left my mouth the police officer grabbed my arm and whipped out his handcuffs. The paramedics protested against him as he tried to put them on me before they were finished bandaging my left wrist. I was completely and utterly shocked that I was being arrested, the handcuffs came without any warning and in my mind, cause.

He then spitefully informed me that attempting suicide was illegal and I could reflect on the pain I caused my mother while sitting in a jail cell. I glanced at her. She was conspicuously calm now and actually smiling. I was accepting the handcuffs, not resisting physically, but I found it almost impossible to remain quiet against his verbal taunts. I was outraged by his demeanour, his blind condemnation of me, and his total lack of insight or compassion. I asked him if he was happy with himself, if he enjoyed locking a girl up in jail for the crime of being abused her entire life, as he patted the abuser on the back. He said I needed to speak to an officer of the law with respect. I said an officer of the law took a vow to be fair, unbiased and protect and serve the innocent and he was choosing not to do that, which forfeited his entitlement to my respect.

In response to my words he pulled me sharply away from the medics still trying to bandage me through the cuffs and slammed me face down into the grass. His entire body, likely all three hundred pounds of it, was on my back. I wasn't made for a body slam like that; I was easily a foot and a half shorter than him, weighed no more than a hundred pounds soaking wet and you could count each of my ribs just by looking at me. To say I was shocked by this sudden physical turn of events would be an understatement of monumental proportions. I was also immediately struggling to breathe, and felt so smothered I began to panic. His entire body was crushing the length of mine and he was pushing my face into the grass and crushing my windpipe into the earth. I couldn't breathe. I heard choking sounds emanating from my throat and felt panicked that I couldn't make it stop. I tried to drag myself out from underneath him by digging my hands in the earth and pulling. By accident and due to the angle at which he held me, my elbow hit him in his upper arm during my attempt to escape. He pulled me up then slammed me down again, harder, and wrenched my arms behind my back. I screamed with pain. I heard a few protests from the medics, but he was like a bull in a rage. Actually, he was much like I'd seen Carol countless times before. The medics were saying I hadn't been properly bandaged yet and asked if we could all take several minutes to calm the situation down, but they went unheard.

He sat up to straddle me and his knee dug into my skinny back as he pulled me backwards by my handcuffed arms. He grabbed a handful of my hair and told me I was a stupid smart ass kid and I was going to get everything I deserved. I couldn't breathe

304

well enough to reply, my head was being held unnaturally far back by my hair, but I wouldn't have said anything even if I could have. I was truly in shock over everything that had happened since I called Carol from Josh's house. The whole situation had escalated so quickly that I was reeling trying to catch up. I was also deeply terrified of the man on my back, having seen the police beat people they were arresting enough times before to know I was only one word away from a punch in the face.

Wonder-Cop pulled me up from the ground, dirt in my mouth and smeared across my face from where he'd rubbed it into the earth. He began to march me towards his police car but at this point the medics became adamant. They insisted I needed hospital treatment and that they would have to take me in the ambulance. Reluctantly he handed me over to them, still handcuffed. His partner, who'd never said a word during the whole of the proceedings, was instructed to accompany me to the hospital, he remained silent in the ambulance.

As I was being walked to the ambulance Josh drove up, slowing his car down as he passed us, his mouth hanging open in disbelief. I shook my head "no" to him to indicate that he wasn't to stop and get involved. He mouthed the words "I'm sorry" to me, and slowly drove on. Wonder-Cop asked me if I knew that person and I said no.

The medic riding in the back of the ambulance with me made attempts at sympathetic conversation with me, asking me if I was okay and saying they could see there was more to the whole situation than what first met the eye. They asked if my wrist hurt very badly, and I replied honestly that I was in more pain all over my body from being slammed onto the ground multiple times. I'd carry the bruises for weeks after. I appreciated that the medics were showing me kindness but inside I was boiling with rage. This was precisely why Troy hated the police and "Lemolians" used to go to him for justice instead of the police. The police hated all of us. The way that officer treated me, from start to finish, seemed an extremely disproportionately harsh and aggressive reaction to a seventeen year old girl's personal moment of crisis, one in which she harmed no one but herself and said nothing but the truth. I couldn't believe the indignity I'd just suffered. I couldn't believe that so soon after facing that endless PROs column I already had grievances to add to it that I didn't know how to recover from. In yet another way I was being viciously punished because of Carol. Yes, I know I'm the one who slit my wrist. But yes, she suggested it to me, and the impact of hearing that from your own mother can't be underestimated. I'd been taking care of myself solely for two years and in the one moment of weakness I had in her presence all power was arbitrarily taken away from me again. Her parental rights were only ever exercised in ways calculated to make me miserable. Without opportunity for that her parenting began and finished with cashing her child support checks and going on weekly shopping sprees.

I remembered the thoughts that brought me out of the placid state of sitting with my arm in a bucket waiting to die while I read a magazine. They were life coursing through every vibrant inch of me, a desire to take revenge, a desire to throw blinding light on every skeleton in our family closet and expose the fact that I wasn't raised by anyone but I managed to grow-up well anyway, despite the constant abuse and neglect. Yes, I was hurting. But I was ready to come out fighting and that was the predominant feeling I had as I listened to the paramedic speak gently to me.

Round Forty Nine

I was taken to the emergency room where I was not very sympathetically stitched up; arriving in handcuffs doesn't endear you to hospital staff. The man who stitched my wrist told me I'd cut in the wrong direction. He said the most common mistake attempted suicides made was making the cut horizontally and not vertically, as a vertical cut was the one more likely to hit an artery. I felt surprisingly stupid for not knowing that and embarrassed that I made my one attempt at suicide incorrectly, but I filed the information away for future reference.

Can you understand how I might have felt the universe was telling me to kill myself? Earlier in the day it had been suggested to me by my mother and later I was told the more efficient way to carry it out by the man entrusted with the job of healing me. Not to mention the general tone of my life up to that day... It took an enormous amount of willpower to banish all thoughts of death and focus on succeeding. No matter how unlikely that looked at that time I was surer than ever that I would, somehow.

From the emergency room I was driven by the police to... Highland. I thought it was a little boring and predictable of the authorities to send me there but that wasn't really relevant. To be honest, I didn't really mind anywhere near as much as I did the first time. I knew the routine well and how to work it, and it would be a steady place to stay for a while which my parents would have to pay for.

Most of the staff remembered me and I was given a warm, almost homely welcome. It was quite nice actually. They were eager to hear about everything that happened in my life since my previous stay, and it was nice for me to get it all off my chest. I didn't resist the counselling as hard as I had before, realising it was good for me to finally uncork everything and talk frankly about what I had been through. But I stopped short of ever expressing any thoughts that could be deemed morbid, suicidal or dangerous to me or anyone else. I knew the red flags that they looked for in therapy sessions and I knew showing any of them would not only decrease the privacy and freedoms that I was allowed but would also extend my stay indefinitely.

I tried to look at this stay in Highland a little bit like a holiday. I had a private bedroom and bathroom including room and maid service and decent enough food if you overlooked the peas. My fellow holiday makers were inevitably full of entertainment and there was a library to pillage. The staff really liked me and I often sat with the nurses in their station into the wee hours of the morning, chatting and sharing stories. In general, being in Highland the second time was a cheerful, relaxing experience instead of the punishment it was intended to be. I knew how to light a cigarette, I knew it paid to be friends with the janitor, I knew that actually, if I wasn't there they wouldn't be getting paid. There was a system to work, just as there was everywhere.

Neither of my parents came to see me while I was there this time the staff knew better than to expect them to. I was happy about that and not at all surprised. I hated Carol, Lawrence and to a slightly lesser extent, Karen, with fresh vehemence. It was obvious there were the Haves and the Have Not's, and although my parents were on one side of the line, I was growing up on the other. The most basic reason for that was that none of them wanted to be parents and they all demonstrated it in different ways. I never ceased marvelling over the fact that Carol and Lawrence had tried to conceive a second child for four years before my appearance, but the second I came into the world they both suddenly decided being parents was something too unpalatable to face. It was hard not to take that personally and develop a complex over it. I felt enough contempt for them that I was ultimately happier raising myself than I would have been living with them, but I never stopped feeling the injustice of it all. They'd brought me into this world then made every attempt to steam-roll over my existence.

While I was in Highland again I managed to find the Muslim psychiatrist who had gently but firmly put me in my place when I threw Troy's tattoos at him. He was working on a different ward to mine but after I ran into him on the way to lunch one day and spoke to him he dabbled a little with the doctors assigned to me. I told him that Troy had died shortly after my last release, gestured to my arm and said "I didn't handle it well". I said I still loved Troy as I always had, but that I was very sorry for what I had said to him. I added that I thought Nazis and Skinheads were awful people and I would make it one of my goals in life to stand against them. Not only for the predominant moral reason but also because it was personal. It was people who held those beliefs who had abused Troy throughout his childhood and contributed to the end of his life. I had much to make right. I thanked the doctor for reacting to me as he did. He smiled at me, patted my shoulder and said he understood better than I might know, and he held no grudges. He said he hoped that I would find my peace and place in life and that I would carry on working to achieve everything I set out to. We said a formal but fond goodbye.

They only kept me in for around two weeks this time. When they told me I was free to go home I was slightly more disappointed than they expected. I didn't want to stay there forever, but I also didn't feel ready to go back to the frightening outside world. I didn't feel capable of doing everything I knew I would have to do again; I didn't feel capable of surviving alone. But there wasn't anything to be done about it and I knew I'd have to face reality again eventually, so I may as well get it over with.

Upon my discharge the staff told me that they liked me very much but they sincerely hoped never to see me again, as that would mean I was still struggling. They wished me all the very best. I was still underage so legally they had to release me to one of my parents. Because my father simply refused to be involved in any way, and I was indirectly sent in because of my mother, they insisted she do her legal duty by me. The staff knew I wasn't going to be living with her again, but she had to come, sign me out and drive me away. This time Carol was given no friendly reception and the nurses glared at her as they brushed past. The doctor turned his back and refused to acknowledge her but gave me a very fond farewell. After she signed the forms she threw the pen on the desk in anger and stomped out. I dragged my bags behind her. As I was leaving the ward I heard the doctor direct one of the nurses to follow us and ensure I was safely seen into the car. A few of them stood in the outer door and waved goodbye to me. Inside the car, Carol swore at them and me as we drove off.

I didn't know what to say when she and I were alone together. She was the first one to speak, asking me where I wanted to be dropped off. For a moment I didn't answer, marvelling at her sheer hypocrisy and cruelty, consigning me to homelessness without remorse while playing the wounded dove with the rest of the world. I gave myself a mental slap in the face because the very fact that she could still surprise and hurt me meant I still cared too much about her opinion. I had learned that indifference was more powerful than hate and closer to the opposite of love, and I had to be indifferent to her. I directed her to take me to Eat-Rite. Nothing else was said.

She pulled into Eat-Rite's car park. I gathered my things and got out of the car, shutting the door behind me without either of us saying goodbye. When I walked into the diner, wrist bandaged and carrying all my worldly belongings, Tammy set down a plate of eggs and beans and took a good long look at me. Her eyes misted over. Arms out, she walked to me and wrapped them around me, holding me there in the middle of the restaurant and petting me as if I was a child. With a word mumbled over my shoulder she told the cook to carry my bags into the staff room and she walked me there, leading me to a small bed the staff used during overnight shifts. We sat down on it side by side and she held me as I shook and cried.

Round Fifty

After a long, thorough cry, I slept for hours on the cot in the Eat-Rite staff room. I was awakened by the deliberately loud huffs and stomps from the disgruntled dishwasher. It was clearly someone else's turn to use the room to rest... I gathered my belongings and headed to my regular table in the corner. After spending some time collecting my thoughts, I dug a few quarters out of my wallet. I went to the payphone to call Vianne. I'd lost track of the days somewhat but I thought she might be home from her holiday by then. I was correct, but she did not respond to me as I expected or hoped. I hoped she and Josh would come and collect me and I'd go back to staying at her house. It wasn't a case of using her at all; I loved her with all of my heart and wouldn't have wanted to stay with anyone who I wasn't as close to. But I thought that part of how she loved me was that she understood the burden I carried of having no home and she was happy to alleviate that when possible.

I forgot to take into account Vianne's expectation of perfect mental health and behaviour in everyone around her, no matter how she behaved. She came on the phone screaming obscenities and abuse at me for cutting myself. It was funny in a way, only the month before I caught her slashing her upper thigh in her bathroom. When I walked in and discovered her covered in blood I tenderly washed and bandaged her, then held her while she cried it out. It seems a similar sort of compassion was not to be extended to me. The eternal guest has to be on eternally best behaviour, right? I listened, numb and knowing there was no point in arguing with her when she was in this kind of self-righteous rage. I was in such a twist of emotional pain as I heard my best and only friend then in St. Louis say things to me that were painfully similar to what Carol had said the day I slit my wrist. Vianne was screaming that if I'd been

313

sufficiently grateful for the fact that I'd been allowed to stay at her house as often as I had, I never would have tried to kill myself, so I didn't deserve her house and time now. She missed the irony that I'd had a crisis of homelessness (and all it entailed) during the time I'd been unceremoniously booted out of her house so she could tour Europe in a series of five star hotels. Not for the first time, she was behaving like the essentially spoiled little rich girl that she was, and I was almost as angry at her for that as she was angry at me. I could hear Josh and her mother trying to calm her on the other end of the line. It was a scene I could easily picture as I'd witnessed it many times before, though other people had been the targets then and I was the one trying to calm her down.

Then she spat out that I should have done a better job of killing myself. She said she wished I had been successful in my attempt and that I may as well have because I was dead to her from that point on. Those were the words that felt like a sucker punch. She knew the enormity of what she meant to me and was still prepared to say that.

I got it. It was her personality and she'd never change, no matter how many times she felt remorseful after flying into one of these rages. It wasn't so very different to dealing with Carol, the only difference being that Carol never felt remorse over her rage; she simply chose to pretend it never happened. When her screaming finally ran out of steam, I quietly asked Vianne if she'd like to hear my side of things, how I was feeling and what had happened when I made that abortive suicide attempt. My words just whipped her into a fresh frenzy of mind ripping abuse. I listened, but only for a couple of moments when I finally just put the phone down. Well, that was over.

Not being able to stay at Vianne's house was the least of my pain that day. It was the loss of her and the horrible things she'd said to me. I loved her so much. She and her family had become more mine than my own. It did cross my mind briefly that perhaps she and Carol were right and I should have succeeded in killing myself. But then I began to feel angrier instead of hurt, and anger generally drives me out of any self-destructive thoughts. I knew I'd messed up, I knew I'd done a stupid thing. And I'd paid for it dearly. I knew that no matter what, if the roles were reversed I never would have turned Vianne away. I would have done anything for her because that's what I did and still do for the people in my life who I love with every ounce of my being. I was tired of friends thinking that because they let me sleep in their house when it was convenient to them, that they held some sort of committee position of authority over my life. I wasn't as conditional in the love and friendship that I gave and I resented that absolutely no one was there to return that. Vianne broke my heart, but after that I wasn't so very keen to see her either and I wouldn't have returned to her house if she'd shown up at Eat-Rite and begged.

I didn't have a solution as to where I was going to live but after hanging up the phone with Vianne it was no longer the most prominent thing in my mind. All I wanted to do was write until I was exhausted. I returned to my table, put my headphones on, pulled out my notebook and pen and wrote for ten hours straight. Tammy and then the waitress who took over on the morning shift gave me endless refills of coffee and seemed to understand that I was in my own world, as they didn't stop to talk to me like they normally would have.

When I was done, the very first draft of this book was written and I realised I'd just spent the night successfully, safely inside the diner. As if writing opened me up to divine inspiration, I discovered that I could live at Eat-Rite.

Round Fifty One

The first days ticked over as I adjusted to a new routine. I spent most of my day writing, furiously and likely often incoherently, writing. Putting on paper every accusation, heartbreak and event I'd lived through. It was erratic and full of so many memories, angry rants, and desperate pages praying for deliverance or death. When I got tired of writing I read from the small library I carried with me wherever I went. Almost always I had my headphones on, playing tape after tape. I carried several dozen cassettes in my backpack, along with all my books and notebooks so it was extremely heavy. When I needed to wash myself I made use of Eat-Rite's ladies' bathroom which doubled as the wheel chair accessible toilet. It was roomy enough to spread out, use as a changing room and do some freshening up. If I waited until the right time of night I could stay in there uninterrupted for long enough to do a very thorough grooming routine, including washing my hair and cleaning the row of stitches on my wrist.

As the days rolled into more days and then the week into weeks, I perfected the art of sleeping shallowly and upright, or with my head only slightly down on one arm. All of the diner employees knew I was living there but Tammy had a private word with me and explained that we couldn't let the information reach the owners. Therefore it was important that the other diner patrons didn't see me spread out asleep across the table. I was careful to keep my bags hidden under the table and keep all of my belongings tidied away in them as much as possible.

Time passed while I stalled, wondering what I would do next. It crossed my mind that I might try throwing myself on the mercy of Leah's parents, who I knew to be good, kind people. But I couldn't bring myself to do it. I could never tell if they liked me or not, but I believed they'd feel obliged to allow me to stay at their house. However I didn't think they would in truth want me there, and I'd ruled out ever being an unwanted burden again. There weren't really any other options, so I came to the conclusion that I'd simply have to continue as I was. The diner showed no signs of kicking me out, so I'd make the most of that while I could. It was uncomfortable and inconvenient to live in a hard chair at a table but it would do. Words can't express how much I didn't want to be the unwanted houseguest anymore, able to be turned out at a moment's notice. Countless people knew I was homeless, and even openly admired me for my fortitude. They admired as they walked away from my plight. I was like a bit of unclaimed baggage, endlessly circling on the belt hoping to be lifted off.

Round Fifty Two

Eat-Rite had many regulars, all eccentric in one way or another. I was friends with pretty much all of them and my permanent presence made me become much more familiar with some that had previously passed slightly under my radar. It soon became obvious that a girl who came in every day for lunch was extremely interested in me. I knew who she was but I'd never spoken to her before beyond a polite hello. She was amongst the group of young Christians who often met in Eat-Rite to socialise and philosophise together.

Every day she asked if she could sit with me and for a while I said no and that I wished to be alone. I assumed if I gave her a minute of my time she'd begin preaching and I'd never be able to escape the conversation without resorting to rudeness. But she was so friendly and persistent that after a while I felt I was being rude to carry on refusing her company, so finally I said yes. Her name was Kim and she was newly married to a softly spoken pacifist called Dan. I was then seventeen and they were nineteen and twenty respectively. If I had to sum them up with music as I often do with people, I'd use Nivana's "Incesticide", Counting Crows, "August and Everything After" with something akin to Sarah McLachlan mixed in. A little vanilla for my tastes, excepting Nirvana, but nothing offensive.

At night Eat-Rite was full of kids more or less my age, all debating over subjects they were covering in college, church or whatever. Eat-Rite had an odd ability to host people of wildly different morals, views and habits and make the combination exciting rather than combative. The days at Eat-Rite were quiet and typically reserved for the old men sitting at the counter and me sitting on my table writing. Kim kept appearing during the day trying to make conversation and I would search for a way to politely explain there were hours for that sort of thing. Her persistence to join me during the day, every day, was certainly an intrusion into my calm routine at first, but it eventually became something I came to look forward to. She was a devout Christian, but in a way I'd never seen or imagined before. It was still very easy to relate to her. To be fair, she was a recent convert and had a very sordid past, so we had more in common than what was obvious to the naked eye.

After a week or so of cautiously talking to each other during the day, both of us avoiding sensitive subjects, she finally came to the point that she was there to make. She looked pointedly at the stitches in my wrist and the bags around my chair, overflowing with clothes, books and cosmetics. Then she asked me if I actually *lived anywhere*. She said she'd come to Eat-Rite every day at different hours of the day and I was always there. Did I ever go anywhere?

Initially I was slightly insulted by her nosiness, but then I figured she was just pointing out the obvious and I admired her forthrightness. So I told her the truth, which was that I lived at Eat-Rite. She wanted to know about my life and so for the next hour or two I told her a brief history of me. She was speechless when I finished, and said it was a miracle that I was sitting there talking to her as sanely as I was. I laughed. Then she completely shocked me by asking out of the blue if I would please come home with her and live with her and her husband, in their spare room. She said I could stay there as long as I wanted with no conditions asked for in return. She just didn't want me to be homeless anymore.

I was truly speechless. It was an astonishingly kind offer from someone I barely knew. And it was for that very reason that I was obliged to say "thank you, but no". She was offering out of a sense of Christian charity, and I didn't want to take advantage of an impulse she'd no doubt regret later on. Kim and Dan had only been married for two months. I didn't want to intrude on newlyweds. I didn't want to live at the mercy of other people anymore, and I didn't want to be pressured to convert to Christianity. I also wasn't sure she understood exactly what she was offering. I'd lost my job at Steak 'n Shake when I'd recently been admitted to Highland, and she was saying she and Dan were happy to provide for me in all ways. She wanted me to live with them, and first take a long rest where I focused on processing the grief accrued throughout my life. She said after I'd had as much time as was required to do that, then I could look for a job *if I wanted to* and contribute to their household expenses, *if I wanted to*. Not even my parents had ever offered me as much. It was without a doubt the kindest, most selfless offer I'd ever been given, and it made my heart feel full to bursting. It was largely because I thought she was so naively kind that I was obliged to say no, out of my own kindness. I didn't think it would work and I wasn't willing to take advantage or even to be perceived of taking advantage of a mistaken offer made in kindness.

Kim was disappointed and visibly upset, but not terribly surprised that I declined her offer. I emphasised to her that I was very grateful but that I didn't think it would work out well. I tried to explain that it wasn't personal; I just didn't want to live with other people anymore. I was tired of being taken in and put out again like a garbage can. She seemed to understand, but she came back every day after that, and repeated her offer as often as she could get away with before I became annoyed. There were days when she'd come close to tears when I had to say once again that I wouldn't go home with her, and I was very sorry for her. I was genuinely coming to like her but I was not going to budge on the issue. I thought she was a little naïve, and that I had to protect her from her own well intentioned actions. It was an odd sort of blooming friendship.

Round Fifty Three

Despite the fine accommodation and company Eat-Rite offered, I became mind numbingly bored of seeing nothing but those four walls for over a month. The furthest from my table that I'd ventured since the day I was released from Highland were trips to the parking lot to stretch my limbs. I enjoyed the socialisation that I had at Eat-Rite, but I was also becoming self-conscious that it was now obvious to everyone else, in addition to Kim, that I didn't just happen to be there uncannily often, but that I lived there. They all had such lovely lives, with loving families and homes. A day came when I felt too out of place, so I decided I had to move on. Eat-Rite wasn't the only twenty-four hour diner that would offer me sanctuary. So I got a lift off a truck driver to the Lemay Steak 'n Shake.

Although I wasn't employed there anymore, I knew I could count on everyone there being happy to see me. I was welcomed with a round of cheers when I walked through the door which was as heartening as it was embarrassing. They had a backroom too and my friend Perry was then the manager in all but name. The other managers were the same ones I'd worked under and were happy to let me stay and even help out when necessary. I intended to stay there as I had at Eat-Rite but as soon as I announced my intentions, Candy, the waitress I was closest to, insisted she'd accept nothing less than me coming home with her. She said I was the daughter she'd never had and if I didn't want to break her heart I had to stay with her. It was very sweet, and easier to say yes to than the offer from Kim. Kim, I was sure didn't know what she was trying to get herself into. Candy, on the other hand, had known me since I'd been with Troy and lived like all Lemolians did, expecting regular trouble. In Lemay I didn't get the feeling I sometimes had elsewhere, that I was polluting the place. I felt at home.

The only reservation I had about moving in with Candy was that it was well known her husband beat her, and I wasn't sure I'd be able to stop myself fighting him if he hurt her in my presence. But then I decided I'd capitalise on spending so much time with her, and spend every moment in an effort to help her escape him. After giving the matter a little thought, I said yes and at the end of her shift, Candy and I went home together. She made me a bed on her sofa and fussed about me, trying to make me comfortable and getting me to fill her in on all the developments in my life since we'd last seen each other. It felt so good to be home again in Lemay.

Candy had qualified as a nurse years ago; I'm not sure how she'd gone from that to waitressing. She asked me how long the stitches had been in my wrist, and it occurred to me that when I'd been discharged from Highland weeks earlier, no one had given me instructions as to how to care for my stitches, nor how or when to get them removed. I'd used common sense and kept them clean but I hadn't given the issue any thought beyond that until Candy brought it up. I gave Candy the date that the stitches were put in and she said they were overdue to come out. The wound did look very well healed, so I agreed we could remove them. I'd become so used to seeing a row of neat black crosses made of thread holding my wrist together that it almost felt like removing a permanent part of myself and my identity. It was daunting, but I looked forward to the wound being less visible to others.

We were in her little living room, now doubling up as my bedroom. I was sitting on the sofa and she sat on the coffee table opposite me. My senses were awake to everything around me; I was entirely and wholly in the present moment. My world shrunk down to the dim room with false wood panelled walls, the hum of the window air-conditioning unit, the feeling of the brown cord of her sofa on the skin of my legs. We were both concentrating intensely on the task at hand. I rested my wrist facing upwards on her thigh, and she began to carefully snip and pluck the threads out, one after the other. I watched, mesmerised to see the skin that had been torn apart hold together as the stitches were removed; I think I half expected that the cut would open and start bleeding again.

When she was about a third of the way through the job I said "Stop," and gently took the scissors from her with my right hand. She handed them over and held my left hand both for comfort and to keep it still. She watched as I continued removing my stitches, and occasionally murmured words of encouragement and praise. My eyes were wide with wonder over how competently I was preforming a medical task and taking care of myself. I slowly and carefully snipped and pulled over twenty more stitches out of my own skin without feeling the slightest bit queasy. My breathing was calm. I didn't feel like a fully physical creature, somehow I felt more than that, and the part of me that was more rejoiced over its dominance of the physical. It was enchanting.

When I completed the job I felt exultant, like a champion over myself. I shared a huge smile with Candy. And then, like a rain cloud quickly passing over a sunny day, my face crumpled into tears. I felt deflated, thrown out of my moment of perfection. I cried so hard my ribs were hurting and I was struggling to breathe. Candy lowered me onto my bed on the sofa. She held and rocked me while I cried, and most importantly, she completely understood why I was crying without needing me to explain. Yes, I was very proud that I'd just removed my own stitches. That was something usually done by trained professionals and I'd done a great job at it. I was crying because I *needed* to do it. Because despite being covered by insurance that would have paid for any treatment in America, it was inaccessible to me, and the people who were actually designated to my care by nature and by law never bothered to wonder if my wrist had even healed, or how I might handle the stitches.

It was a moment of triumph, no doubt, when I removed my own stitches. It made me feel accomplished for the first time in a very long time, and it made me feel I was growing competent enough to make wise decisions and actions for myself. But it also made me very lonely because I belonged to nobody. It made me indescribably sad when I considered that the burden of my care was always mine to enjoy, and depended so much on the random kindness of others.

Round Fifty Four

While I stayed with Candy, I settled into yet another new routine. She and I would spend time together at her house until it was time for her to go to work. She didn't think I'd be safe from her husband if I was at her house alone, so whenever she went to work I went with her. I spent her shifts at Steak 'n Shake doing a variety of things. Most of the time I read and wrote while drinking coffee at the counter, but during especially busy times I'd put an apron on and help out. When I got restless I'd walk around Lemay, sometimes standing across the street from Troy's house and staring at his bedroom window, sometimes just wandering aimlessly.

Many times during my stay with her I witnessed violent arguments between Candy and her husband. He was an out of work alcoholic, and he constantly harangued Candy to work more hours, bring in more money, do more housework and so on. She usually tried to remain quiet and ignore his rants, but sometimes she'd snap and argue back, at which point he'd hit her. My presence during these intimately abusive moments diffused them somewhat; Candy would often remind him he was doing all of this in front of me, which seemed to snap him out of it a bit. Then he'd look at me, with eyes full of hatred. Each time, I stubbornly refused to break eye contact with him. I wondered if he would eventually break down and attack me too, but I wasn't willing to cower before him, which is exactly what every bully hopes to achieve. Almost every dispute between them would end with him storming out the door and driving away, and Candy and I collapsing in relief. If necessary I'd fetch an ice pack or anything else she might need, and we'd discuss the possibility of her leaving him. She didn't depend on him financially, so I found it frustrating that it was so difficult to convince her that it was the right thing to do.

We did talk daily about her leaving him, I even met her mother and asked her mother to join me in encouraging Candy to leave, which she did. Each time I tried to get her to commit to leaving she'd say that she would do it one day, just not yet. It was always "not yet", and I couldn't see what she was waiting for. I decided the best I could do was carrying on offering Candy advice and support and be ready when she was. She was helping me, and I sincerely wanted to help her.

Almost three weeks into staying at Candy's and much to my shock, Kim crossed over from my Eat-Rite world into my Steak 'n Shake world, worlds that had hitherto been compartmentalised. The day Kim found me at Steak 'n Shake I was having a picnic under a tree in the grassy area beyond the car park. I looked up from my book and saw her approaching me, carrying a carton of cigarettes. They were a present for me and an instant endearment since I was completely broke. The small amount of money I had came from tips earned while unofficially helping in the restaurant. I had to pay for all of my expenses except housing, which were predominantly food and cigarettes. At that time I depended more on the cigarettes than the food.

My first thought when I saw Kim? "My god she's persistent!" I asked her how she knew where I was and she said someone at Eat Rite told her that if I wasn't there I was probably here. I rolled my eyes and threw my apple core at a tree. I gratefully took the carton of cigarettes and tore into a pack, lighting one and sucking in in ecstasy. We smiled at each other, and I teased her a little bit, saying that if I'd wanted to be found I would have told her where I was going before I'd gone, but seeing as she was there any way we may as well hang out. I was actually happy to see her, and she knew that.

Once again, she wasted no time in coming to the point. She asked me earnestly, in her most serious tone, if I would *please* move in with her and Dan. She swore on her god, which I knew meant everything to her, that contrary to it being a burden, she and Dan were incredibly eager for me to live with them and very sad that I wasn't. She said it was a burden to them that I'd said no for so long. She was a little hurt, and asked me why I was willing to live with Candy when I had said no to her so many times. The simplest answer was that when Candy offered I knew I could make myself useful to her, but more to the point, I knew she fully understood what she was offering. Half of Lemay had been homeless at one time or another and it was usual to offer hospitality to friends without accommodation. It was the way of life and everyone understood how it worked. I'd always felt that Kim and Dan were genuine but too naïve, promising more than what could be realistically achieved.

However, I wasn't so quick to brush her off this time. The night before, I'd woken in the middle of the night to the sounds of Candy's husband beating her in their bedroom. I lay on my sofa, frantically trying to think of what I should do that wouldn't hurt Candy any more, or me more than I could handle. It seemed my only options were calling the police, which Candy had sternly instructed me never to do, or barge in and try to beat him off of her. I knew he could quickly overpower me but I thought together Candy and I might have a chance. I was very scared. Unsure about what to do, but knowing I had to do something. I decided to first try to stop the assault without adding my physical presence to it. I got up and slammed the bathroom door as loud as I could so they'd know I was awake and hearing it. If that didn't stop him, I was resolved to grab a blunt object and hit him over the head with it. Thankfully I was relieved from the obligation to do so. As soon as I slammed the door, all went quiet in their bedroom. I stood; chest heaving with fear as Candy's husband came storming out of their bedroom, pulling a shirt on as he walked. As he passed by me, he told me to stay the fuck away from him or he'd take me down a few pegs. I didn't reply. As soon as I heard his truck tear out of the drive I ran into their bedroom to take care of Candy.

I wasn't willing to abandon Candy, but in the weeks I'd been living with her I hadn't managed to make any headway in convincing her to leave him. In addition, he was growing more familiar and rough in the way that he spoke to me. As I became a fixture in his household, where he held jurisdiction, I was beginning to feel it was only a matter of time before he felt able to treat me the way he treated her. I wanted stability and safety, but I was torn over what was the right thing to do. I felt obliged to do right by Candy, but Kim seemed the safer option. They were equally willing to keep me.

Finally I came to a decision. I asked Kim to wait for me while I went to speak with Candy. I decided to try to persuade her once more in the strongest possible terms to leave her husband. I told her that if she'd leave him I'd stay with her and do everything in my power to help her rebuild her life, and mine too. If she said yes, I would tell Kim no without regret. But she said no. She said that she loved him despite it all and wasn't going to leave him then or ever. She knew the disturbing events of the night before had made a huge impact on me, and she said she wouldn't blame me for going somewhere better. It was very hard; I didn't want to betray this woman who'd been so kind to me. But her adamant statement that she wasn't ever going to leave him made me feel that there was little point in living there just to be available when she was ready to go. Presumably that day would never come, and all the while I would be endangering myself for a hopeless cause. I promised Candy I would stay in touch and be there in a heartbeat if she ever changed her mind. Although she never did choose to leave him, we did remain close. But we weren't going to be living together anymore. I'd finally decided to accept the offer Kim and Dan had first made around two months earlier.

When I returned to Kim, I thanked her again for her offer of a home and said that I would be pleased to accept it. She did a little victory dance and song, which made me look at her as though she'd lost her marbles. I said she was a very strange person to be so excited over taking a penniless waif into her love nest. She grinned during the entire drive to her apartment, gleefully recounting all the things we'd do together. I thought she was slightly insane, but despite myself I began to feel some of her excitement rubbing off on me. Another new world was opening up to me, and maybe this one was where I was destined to belong.

Round Fifty Five

Kim and Dan were extremely generous to me. They offered me my own room, which was a sort of enclosed porch off their kitchen. They didn't expect any rent and were happy to pay for my food and even cigarettes. Basically, they would provide anything I needed. It was overwhelming and unprecedented, and I worked very hard to take as little from them as possible. They were adamant that I should take a significant amount of time off before looking for a job, believing I needed time to heal from everything I'd been through. I was very grateful for that, but I couldn't bring myself to wait for very long before I began looking for work within walking distance of their apartment. By the end of three weeks I'd found a job, whereas they had suggested I take six months or more. I did love having some time where I could do only what I wanted to, never anything I was obliged to do. It felt like I'd been working in one form or another for as long as I could remember, so it was a luxury beyond explanation to sleep for as long as I wanted in my very own bedroom, to lounge on a sofa and read for hours, take hour long baths and generally relax.

I loved it, so much, and I knew Kim and Dan couldn't fully grasp how wonderful the gift they were giving me was. I came to love *them* very quickly; I don't know how I couldn't have in the face of so much kindness. I wanted to make sure they'd never suffer for their kindness to me, so I felt it was important not to lean on them financially any longer than necessary. My work-free time in their apartment was lovely, but I couldn't help but continually calculate how much I was costing them. I applied to a McDonald's around the corner from their apartment in South St. Louis City and was hired the same day. I went back to the apartment proud to announce my surprise news to Kim and Dan, thrilled that I was showing them through actions that I wasn't a waste of time, and I was a hard worker who wanted to give back as much as they were giving me. I wanted them to know that their act of kindness hadn't been wasted on me, that I would take the opportunity they were giving me to make my life as good and productive as possible.

As soon as I moved in, Kim made the delightful decision that I should have the singular dignity of having all of my possessions together in that one sacred bedroom. Since I'd left home at fifteen I'd generally travelled around with only a backpack and extra bag, but I had several boxes of books stored at Carol's house and my precious black trunk still at Vianne's. I didn't want to see either of those two people, but I was finally feeling good enough about myself that I could deal with them without approaching the situation with terror. It made the world of difference that Kim was going with me to both locations to collect my things. I felt supported by her, and she knew the huge emotional toll meeting both Carol and Vianne would take from me, no matter how I tried to prepare myself beforehand. Collecting from Carol's house was easy in the end, because we didn't speak to each other at all. Carol asked Kim why she'd taken me in. Kim replied that it was because I was worth taking in and she enjoyed my company. When we got back into Kim's car, she said "I hope this doesn't offend you, but your mother is a very strange woman." I laughed and said no, I wasn't offended, and yes, she was.

Seeing Vianne wasn't going to be so simple. I'd made the arrangements to collect my things with her mother, and I was hoping Vianne wouldn't be there. The trunk that was still at her house held my most precious objects: mementos from Troy, my nephew and my grandparents; countless notebooks full of my writing. I prayed she wouldn't be so malicious as to destroy it, and grateful for its padlock and sturdy metal frame.

When Kim and I pulled up to Vianne's house, she was sitting on her front porch with Josh, my belongings piled up on the grass. I should have known better than to hope Vianne would let me collect my things in peace. I should have known she would never pass up an opportunity to twist the knife inside someone after she'd stabbed them with it. The intended point was clear; I was being treated like a leper, not even fit to step foot inside her house that I'd once called home. I took a deep breath, and getting out of the car, began walking with Kim at my side across the lawn to them. Josh avoided making eye contact with me but I forced it by staring at his face, wanting him to see in my eyes the behaviour he was condoning. In the short second he looked at me, he attempted an apologetic, sympathetic smile. I didn't smile back. I hadn't just lost Vianne, I'd also lost Josh who I'd been very close to and trusted implicitly. His lack of backbone in dealing with Vianne's hypocritical, harsh and controlling behaviour caused me to lose all respect for him.

Kim and I gathered my belongings and I said "Well goodbye then" which were the first words uttered by anyone since our arrival. And then Vianne showed me precisely how low and sadistic she could go. She pointed to my boots. As she pointed to the boots that I thought were mine, she said "Those boots are mine. I want them back, now." She had given me those boots - over a year earlier. They were my only pair of shoes. She'd given them to me because she thought they were ugly, and she had over fifty pairs of boots and shoes housed in a walk in closet larger than my current bedroom. She'd declared at the time of giving them to me that she neither wanted nor needed them. She knew they were my only footwear. She didn't even want them for herself; she just wanted to control and hurt me.

I was beyond stunned. Kim and even Josh's jaws dropped. Josh murmured to Vianne, saying maybe she should let it go and let me keep them, that maybe she needed some time to calm down. She snapped at him, replying that if he had a problem with what she was doing then he could leave with me, which promptly shut him up. I could not believe that the girl I'd lived with so intimately and loved so dearly was going so far out of her way to devastate me. For a second I thought of refusing to hand over the boots and just walk away. They had been given to me, not loaned. I'd had them for over a year and she had no right to them. I went through my life trying to pay every debt I had, but this was no debt. This was her striking out at me.

I hated her so much in that moment I didn't want to leave that situation feeling like I was indebted to her for a single thing. I didn't want to have her to thank every morning when I put my shoes on. Instead, I wanted to give her the chance to reflect on how sick she was. I stared at her face as if I was studying her for the first time, as if we hadn't spent entire days lying in bed together talking and staring into each other's eyes. I was searching for the traces of self-absorbed tyranny that I'd missed before. I looked at her like she was an unpleasant curiosity. I sat down on the grass and one at a time unlaced and removed my boots, all the while looking at her. When I had them off I stood again and dropped them at her feet. I said "Well done!", and smiled, because her cruelty gave me the chance to rise above it. She lunged up out of her chair as if to attack me and Josh held her back. Kim and I returned to her car carrying the rest of my worldly belongings, except my boots. My socks, full of holes, were soaked through from the grass.

When I closed the car door, my self-control threatened to vanish. The indignity I'd just suffered choked me. The mixture of emotions I felt while I walked away from Vianne, so spoiled, sitting in front of her mansion while I wore only socks with holes in the toes, couldn't be conveyed if I devoted five thousand words to the subject. It was painful and wrong on every level, and it caused a sudden and drastic change in my mood. I felt I was the moral victor in that situation, but moral victories are hard to enthusiastically celebrate when your feet are wet and you've just been demeaned as a human being before an audience.

Living with Kim and Dan, such very kind people, had made me feel better and more myself than I had since before Troy died. For the first time in so long, I had real, solid grounds on which to build my future and hope for a greater life. I'd felt buoyant, which was a new and different sensation from my usual focus: survival. Vianne struck a severe blow that day. It was hard work to stop the vindictiveness, insult and humiliation of it all from consuming me. Kim and I drove away in silence; she understood I was unable to speak. I was trying to regulate my breathing and pull myself back from that place where I knew it was possible for me to tip over the edge.

After much internal struggle I managed to get to a point where I could breathe normally and feel okay about what happened. I'd been in danger of hitting a new low over the incident, but instead I turned it around and added it to my list of motivations to succeed. I didn't want to talk about it, but I wanted Kim to know I was okay and that I was grateful for her support. So eventually I broke the silence by saying "Well, that was interesting! Aren't we glad it's over?" She smiled at me, but wiped a little tear out of the corner of her eye. She said "Erin, I'm so proud of you. You've been through so much and you handle everything with such grace. I don't think I could do what you've had to do." I was embarrassed and humbled by her words, so I shook my head in response.

We returned to our apartment and began unpacking all of my things into my little room. I enjoyed setting up my few ornaments, hanging pictures up (just so!) and organising my books, tapes, CDs and records. While I was decorating my room Kim came in bearing a pair of boots. They were one of her pairs, and she insisted they didn't fit her so would go to waste if I didn't accept them. It was an exceptionally thoughtful gesture. They were a pinch small for me but I accepted them gratefully. It had certainly been a difficult day, but I'd gone through it with a friend at my side and my head held high. And best of all, as I went through it I had the confidence and good feeling that comes from knowing I had my own room to return to, somewhere where I was wanted.

Round Fifty Six

I loved my new room. Because our apartment was on the second floor and my room was actually an enclosed porch dangling off the back of the building, it felt like I was sleeping in a magical tree house. With no air conditioning, the room was an oven in the St. Louis heat. But it was my oven. I slept with the windows open and a cool breeze floated through every night, caressing my skin and making me feel glorious. Kim and Dan were beyond reproach as hosts and roommates. They went out of their way to include me and make me feel wanted and comfortable.

There was only one problem, and it was one of the most important reasons I'd refused their invitation to live with them for as long as I did. It was awkward living with newlyweds, and it was made worse by their refusal to be honest with me about what they needed for themselves and their relationship. They were so *very* nice that I constantly worried that they felt obliged to include me in everything and were too polite to acknowledge that I was a third wheel. I couldn't get past the fact that they'd only been married for six months, and I rather thought they'd like some time to romp around their apartment naked (with each other). Even relaxing alone together listening to music was impossible if I was always around, and I knew couples need that kind of time. I wanted clear guidelines regarding what they needed out of this living arrangement, but they insisted they had no needs. Which wasn't a very helpful answer, to be honest. It put me in the constant position of trying to judge when they wanted company and when they wanted to be alone but wouldn't say so, because there were certainly many times when I'd enter a room and clearly be interrupting something.

A peculiarity of many shot-gun style apartments in South St. Louis is that most rooms lack inner doors. When I tip-toed to the bathroom (next to their bedroom) in the middle of the night, I was terrified I'd interrupt them having sex. I tried to spend a good part of the day in my room so they could have time alone together, but this created another

339

problem. Sometimes I know they misunderstood my efforts to give them privacy and thought I simply didn't want to spend time with them. That upset me a lot, and I struggled to get the balance right. I wanted to show them how much I cared about them, but I didn't want to intrude on all those intimate moments common in a new marriage. It felt very awkward if, for example, I entered the living room to find them rolling around kissing on the floor. They'd insist I should stay but I just cringed, knowing that if I wasn't there they'd probably be having sex by then.

As my job at McDonald's commenced I began paying an amount towards apartment expenses, as well as paying for my own things, such as cigarettes! It was a new and stable way of living for me. It was wonderful to feel a sense of entitlement to living somewhere, and a total sense of security that I would not suddenly be cast out of my accommodation. The three of us went to Eat-Rite together most evenings, and it was even odd for me to go there only to socialise, without needing it for accommodation. I felt almost normal at the end of the night, when the three of us would pile into their car and drive home to our apartment, say goodnight and head to our respective beds.

Leah and I stayed in touch as usual, but she was still in Michigan. Cora and Perry were not quite back yet from living in Texas, and of course Vianne and I were no longer friends. When I left the club scene I'd made a conscious effort to trim everyone out of my life who I felt was either a negative influence or just not that important to me.

Instead, I chose to focus on the few people I was close to, rather than spreading myself thinly as a social butterfly. Now I was learning to make new friends in a brave new world.

The first and most important friends I made besides Kim and Dan were their two best friends, an engaged couple named Isaiah Miller and Jennifer "Soon-to-Be the Same". Kim, Dan, Isaiah, and Jennifer had all attended a small Christian college together and they all attended the same small non-denominational church that Isaiah's Father was an Elder. Many non-denominational churches have a group of "Godly men" act as Elders, rather than one priest or pastor. The concept is that having a small group leading the congregation together creates a sort of checks and balances situation, where the Elders are held to spiritual accountability by each other, and preventing any one person stamping their personality over the word of God.

Soon I was introduced to Isaiah's family, who were fascinating and almost unfairly beautiful people. Mother (Linda) and Father (Bill) had six children, boy (Isaiah), girl, boy, girl, boy, girl, with never more than a three year gap between any of them. They were all beautiful, brilliant, clever and kind, like an incredibly successful experiment in breeding. To know them was truthfully to be at least a little in awe of them. They exuded energy, innocence, intellectual stimulation and most intoxicating of all, family. I came to love them almost slavishly, though they would forever seem to be a totally different species from myself.

The day I met the extended Miller family was an overwhelming one for me. His mother greeted me, and she was so utterly beautiful I could not believe she'd had six children, the eldest old enough to be planning a wedding. One of the things that amazed me the most was how very much they all enjoyed each other's company. There were no screaming matches or disowned daughters. They had so much love for each other, and fun, too. Linda led me to the kitchen table and made me a drink, fussing over me like I was a bird who'd fallen out of its nest. Lunch was served and everyone automatically bowed their heads as Bill began to pray. I jerked my head down in shock and embarrassment as I'd been on the point of beginning to eat, not realising they prayed before meals. I wanted to show respect for them and although I didn't pray along with them I felt it was no skin off my back to be polite and lower my head.

After Bill said "amen" I raised my head and felt slightly dizzy from the action, as if I'd only just realised where I was and what I was doing. I was no longer a confirmed Nihilist, but I had been and the effects of it were carved into my skin. Having turned away from Nihilism, I was then back in the same sort of mind-set that I'd had up until Troy died. I felt wonder and awe for the universe and a sense that something I couldn't understand had a hand in all life, but I felt no urge to try to pin down those vague feelings into a religion. On the contrary, I thought religion was little more than another

342

system society set up to prevent people from reaching out, expanding themselves and by extension propelling humanity onwards from barbarism to enlightenment. I couldn't quite believe I was a guest in a house as pious as the Miller's, and thought it was slightly ironic. I admired them for inviting and including me, despite how I looked and what they knew of my past. They didn't seem to mind all of those more superficial things, but rather seemed to care about me as a human, and believed I was a good human, too.

While still living with Kim and Dan, I began visiting the Miller family any time I wasn't either working or at Eat-Rite. This was largely because Isaiah's fiancé, Jennifer, and I became extremely close, and by extension I also got to know Isaiah much better. In addition, the Millers constantly invited me over to spend family time with them. They were so very lovely, loving, and fun to be with I was always eager to say yes. It was an exciting new joy to not only socialise with the older kids close to my age, but also to play with the younger children in their family. But the very best thing of all was those moments when Linda or Bill came up and hugged me, or rested an affectionate hand on my arm while speaking to me. I felt loved and welcomed into the warmth of a happy, busy home, which was unprecedented.

An unfortunate side effect of the greater amount of time I was spending at the Miller's was that Kim felt hurt that I wasn't choosing to spend that time with her and Dan at their apartment, where I was still living. I understood why they felt that way, so I made a big effort to spread myself between where my heart really wanted to be, and where I felt my sense of loyalty telling me where I ought to be.

Round Fifty Seven

It was inevitable that I would learn about the Christianity my new friends followed. I regularly reminded them, kindly but firmly, that while I was curious about their beliefs, I had no intention of converting. They universally said that was absolutely fine, that they were just pleased I was willing to listen and discuss these ideas with them. I've never been short of opinions or philosophical thoughts or theories, and I enjoyed having people to flex those muscles with, irrespective of the fact that we approached each debate from almost polar opposite perspectives.

Although their church was technically non-denominational, in truth it was strictly Calvinist. For a full definition of Calvinism I suggest you look elsewhere, but I'll attempt to sum up some of the key points to the best of my abilities. Calvinism is a fairly literal interpretation of the Bible, based on the interpretations and influence of John Calvin, an early Protestant reformer. It involves several non-negotiable rules regarding salvation, summarised in the "Five Points of Calvinism". They rely heavily on the belief of absolute depravity, predestination, the total atonement offered through

Christ's sacrifice, and the Holy Spirit inhabiting the souls of those "saved".

Everyone I was then surrounded by was praying that I would accept Christ in my heart and be saved. They all did everything they could to contribute to that final result. However it was probably Bill and Linda who had the greatest impact on me. I'd wanted a family more than anything else for my entire life. Bill and Linda were quickly becoming father/mother figures to me. At the same time the rest of the family was becoming equally fond of me. Bill took on the job of having the many, many philosophical debates it would take to try to convert me to Christianity.

I enjoyed participating in those conversations with him, firstly because I was basking in his fatherly attention, and secondly because I did, and still do, find discussing any philosophical theories utterly fascinating. I enjoyed the chance to put my thoughts forward as much as he enjoyed teaching me his. I greatly appreciated that he listened to my ideas and questions with respect, curiosity and honesty. There was much we debated over. We never argued, although we often passionately expressed ideas that were totally antagonistic to each other. I was told of the redemption I could receive in Christ, but I studied the Bible as if it were just another book that I might or might not like and agree with. After reading passages that he suggested, I came back to Bill with the Bible I'd been given, having highlighted everything I had a question about or strongly disagreed with.

That the unsaved went to hell, and that the definition of those who were saved was so narrow, was something I could never accept -- especially when I learned it also applied to babies, young children and severely intellectually disabled people, who, lacking the ability to comprehend the concept of Christ's redemption, were therefore excluded from it. It damns huge swathes of the earth's population simply because they may never even hear the Gospel of Christ, and of course discounts everyone else, no matter how moral or devout in other religions. Easily, it was the concept of a God willing to damn so many to hell that was my greatest objection. It was impossible for me not to draw the obvious conclusion that if what the Bible said was true, Troy was in hell. I didn't believe that, no matter what, because I'd felt him surround me too many times since his death. I tried to stop thinking of the subject of Hell but I never stopped wrestling with it inside my head.

The roles assigned to men and women made me indignant; women weren't allowed to speak in their church and had to wear head coverings whenever they were worshipping God in a church service. That was because of a verse in Corinthians that says a woman's hair is her glory and she should hide her glory in the presence of God. I pointed out that if what they said about God's omnipotence was true then we are always in the presence of God. So why only cover a woman's hair at church, why not twenty-four hours a day? There was much more to their teachings on gender difference that I disagreed with.

To every point I brought up Bill replied with a similar message. That he knew it was difficult and confusing for me, but that we humans couldn't possibly understand God's plan. We had to have faith in Him and His word and trust Him even when the ramifications of His word drove against our human instinct. We spent hours using *Strongs Strongest Concordance*, translating the words in the Bible back into the original Hebrew or Greek it was written in to better understand some of the meanings that had been lost in time. I was amused to discover that in the original writing of the book of Genesis, it is a pear, not an apple, which Adam and Eve ate in the Garden of Eden. I tried to explain to Bill that I was incapable of having faith to that degree, that I needed proof. I said that despite wanting to please them all very much, I couldn't just declare myself a Christian when not only did I not believe it but I actively disliked it, just because they wanted me to. Bill would always say, "That's fine, just please keep an open mind and keep talking to me." I agreed. I didn't think my soul was in any real danger of being saved.

Linda was incredibly warm and affectionate with me. Her maternal instincts were appalled as she learned more about my life up to then. She made a point of pouring love into me, at least for a while. I fell in love with her as a mother. I adored her so much I would have walked over hot coals for the privilege of curling up on her cosy bed and chatting about life. The whole family made me feel so welcome that I felt as if I had gently landed on a soft feather pillow. I was beginning to want to believe in Christ, just so that all of that could be mine by rights, not as a guest. Various hints, dropped like bombs, informed me that if I did believe in Christ as my saviour, that I would have a home with the Miller family. Not just until I could move on somewhere else, but *forever*. I wanted that so badly I could taste it, but I couldn't lie about what I believed, even for that.

I think I wanted to be convinced because I wanted to be considered a good person, pure again despite everything, as well as a member of that family. But I could not find it in my heart, no matter how hard I tried, to feel any faith in Jesus as my Saviour. I hoped that if I could believe just that one thing, maybe I'd be given insight and peace regarding the other issues I so vehemently disagreed with. Strangely, it was my very inability to tell a lie and pretend to believe what I didn't that most endeared me to Bill and made him ever more determined that he would lead me into the Light. He told me that if I truly wanted to know if God was real, that He loved me and that I was meant to live by His Word that I needed to pray with all my heart and ask God to reveal Himself to me. Bill said that if I asked in a spirit of open-mindedness to know God that God would not turn away from me. God would give me the faith I couldn't summon on my own, and I'd have all the answers I'd always sought once and for all.

I considered his advice and decided that it was no skin off my back to try it - sometime. I viewed it much like a scientific experiment. The day after Mr. Miller and I had this conversation, I was badly in need of a miracle. I decided it was the perfect time to experiment.

Round Fifty Eight

Several months into living with Kim and Dan, a piece of post caught up with me. When I opened it I felt faint with horror and indignation. All that time I'd thought I was putting the past behind me and working so hard to be productive and good, I was in truth being ground through the wheels of justice. The letter announced that the Wonder-Cop police officer who'd arrested me the day I slit my wrist was independently pressing charges against me for **assaulting a police officer and attempting suicide**. There was no doubt I'd committed the second crime, though I hadn't known it was illegal when I did it. But the first, and most important charge against me? Assaulting a police officer? His claim was based on a moment I hadn't given a second thought to. When I read the letter I replayed the events of that day, searching for the moment when I'd "attempted to elbow the police officer in the face". I realised it was when I tried to pull myself out from underneath him, when I couldn't breathe, and my elbow grazed his shoulder. That was what constituted "assaulting a police officer".

He had assaulted me by reacting totally out of proportion to the situation, but because that was taken as a matter of course during arrests, I'd suppressed my feelings on the matter, and avoided discussing or thinking of it. In truth, I felt violated when I remembered what he did to me that day. Having a man, any man, even a police officer, throw me to the ground and drive his body into mine, threaten me and cover me with bruises while I choked, was a memory I couldn't visit without feeling ashamed, afraid, vulnerable, used for a power thrill and abused. It was before the time of camera phones being on every corner. Perhaps if it had happened today there would have been an investigation into his conduct rather than mine. But that wasn't my life or reality.

I thought it was the most audacious thing in the world that because of a natural instinct to move my body to a place where I could breathe, I was being legally accused of assaulting a police officer, and he hadn't even been injured. I knew I'd *talked* back to him, but that was the key point. I'd *talked*, and even that only after he came charging at me firing off unfounded insults based on a total lack of objectivity. Surely police were trained that in many family disputes there were many sides to one story and not everything is as first meets the eye? I hadn't shouted or screamed at him, though I did swear once. I thought it was an act of madness that what I did that day constituted assaulting an officer. If I felt unprotected by the system before, now I felt actively persecuted. As far as I could see, the world was predominantly run by violent, sexually frustrated, misogynistic, racist men. I remain hopeful that one day society will surprise me.

The letter informed me that if convicted, the minimum sentence would be one year in prison. I was speechless. I was physically unable to face the reality of going into prison, becoming a prisoner and everything it would entail for my future. I knew that if I went into prison, I would come out utterly ruined, if I even came out at all. The time inside would destroy my spirit and character, and when I was released I would have nothing and no one left, not even me as I knew myself to be. I'd be unemployable. My life would be over before the age of nineteen. I decided that no matter what I had to do, I would not be going to prison.

The letter explained that if I was found guilty I wouldn't be taken into immediate custody. I'd have twenty-four hours to report to my local police department to begin the processing into prison. I vowed that if I was convicted, I would kill myself in that twenty-four hour window. This time I didn't even feel a shred of guilt about my intention. Something greater trumped guilt and the doubts it fosters. Of course I was careful not to tell anyone of my vow, but I did begin making preparations in secret. It would be irresponsible for me to describe my plan here, but it was precise and well-researched and lethal, and I was sure that this time, if I had to do it, I'd be successful. However, I spent every spare moment of thought silently, desperately, incoherently praying and begging that it wouldn't be required.

That was why on the morning of my court date I decided it was time for me to ask God if He was there. I had breakfast in my tree house room and then nervously got on my knees and tried earnestly to pray. I wasn't sure what to say, and there was much clearing of my throat as I began, rather like trying to take off on a bike when you haven't ridden in twenty years. My prayer went something like this:

"Dear God. It's Erin. I guess you know that, if you're real. Mr. Miller said that if I asked for you to reveal yourself to me that you would. So I'm asking. I really need you to do that now if you're ever going to. Obviously you know I'm going to court today, and you know what my plans are. If you want me to be yours, and to live, then please save me. Thanks very much. I guess if you're real then we might be talking again. As you know I haven't done this before, so I hope I did okay. Right. Okay. Thank you. Amen, Erin"

I stood, dusting off my knees and looking around the room self-consciously. I supposed that I was as well prepared for the court date as I could be. I was ready to get it over with.

Round Fifty Nine

Isaiah and Jennifer drove me to the courthouse for my appearance. I didn't even know if I would have legal representation when I arrived. That hadn't been covered in the letter I'd received. I hoped there would be a lawyer who I could explain the situation to before it was my turn to stand before the judge.

As the three of us waited for an hour or so, I watched the cases ahead of me take place. None of them were conferring with lawyers, so I made the correct assumption that I would not either. The judge was simply reviewing papers on each case and then questioning the defendant until he came to a decision. I was very afraid that I would not be able to answer or explain myself well enough because my nerves were almost overtaking me.

Finally the clerk called my name out, it was my turn. This stranger, this judge was about to alter the rest of my life. Isaiah and Jennifer squeezed my hand in support. I stood, legs shaking, and walked to the stand in front of the judge. Weeks of waking up in cold sweats of terror of the outcome of this day were about to end, one way or another. As the clerk handed the judge my file I heard him say "Statements from EMTs and the police officer in question." I waited as the judge read them, concentrating on not fainting. My legs were locked in an upright position. I was deathly pale as I waited for him to begin questioning me. Now I was praying to anyone who might hear for salvation from this.

It was several minutes before the judge looked up. He squinted at me as I stood opposite him, halfway across the large room. I wondered if he was looking to see what kind of horrible monster would assault a police officer. I thought I was going to collapse from terror, I don't think it ever occurred to me that he would let me off easily.

As if shifting into a parallel reality, I watched as he made no effort to disguise the rolling of his eyes. He muttered something unintelligible under his breath and tossed my file back to the clerk. He was looking at me again when he said two words "Case dismissed."

I was stunned and unsure what I was supposed to do. "Case dismissed" sounded tantalisingly promising, but was I allowed to just walk away? I was bewildered; I hadn't even put my carefully prepared case forward. In fact I hadn't even said a word at all. I believe I stood there for a moment too long, causing the judge to look up again from his papers and say, "You may go." I wasted no time in obeying him, scurrying out of the centre of the courtroom and heading towards the door where Isaiah and Jennifer were waiting for me. I couldn't speak. I was overwhelmed and confused in equal measure.

They supported me as I walked dazed out of the courtroom. Automatically I put one foot in front of the other without quite knowing what I was doing or what direction I was walking in. Could it possibly be that easy? Why wasn't I questioned? What was written in the statements the judge read? Why did he decide to instantly dismiss the case like that? I knew that I hadn't done anything as extreme as "assaulting a police officer", but how did *he* know that?

I was still in this state of stunned, mute gratitude and confusion when the three of us reached Isaiah's van. Jennifer stopped and asked that before we leave, we took a moment to pray together to give thanks to God for giving the judge wisdom, and me freedom. I readily agreed. It was during that prayer, led by Isaiah, when I suddenly remembered the prayer I made that morning, asking for a sign that God existed, loved me and was the truth I was meant to follow. In that prayer I promised that if he showed himself to me, I would give him my trust and faith.

Jennifer was clearly thinking along the same lines. She knew I'd prayed that morning and as soon as Isaiah finished thanking God, she excitedly said "Erin, your prayer has been answered!" I felt a small sense of foreboding, a concern that although it did appear that my prayer had been answered I still didn't feel the sensation of faith that had been described to me, and I disagreed with too much within Christianity. But no matter what else I have been, I am a person who stands by their word. I had promised my loyalty to God if God showed me He loved me and it did seem that he had done so.

Considering I'd attended that court date fully expecting to be committing suicide later that evening, and considering the bizarre manner in which the judge dismissed the case against me, it was hard to deny that God had carried out his end of the bargain. Now it was time for me to do mine. I vowed to myself that somehow, the faith would come with practise and I'd be granted an understanding of Christianity that would resolve my doubts. I announced then and there that I would believe in God, I would put my faith in him and the sacrifice of Christ. I announced that I was a Christian, to great rejoicing.

Round Sixty

Kim and Dan were gathered at the Miller house to hear the outcome of my case. They'd all been in constant prayer that I'd be given mercy at court. When Isaiah, Jennifer and I returned we were giddy and triumphant. Jennifer especially was bursting with joy and excitement. I was still in a daze, trying to digest not only the events at court but also my sudden decision to convert. The decision was based on what seemed to be irrefutable proof, but it was still sudden. Between the three of us we managed to relay the events of the day. We filled everyone in on every detail, but most importantly, we announced that I had given my life to Christ. Given in thanks, acceptance and gratitude that He had revealed Himself to me in such a life transforming way. Everyone was overjoyed; I was happily smothered in hugs and kisses. Bill led the family in a prayer of gratitude for my conversion and freedom. Linda clutched me to her chest and tears of love fell from her eyes onto me. I never wanted to let go of her, and I loved her more than I could possibly express.

Within a week I was invited to move in with the Miller family. It was an extraordinary offer. Like Kim and Dan, who had given me a home and asked nothing in return, the Millers wanted me to live with them *as a daughter*. I was eighteen, and could no longer be legally adopted. But they offered me their last name, and to live with them under the same terms their children did. I was incredulous. I'd been a guest of many people, and most recently a roommate. But never had I been offered a permanent place in a family. It was irresistible.

I knew Kim would be hurt if I chose to move out of her apartment, and announcing my decision to her was a very painful thing to do. I had to explain that what I'd always wanted was a loving family, and I couldn't just turn away from one when it was offered to me. I tried to make her see how nice it would be for her and Dan to have their privacy back. None of it took away the hurt. I felt awful. I reassured Kim that I still loved her as a friend. I tried to explain that the two living situations I was then in the position to choose between were totally different. With her and Dan I was an adult roommate, and often an awkward one at that. With the Millers I would be a daughter, I'd live in a family as an integral part of it until nature moved me onwards in the growing up process. She was sad I was leaving, and I believe there was an element of her feeling that the Millers, namely Jennifer, had poached from her, just a little bit. But she said she was happy for me, and we remained close friends for a long time afterwards.

The day I moved into the Milheims' home, I threw my arms around Linda and Bill and cried, "Mom! Dad!" It felt exquisite. I was given a rose and a "certificate of adoption" that they had printed, which every member of the family signed. I framed it and hung it up in my room. My new room, though, was the one thorn on the rose. All of the bedrooms were taken by the biological Miller children, and rather than make one share I was put in the basement. They didn't know of the bad experiences I'd had in previous basements, but my heart sank when I saw where they'd arranged my bed.

I have an inbuilt terror of basements. And theirs was full of crickets that never stopped chirping and would leap on my face while I slept, climb in my hair and crawl all over my body. I hated walking down the basement stairs each time I was obliged to go to my bedroom and dreaded sleep each night. Sometimes I reflected bitterly that they expected me to sleep in conditions that they would have considered unacceptable for their biological children. But then I'd give myself a mental slap across the face and remind myself to be grateful I had a family who loved me. They hadn't just given me their surname; they'd even added me to their family health insurance. They weren't toying with me. I had a home, finally, and many blessings to count.

I had a new name and a new religion. I was a new person. I was also exactly the same person I'd always been, and the two would forever be at war. I would be living a very different life as a Miller to how I'd ever lived before. Suddenly I had to learn a whole new set of rules. How to dress, how to speak, how to study, how to behave in church, and, not least, how to go from living alone and accountable to no one, to living in a large family with participating parents. I couldn't change quickly enough, or well enough. I tried. I truly did. But going from a life lived in almost constant movement to having a world that shrunk down to one house and one church required a great deal of stillness from me, something I've never been good at. So many days it seemed no matter how hard I tried I couldn't be ladylike, pious, civilised, or calm enough, and Linda would bristle with annoyance. I hated disappointing her so I worked harder at being what she wanted me to be. I was more afraid of the repercussions of my actions than I ever had been. I agonised over every action, analysing it for missteps before I did anything. Then I'd do what I thought was right, and find it was in fact wrong. This time it wasn't a mere roof over my head at stake, it was the love of the mother my heart had always craved, and a position in the family I desired.

To say I wanted to be one of them would be such an understatement that it would cheapen the sentiment behind the words. It means a great deal to belong, especially to a child. While I was not a child at eighteen, and I had a great deal more experience

359

than anyone I knew who was my age, in many ways I was still unfinished. There was a child that had remained within me. She'd been left starving for so long, and she still wanted to be fed. I wanted to be cuddled and loved, to feel my hair stroked and a soft voice tell me I was loved. Despite how I was required to live, I was also as immature as any other eighteen year old person might be expected to be. They're not generally known for possessing the wisdom that (hopefully) comes with adulthood. I did still want a family to care for me; I did still want to belong somewhere, to no longer be alone.

Throughout my entire life, I'd only ever felt "owned" by my Grandparents, so long ago, and then later, Troy. With those two exceptions I'd been on my own and was expected to fend for myself. No one claimed me as theirs. To be owned by such spectacular people, forever, blew my mind. Very few days went by when I didn't regret the fact that I couldn't mould myself after them better than I was. It created a situation where I was a constant failure, as no matter how many times I was told I'd done wrong I just didn't know how to navigate their world and rules because I hadn't been raised in them. I put endless effort into looking, speaking and behaving like them, the way they wanted me to, and it was often very stressful. Whenever I felt I couldn't and shouldn't do it, I reminded myself of the miracle that brought me into their family, and I carried on trying to deserve them.

Round Sixty One

After I settled into my new home I began using much of my free time working on the earliest versions of this book, which I had begun while living at Eat-Rite. My writing was extremely immature and irregular and often spiked off into rants, but it was heartfelt and I loved the challenge it presented. I wrote and wrote, filling several notebooks, finally completing the story of me, from birth to Miller. Naively, I thought my story had reached its Happily Ever After. I dreamt of one day publishing the book with a CD full of music matching each section, a sort of soundtrack to my life. I wanted my book to be a sensory experience that would immerse the reader in my world, my mind. If I could have reached out from the page and pulled you into my world, I would have, to make you feel, taste and see as I had.

Linda said it would upset her too much to read it, which was a relief to me as I didn't want her to know everything I'd done. Bill asked if he could read it, and I said yes, although I was very nervous that his opinion of me would lower upon knowing more about me. I sat watching him as he finished reading, anxiously waiting for his verdict. When he turned the final page, he was frustratingly silent for a very long time. I was wondering if I was going to be kicked out of the house immediately. Finally, he said "Well you're a talented writer, though you need more practice and discipline. You've had a very unfortunate life. I'm glad you're with us now, and you have the chance for a new beginning. As to this" – he gestured to the book – "I would put this all behind you. I don't think you should carry on writing about it. It's essentially very self-centred to write so much about yourself, no matter how much has happened to you. It won't help you move on from all of this if you're still thinking about it."

I was mainly relieved by his reaction. I still had his love and respect, his surname and home. I was a little hurt that he didn't approve of the existence of the book, and alarmed that he was suggesting I put it and my entire past behind me. I wasn't sure that was possible, even if I attempted it. I was compelled to write what I did, over and over again. It helped anchor me to sanity to go through that process of understanding what happened to me, what I did, who I was and how I became that. But because I loved him, I resolved to do as he asked. I still wrote, but if my writing veered to the subject of myself I shredded it, trying to learn to keep my focus on any subject but me.

Jennifer also read the book. She and I were becoming inseparable. I adored her; she radiated angelic qualities as well as an intriguing sense of fun and naughtiness. As she was reading the end of the book I was again waiting anxiously next to her. When she finished, she took my hands in hers, and with tears running down her cheeks, she said "Erin, I want you to know you're a very good girl. I know you are. Anyone who knows you should know you are. You're a very good girl." It took my breath away. It felt like divine absolution, being told by *her,* who was so blatantly good, that I was a good girl, something that almost no one had ever thought to call me.

Round Sixty Two

Of course from the beginning I attended church with my new family. There finally came a time when I had to wrestle with the last nail in my Calvinist coffin; St. Paul's beloved head covering. The Corinthian letters were written by Paul as a none too gentle rebuke to the Corinthian Church, which had become (by Paul's reckoning) too materialistic, showy and full of self-glory than was appropriate for a temple of the Lord. He wrote to them for the express purpose of putting them in check, outlining, you might say, a refresher course of what should and should not be done in church and out of it. There has been much debate over whether Paul's admonition to the women to cover their hair was directed solely at the Corinthians of that time, or the entire Christian flock forevermore, but Calvinists err on the side of caution. A Calvinist Christian would say that a woman who calls herself Christian but neglects the head covering is cherry picking which verses to obey and which to flout in the name of fashion.

Even after attending the church for a couple of months I baulked at wearing a head covering. They were terribly romantic in appearance; beautiful long lengths of lace that the ladies elegantly draped over their hair when they sat down to in church. I understood the logic that if I was going to call myself a Christian I couldn't pick and choose when to obey God and when to ignore him, but I still felt resentment regarding the restrictions put on women in my new world. It all ran directly contrary to everything I'd thought before the advent of Christianity in my life. When I expressed these feelings I was told that God created men and women equal, but different. Our strengths and weaknesses, and by extension our duties, complimented each other but were not the same. Apples and oranges, and so on. It still rankled, and it also rang false. The head covering symbolised all of that for me.

Eventually Bill told me gravely that we needed to have a private talk. He told me that some people at church were offended by my conspicuous refusal to participate in the wearing of a head covering. They took it as implied condemnation of their practise, as well as ungodly behaviour on my part. There was resentment amongst some people, saying I was being permitted to go without one because I was part of the family of an Elder. He told me I couldn't carry on like that anymore. He asked me if I believed in God, and I said yes. He asked me if I wanted to please God, I said yes. He asked me if I wanted to please the family and have good relations with my fellow churchgoers, I said yes. Then he said that if my answer to all those questions was truly "yes" then I knew what I needed to do.

That night, I asked Linda to get me a head covering. She was overjoyed, and said that she'd make me one herself. All of the head coverings in church were cream or white, but when Linda presented mine to me, I saw it was made out of black lace. I assumed she made it that colour as a nod to my individuality, so I tried not to be hurt. If I was going to have a head covering, I wanted it to be as it should be, as everyone else's was, everyone I was trying so hard to fit in with. Every time I put it over my hair I felt conspicuous. I felt like a widow again. I even heard a few malicious women tut over it, saying I was perverting the point of the head covering, drawing attention to myself by wearing a black one. I overheard that, and I wanted to rush in and say I hadn't even chosen it, that their precious, perfect Linda had! But I couldn't do such a thing. Sometimes it seemed that no matter how hard I tried or how much I compromised I was doomed to be a failure at this new attempt at life.

Round Sixty Three

Bill helped get me a job working at the photo lab his cousin, Fred owned. I was finally elevated from the ranks of fast food, and I loved my new job. I learned to develop film the old fashioned way, blind and with skill, and I gained an intoxicating sense of achievement each day spent in the lab. The smell of developing fluids still thrills me. Balanced on top of the printer was a little CD player that I was given full rights over. I was almost always alone in the shop unless a customer came in, so I spent most of my work days singing at the top of my lungs as I developed rolls of film and span around the room on my wheely chair. It was the best job in the whole world.

One of our regular contracts was with the local police department. We developed their mug shots and crime scene photos, and I took a wry enjoyment in looking through the pictures for familiar faces. Our largest group of regular clients consisted of independent private investigators. Their films were fascinating to develop, I loved following the cases they were piecing together and chatting to them about things they never should be telling me. I had one odd young man who asked me out when he dropped off his rolls of film. I wasn't interested, so I said a friendly no thank you, giving a general excuse that I wasn't available. He smiled, and said maybe I'd change my mind after I developed the film. I wasn't sure what he meant by that. Imagine my surprise when I developed his film to see hundreds of pictures of him defecating in an apparent trek across India, as well as several dozen pictures of his cock. Needless to say I made myself absent when he came to collect his pictures.

Round Sixty Four

I lived with the Miller's for a year and a half. It was the longest I'd lived in any one place since I left Carol's house. For a while it was deliriously good. For a long time before I finally left it went very badly but nobody wanted to acknowledge or talk about it. In the end, it was excruciating for all of us. It wasn't any one thing that made it impossible for us to live with me as a member of their family. Ultimately the cause of everything that went wrong was that I didn't do well enough transforming myself, and too many traps and lies were laid out for me to navigate. My tongue slipped too many times, my toes tapped in prayer, I dressed badly.

One day, about nine months after becoming a Miller, I came home after a trip to the bookstore. Linda asked to see what I'd bought and I was excited to show her. Books had always been a passion of mine but before living with the Millers I wasn't usually able to afford them. It was a great luxury to have spending money for things that I enjoyed. Among several others I bought was *Lady Chatterley's Lover*. I knew nothing about the book but that it was a classic, and I was working my way through the classics. Linda was furious and looked at me as if I'd just had an orgy with forty men on her kitchen floor. She told me the book was pornographic and to return it immediately. I was shocked and upset. I fell over myself apologising to her and promised I would get rid of it. She accepted my obedience, but I was not forgiven for making the mistake. Not that one, nor any of the others. I secretly thought it was wrong of her to censor my reading to such an extent but I was resigned to obeying her because it was her house and she was the parent. I was hurt that despite my instant obedience she remained angry at me. I felt it was very unfair that I was being punished for failing to live up to standards I'd never been educated in. Everything was unravelling and the faster I tried to catch it the more it slipped through my hands. Eventually, I suppose I lost the will to keep trying.

Jennifer turned against me as her wedding with Isaiah approached. She became irrationally jealous that he and I lived in the same house and demanded we never spend time alone together. Then Linda decided I also should no longer be left alone with the second eldest Miller boy. I'd been suffering under the illusion that both boys were my brothers, because I'd thrown every part of my heart into that farce of an adoption. Not even to mention the fact that I wouldn't have wanted Isaiah even if he was single. Jennifer's sudden about face was as mind boggling as it was ridiculous and hurtful.

Jennifer had long standing problems of feeling unattractive and overweight. I thought she was stunning, and clearly, so did Isaiah. But almost overnight she went from being my best friend to accusing me of trying to usurp her and participating in countless sins. Some of the things she chastised me for were true. I still hadn't been able to quit smoking, I listened to lots of "bad music" though I'd made an effort to weed out the worst of it. I dressed far, far more modestly than I ever had before but I still enjoyed making myself pretty enough to make me vain, and when I was fully covered I was criticised because I was usually wearing all black, a habit of mine for many years that stemmed from a deep insecurity.

The point is, I wasn't just like them, but the other point is, I never had been.

Apparently I was acceptable for a while, enough to merit the offer of adoption, but not anymore. There'd been an unannounced time limit for me to become a totally different person, and I was just catching onto that. I found myself both trying to please and (re)ingratiate myself with the family as well as resentful that it was even required of me. Jennifer constantly carried tales of my misbehaviour to Linda, who began to view me with something like repugnance, as if I were infecting her sacred home. When I was pushed, I let myself be pushed for a very long time, because I loved them. But eventually I began to push back and make less of an effort to blend in. My sins were not knowing how to or being capable of operating life as a model Christian teenager on the surface level, it's true; I was very bad at being that. I did not know how to operate life as a model Christian teenager, and I doubt that I could have succeeded in doing so even if I had. What is also true is that my heart was in the right place, that I was trying, that I was often set up for failure, and that my constant goal was to find a way to make the family feel the same way they'd felt towards me in the beginning. There was absolutely nothing malicious or seductive happening in my thoughts or actions. That wasn't enough.

Linda froze towards me. Jennifer froze towards me. On several occasions they even whispered to each other about me right in front of me, which hurt and enraged me so much that I would stomp off, purportedly proving that I was guilty of whatever it was they were saying. Despite how much I disliked my basement room, I began spending

369

most of my time in it when I wasn't directly required to be with the family. That was also the wrong thing to do. Soon Jennifer confronted me in tears, a hand over her heart, asking me what awful things I got up to down there. I couldn't even respond, I thought she was losing her mind. What did she think I was doing, sacrificing goats on the altar of Satan? I was reading, listening to music, and yes, praying for help. My door was never locked, anyone could have walked in whenever they chose. Somehow this impression that I was doing something terrible in my room moved onto Linda, and I was told I was no longer allowed to close my bedroom door. It was too many insults to handle, from the very same people I wanted to love me the most.

I had tried so very hard to be what they wanted. I'd even gone against my own conscience. But everything I did was translated in the worst possible light. For a while I'd felt truly loved by them, and when that was taken away it was almost more than I could bear. I instinctively knew my time at their house was coming to an end, realising that it had ultimately been nothing more than a dressed-up version of the old, constant couch surfing.

Round Sixty Five

Several straws broke the camel's back. For me, the first one was a trip to the doctor. While I'd been living with the Millers I continued to experience the random physical attacks that I mentioned earlier: severe, blinding head pain, and physically dropping to the floor and going into seizures. It wasn't something I could pursue when I had no address or assistance in getting a doctor. When I initially moved into the Miller house I tried to chalk the events up to the stress of living without a home, and I optimistically hoped they'd stop now that I was settled. For a short time they did, but then they began again. I kept them secret for a while, but soon it was happening frequently enough that I asked to see a neurologist. This was towards the end of my time living with the family, and for some reason, I was no longer covered under their insurance, so I arranged the appointment through Medicare.

Linda and Jennifer came with me. I took it for granted that I'd be going with Linda, as she took all the kids to their doctor's appointments and I couldn't drive. But Jennifer coming along alarmed me. She hated me, and I was nervous enough about the appointment without having to navigate a constantly hostile conversation. I remained quiet during the ride there.

When I met the neurologist Linda and Jennifer came in with me. The neurologist began asking me questions about the episodes I was having and I answered as best I could. I hadn't vocalised the symptoms very often before, and I found them a little difficult to explain without much stuttering, pauses and embarrassment.   When I finished answering his questions, Linda turned to me and ordered me to leave the room and wait for her and Jennifer outside. I hesitated, it didn't seem right that I was being kicked out of my own doctor's appointment and I didn't know why they wanted to speak to the neurologist without me present. I was well enough conditioned to obey, though, covered in a shame whose origin I couldn't understand.

Around fifteen minutes later I was called back in to the room. The neurologist's demeanour towards me was totally changed. He informed me that he didn't have any time for fakers and that I should be ashamed of myself for putting my adoptive family through such hassle. Jennifer sat looking smug and satisfied. I was speechless. Tears welled up in my eyes. I looked from Linda to Jennifer and shook my head at them, then openly crying that they believed that of me. It seemed like such a vicious thing to do to someone. I looked at Linda with fresh eyes, seeing that helping me set up the appointment had never been in hopes of diagnosing my problem, it was a sham to teach me a lesson.

On the way home in the car Linda lectured me non-stop, saying that I was pretending to have the attacks of pain and seizures. She said I needed to pray and beg God's forgiveness and if I did then I'd be cured of my imaginary disease. I said it wasn't true, that I wasn't faking and I had prayed, but I was too hurt to make any other arguments. There really wasn't any point. I couldn't convince them I was being honest and I couldn't stop them from only looking at me in the light of a failed experiment. I was supposed to be magically turn into a conservative Christian just as I was experiencing a tentative experience with attempting faith, a difficult enough task in itself. I was supposed to use their words, dress like them, move like them, wear make-up like them, without the benefit of growing up indoctrinated in that way of life, knowing it inside out. I tried to copy them and I failed. I tried to have enough faith in God to give me an aura of holiness, and I failed. We got to a point where without anyone making any announcements, it was understood that they no longer considered me a Christian. I had not been saved the night of the court date. I was obliged to agree. I still went through the motions to behave well, but the welcome mat was being yanked back in.

Isaiah, Jennifer, Kim and Dan were advised not to socialise with me. Jennifer was thrilled, Isaiah made a weak attempt at an apology, and Kim and Dan said nothing. Ironically, I was also constantly criticised for remaining close to my few remaining friends from my secular life. As I retreated away from the family, Leah happily came home from Michigan. Perry and Cora were back from Texas and living in Lemay. And most surprising of all, Vianne tracked me down via Eat-Rite and got my new phone number from someone. She called me crying, begging for me to forgive her for her actions a couple of years earlier. She said she knew she had been cruel and unfair and she would do anything to make it right with me. She said life without me had been miserable, and she swore she would never strike out at me again. I listened to her speak, standing in the Miller's kitchen. I'd been taught much about the concept of forgiveness during my time with them, and I still found it as difficult to grapple with as I always had. But I still loved Vianne, and I took her apology as sincere because I knew how much she loathed and avoided making them at all costs.

I knew she was likely to do something very hurtful to me again, because while I was capable of forgiving her, I did not forget. Nevertheless I was happy to have her back in my life. I suppose I factored in her instability as though giving a handicap in golf, and I made room for it in our friendship. There are some people you find in life who you love so much, and know so intimately, that it is almost impossible to turn away from them. I told her I forgave her, that I still loved her and I was very happy to be friends again. She sobbed with gratitude and was at my house thirty minutes later, throwing herself in my arms. My (secular) friends were rallying around me in one supportive circle as I faced the crisis of losing a second family. My scattered friends and I were solidifying in a way we had never done so cohesively before.

Round Sixty Six

I saw my time with my "family" coming to an end, and I was in a state of constant grief over it. But I was powerless to stop it happening. Seeds of hatred had been sown and nothing I did was given as much as a smile. I was insulted in front of the entire family and told to use my previous name. You aren't supposed to say you're adopting a child, even an eighteen year old child, and then shout "TAKE BACK". They had made a rash decision in offering me adoption, and I had mistakenly believed that they were wise enough that I could safely trust them and hand myself over.

The farce that was my attempt at Christianity was over. I went to church out of respect and bowed my head at prayer because I still considered myself adopted and I followed the family rules, but no one suffered under the delusion that my faith went any further. I was beginning to draw myself up, not inch by inch or even centimetre by centimetre but millimetre by millimetre. The Millers gave me something precious indeed, something I can never thank them enough for. They gave me time; time to regroup myself after long years of trauma and constant movement, and time to form a plan. I'd been able to sit for the G.E.D. test while I lived with them, so I finally accomplished my goal of gaining a formal high school accreditation, in the hopes I would be able to enrol in college later on. Yes, living with them was a sort of trauma in its own right. But having to deal with only one trauma at a time gave me the window I needed to come to terms with who I was and learn to like it, irrespective of anyone else.

A series of coincidental events happened that brought this simmering pot to a rapid boil. Perry and Cora decided to move from Lemay to Cincinnati to be closer to Cora's family and also explore a new city. They were getting a two bedroom apartment, and they asked me if I'd like to have the second bedroom. When they first brought it up to me I was very unsure. It was a good idea to be with people I knew well and trusted, and I knew I wasn't welcome at the Miller's anymore, but I was still trying to work out if that living situation could be salvaged. I also felt uncomfortable with the idea of leaving St. Louis; the city was practically my mother. I told Perry and Cora I needed time to think, and they said they were happy to wait. I wasn't particularly excited about the idea of Cincinnati, but I did have a spirit of adventure and a love of exploring, and I thought it would be fun to do that with Perry and Cora. It was also that much closer to Ann Arbor, so I would be able to see Leah much more often.

Simultaneously, Vintage Vinyl in the Loop ran a competition that Vianne persuaded me to enter. She was ineligible because she was still under eighteen (I was nineteen). I thought filling out a piece of paper to win a prize was a waste of time but she cajoled me into it. It was a simple thing; just a basic square of paper asking for name, age, address and phone number. The prize was two all expenses paid VIP tickets to the 1998 MTV music awards, staying in Los Angeles for three nights. I'd just bought a beautiful Joy Division box set and I was eager to get outside and examine it; I hastily scribbled my details, dropped the paper in the box (folded like an accordion) and didn't give it a second thought.

That night when I got home Bill and Linda asked to speak to me privately in their bedroom. I went slowly, knowing what was coming. I was being dismissed. Well, almost. I was going to be given an impossible choice. Bill and Linda took turns speaking, beginning with a list of how many ways I had been a disappointment. I burned with pain, shame, and fury while I listened, my heart breaking in silence as they carried on. They concluded their speech with an ultimatum. I could remain living with them as part of the family, but only if I stopped listening to secular music and reading books besides Christian books, spent an hour a day in prayer, confessed to them regularly, and recommitted myself to Christ. They said I was corrupting their younger children by setting a bad example. That was particularly painful as I loved my "siblings" a great deal and had always tried to behave impeccably around them. My head was swimming from the list of complaints and demands, when they added "You must also cease any contact with any friends who aren't Christian and approved by us." I sagged against the wall and said "Even Leah?" They nodded. I bitterly wanted to tell them that I hadn't been included or welcomed by my Christian "friends and family" for the better part of the last year. I wanted to reveal every lie Jennifer had said about me but it was patently obvious that they would receive that as bad behaviour on my part and not believe me anyway.

Until that final demand was made, I was seriously asking myself if I could do what they were asking. But as soon as those words left their mouths I knew what I had to do. My friendships had trials and bumps in them, but my few friends were the only ones who had actively chosen to stand by me throughout the many twists my life took. They loved me for me, not for what they hoped I'd become, and I loved them the same way. I was not willing to sacrifice them on the altar of this family's name and neurosis. I no longer felt the Millers were acting out of love towards me and I wasn't going to go through a long period of wallowing in shame, grovelling and hypocrisy to gain their love. I was sick of being blamed for things I hadn't done and never given the benefit of the doubt or a chance to explain about the things I had done. I wouldn't ever stop loving the Millers, but they crossed my line of what I could tolerate and I had crossed theirs. There really isn't any more to it than that.

I thought of the bedroom waiting for me in Cincinnati. I made my decision then and there, but I found it impossible to say it out loud. I wanted a night to think it over and be sure I was correct. I asked them if I could take a few days before deciding. They said yes. I left the room and went into my basement room. I sat on the bed, for once oblivious to the constant chirping of the crickets, and absorbed the fact that my time as a member of their family was over, and I had to work out a way of announcing that decision. And apparently, I was going to be moving to Cincinnati as well. It was a lot to take in.

Clearly not the Christian God, but *some* Gods were smiling down on me the day Vianne made me fill in the MTV contest form and Bill and Linda issued their ultimatum. It was a beautiful moment of synchronicity. Three days after hurriedly dropping the form in the box and deciding I had to find a way to announce I was choosing to leave the Miller family, I got a surprise phone call. It was a woman, and she was informing me that I'd won the contest. I thought it was a prank from one of my friends at Vintage, and didn't believe it for several minutes. She was friendly and excited about the contest but I think I slightly exasperated her by asking for so much proof that I had indeed won and she was who she said she was! Finally she convinced me, and said she needed to know the name of my guest to finalise the place tickets. I took her details and said I'd call her back right away to let her know. I would have taken Vianne, since she was the one who persuaded me to enter the competition, but she was under age and therefore ineligible. Leah was busy with college so Cora and I decided it would be an awesome way to kick off being roommates. We were leaving in just over one week.

I was elated! I felt like Cinderella being sent to the ball. It felt so good to get something so amazing out of the blue and it was a much needed lift for my spirits. I'd been mired down in depression, grappling with the reality of losing the family I loved so much and agonising over how to tell them I had to choose my freedom over them. As hurt as I was in many other ways, I was still grateful to them for loving me for a little while, and because I knew how crucial their religion was to them I could almost understand why my existence under their roof horrified them so much. My elation over the win faded somewhat when it dawned on me that the trip was my one way ticket out of the family. I'd been looking for a way to tell them I had to go. Now I could let my stroke of luck do the dirty work for me. They'd given me an ultimatum, and I'd answer them with another, which would settle everything.

These things are best done quickly and ruthlessly, with as much compassion as the situation can allow for. The day I got the phone call telling me I was going to be heading to LA in just over one week I waited patiently for all the Miller children to go to bed. Then I knocked on Bill and Linda's bedroom door. They called me to enter and I stepped in. I stood at the foot of their bed, nervous but making an attempt to sound confident and firm, and most importantly, not afraid or heartbroken. Bypassing the answer they were expecting me to give them, instead I announced that I'd won the trip to LA. I knew that they would disapprove of such an ungodly event. I asked them for permission to go. They said absolutely not. I said I was very sorry. That I had given our previous conversation much thought and had been agonising over what I should do. I forced the words out of my mouth. My chest felt like it was being crushed from the pain in my heart. I said I couldn't give up my friends, I couldn't set aside my passion for the world and I couldn't turn my back on what I believed to be true, no more than they could. I said I loved them more than anything, which was true. I finished by saying I would be going to the music awards in LA and directly to Cincinnati after. I thanked them for the care they had given me and said I was very sorry it hadn't worked out. They didn't respond, so after a long silence I turned and left the room.

I cried all night that night, but I believed I had done the right thing. They were asking too much from me and not returning the love and effort I was giving. I couldn't carry on living in a life where I could never succeed and all my natural talents and passions were forbidden.

Round Sixty Seven

Anticipating leaving St. Louis for Cincinnati was a bag of mixed emotions. I packed my belongings and left the Miller home the day after I told Bill and Linda that I was leaving. In the days between leaving their house and my trip for LA I stayed at Vianne's house, along with Cora. I was inconsolable over the loss of my "family", even though it was a loss I'd chosen and one I maintained was necessary. It hurt no less for that. Most of my time was spent alone, thinking. Everyone knew how much it hurt me to give the Millers up, though I had the strong impression that they were glad I did. It was hard for me to feel any excitement about the upcoming trip to LA. I wondered what life in Cincinnati would be like. Going to Cincinnati was another leap of faith. I needed a new home, at least a residence, with people I trusted and there was nowhere and no one else.

Cora and I overslept on the morning we were meant to catch the plane for LA. We ran around Vianne's house frantically loading our things in the car. As we drove to the airport battling traffic we went from hysterically shrieking, alternating sobbing and screaming at cars, to sitting in devastated silence, watching the clock tick towards our departure time. Arriving at the airport we ran as fast as we could through each part of the boarding process. At the check in desk we were told the plane was already leaving. We asked if we could please try to catch it and they said yes, but they doubted we would. We ran anyway, and finally reached the gate doubled over, breathless.

Assuming we had missed our flight and the whole trip was ruined, Cora and I were close to tears as we approached the stewardesses at the gate with our tickets. They said "You girls have a guardian angel! A man on the flight heard that we were boarding and about to pull away despite the fact that two passengers hadn't shown up yet. He said he'd buy us all coffees if we gave you another ten minutes. You're just in time!" Cora and I looked at each other in amazement, incredulous over our good fortune! We boarded the plane, both of us dishevelled, looking as if we'd just woken up (which we had) and run a mile (which we also had). As we navigated our way down the aisle to our seats we searched every male face wondering who had been our mysterious benefactor. It seemed like our trip to LA was destined to happen.

As we took off and the morning's excitement faded a little, my heart felt heavy. I was looking forward to the experience I'd have in LA, and I was looking forward to the adventure of living with Perry and Cora in Cincinnati. But I lost the family I thought

I'd finally found. I was full of more unanswered questions about the nature of the universe than before I'd met them. I thought I'd finally found where I belonged, where I'd be part of something greater, and I was wrong. I was still essentially alone, for I'd learned well enough that no matter how much love there is between friends, they are largely conditional relationships and offer no guarantees of carrying on forever. My heart was savagely broken, and reasoning that I'd done the right thing was small comfort. I didn't feel capable of anything more than a fleeting, superficial kind of happiness that comes with the determination to have at least that much, but I resolved to milk every moment I could out of LA. I'd voluntarily lived a very restricted life for almost two years, and I was ready to be in the world again. I needed to move on, and as quickly as possible, because every time I remembered that I had been got rid of by them, that they no longer loved or wanted me, madness threatened to creep in. My sense of self-preservation compelled me to try to avoid thinking of the Millers as much as possible.

Round Sixty Eight

A limousine collected us from the airport and drove us to a five star hotel on Sunset Strip. We were given a welcome pack with a schedule of the MTV events we'd be attending, and when we'd have free time. Our room was, I believe, on the eighth floor, and had a balcony that overlooked the famous strip itself. The view was jaw dropping.

People were everywhere, and every kind of person you could imagine was represented. Everything was so vivid and teeming with life, I practically camped out on the balcony to soak up the sights. Directly opposite our hotel was Sunset Strip Tattoos. When I enquired, the hotel staff informed Cora and me that it was where all the stars and musicians had their ink done. My curiosity was piqued.

We had three nights in Los Angeles, centred on the award ceremony and surrounding parties. I only had $25.00 to my name because the several hundred dollars that I'd built up in savings had gone towards my initial moving and rent expenses. I managed to not dip into my remaining $25.00 each day by shovelling my bag full of buffet food and water bottles at each event we went to.

On the night of the awards, the limo came to our hotel and took us to the show. The production was an awesome thing to behold! I was no stranger to big shows; I'd been to three Lallapaloozas, a stupid amount of Nine Inch Nails concerts, The Cure, and countless other shows over the years. But I'd never seen a production made for broadcast TV, nor had I seen anything staged with as much pageantry as the music awards. The atmosphere was electric. I sat in my seat and tried to take all of it in, see every detail, but it was almost too much. I was astonished thinking that anyone in America could have won that contest, but *I* did. That was a very surreal thing to reflect upon.

The night passed like a dream, as did the after party when I got terrifyingly close to the Material Girl herself. She was surrounded by a dozen people, and I was just outside of that circle. Madonna was no more than ten feet away from me; I saw every detail on her face and costume. For a moment I considered breaking through the people surrounding her and asking her to adopt me. At the end of the ceremony and after parties Cora and I returned to the hotel, ears ringing, stomachs churning and both of us so gobsmacked by everything we'd seen that we moved in an automatic daze. It was "an experience".

The second day in LA involved a smaller party; after that Cora and I explored the Strip for hours spotting famous bars and people watching. The last day of our trip was reserved for our own entertainment. My $25.00 remained untouched. I was on the balcony, looking across the road at Sunset Strip tattoos and rubbing my dollar bills between my fingers, wondering how I should spend them. I remembered once when my stomach was aching so badly from hunger that I seriously considered eating several free packets of ketchup from McDonalds. I couldn't bring myself to do it, so I just drank more water. I remembered my longstanding habit of checking the weight in ounces on chocolate bars. If I only had seventy-five cents to spend on food I wanted to get the biggest bang for my *almost*-buck. So I'd find the heaviest candy bar, reasoning it would fill me up more than something smaller. In case you're wondering, in most cases it's a Snickers. I decided – fuck it. I've got a bag full of food carefully smuggled out from the ubiquitous buffets and abundant breakfasts. I've been hungry before and I'll be hungry again. I may as well get something that will last. Cora and I headed across the road to Sunset Strip Tattoos.

It was so quiet, cool and dark within that I wondered if they were actually closed but had left the shop door unlocked by accident. At first the room seemed empty but when our eyes adjusted to the darkness we saw a man sitting at the far end of the room, wearing a strange set of very large white headphones with aerials. He said nothing, just raised his hand in a gesture that meant "wait a moment". We looked around, scanning the hundreds of photographs on the walls. There were indeed countless celebrities in them. Most of the Brat Pack, Johnny Depp, Pamela Anderson and I all have something in common.

After a few minutes the man with the headphones rolled his chair forward and lifting his headphones off one ear, asked what he could do for us. I asked, "How big of a tattoo can I get for $25.00?" He laughed, and didn't bother answering, which irritated me. I said "Well, I must be able to get some size tattoo for $25.00!" He squeezed his thumb and forefinger together until they almost touched. I rolled my eyes. After thinking for a moment, I decided the most appropriate tattoo I could get would be of a music note. After all, I was there because of music, music was one of my greatest passions and one of life's few constants. It wouldn't be something I'd ever regret being on me. I wanted a treble clef but he said I only had enough money for an eighth note. I shrugged and sat down in the chair presenting my left ankle. He uttered a long suffering sigh, but went to work. He was done before I'd finished a cigarette.

I returned to the hotel marvelling that I'd irrevocably changed my body. I'd always wondered if I'd ever want a tattoo and apparently I did! It's small enough that it's been mistaken for a mole on more than one occasion, but it was a badge of my new freedom and intent to create a life on my terms. I was definitely winging it one decision at a time, but I had ideas and desires forming about my future, and I was trying to head in those general directions. Writing this all out is close to being as depressing as living through it was. Being forced to acknowledge the number of times I tried and failed to live the life I wanted to live is embarrassing. I also realise how many times I compromised myself, whether out of hope or desperation. All I can say is that I always did my best, even if it wasn't quite enough at the time, and I hope I've redeemed myself since. I can touch that music note right now. It is a part of me, just as these memories are. It sits on my ankle and says that I chose my life, and I worked for it. Every joy received, such as that given from music, is mine, earned.

Cora and I flew back to St. Louis, collected my belongings, and drove to Cincinnati.

<u>Round Sixty Nine</u>

Settling into Cincinnati was of course a mixed experience. Because Cora and Perry had lived in the apartment together for several months before my arrival, it felt very much as if I was moving into their space, rather than the three of us sharing an apartment equally. They did make a lovely effort to welcome me, but unconsciously routines had been firmly set in place and I had no say in them. Upon my arrival I got a job at Lazarus, the same department store that Cora and Perry both worked at. It was in a shopping mall directly across the road from our apartment building, so ours was a very small world.

Cora, Perry and I wanted somewhere to escape to from the daily circuit of playing Goth Talk in our apartment and working at Lazarus, so we scouted the local club scene. We found one club. It was in a converted grocery store built in the 1970s, and was a long, low building converted in tidy white siding. The car park had neat yellow lines outlining each space; the clubbers even made the effort to park within the lines. The whole affect made you feel you were doing something very respectable and sensible rather than embarking on a night of debauchery. We were used to St. Louis clubs that were appropriately dirty and shabby, located in dodgy, unkempt areas of the city and full of riotous crowds who parked wherever they damn well pleased.

Inside, the management clearly made an attempt at salvaging a sense of atmosphere with black lighting, black painted walls and a concrete floor covered in cigarette ends. They prompted me to wonder if each one had been carefully positioned on the floor to achieve the correct look of casual neglect. But the poles and cages scattered in the middle of the dancefloor gave them away as trying way too hard. There was a large square bar, where the three of us loitered, feeling very depressed, drinking and watching the near empty dance floor. It was pretty immediately clear we hadn't found our second spiritual home, but the three of us had fought over the mirror getting ready all evening, so we were there to stick it out. Even there, standing at the bar in that club, I thought of the Millers, and how much they'd disapprove of what I was doing. Not all, but much of the pain I was going through over leaving the family was morphing into anger, as my pain typically does.

We persevered despondently with the evening, and I met a twenty-six year old man named Ricky. At the end of the night he asked for my phone number. I wasn't attracted to him, but Cora urged me to give him our number in the hopes we'd meet more people through him. I was surprised when he called the next day and asked me out on a date. I didn't know how to politely say no after giving him my phone number the night before, so I said yes.

Round Seventy

As if by accident, I began dating Ricky. I hadn't really had many actual boyfriends. There was obviously Troy, then unfortunately Mark, and now Ricky. He was a direct result of guilt, boredom and peer pressure. I found it almost impossible to break up with him, which I tried several times. He'd cry and I'd feel bad and retract what I said. Perry and Cora wanted me to be with him because they wanted his company and they said I was cruel for breaking up with him when he so adored me. I had absolutely nothing to do but work and sit in our apartment and I felt he was harmless, so I went along with yet another action my heart wasn't in. Thank god I'm almost finished recounting those! One thing Ricky did have going for him for me was he was by far the most "respectable" person I'd ever dated, and I was still suffering from the desire to be seen as a "good girl" rather than the more complicated true me. He came from a good Catholic family and still lived at home. He was extremely naïve compared to me and we usually found each other inscrutable. I enjoyed dating someone who at least had a real job and car, and he enjoyed dating someone who was thought to be "pretty and witty and gay". Well, one of us was gay at least!

He had the most annoying habit, obsession actually, of constantly dropping into conversation lists of products either manufactured or invented in Cincinnati, or any famous people with a remote connection to the city. He'd only left Cincinnati a few times in his entire life, and was abnormally enthusiastic about it, as if Cincinnati were the centre and beginning of the civilised world. If I could erase his arrogance, his enthusiasm for underestimating my intelligence, and his tendency to utterly bore me senseless the moment he entered a room, I might have had a chance of at least enjoying his company as a friend. Few couples have been less interested in each other than we were. I knew why I was still dating him, but it took me a while to work out why he was still dating me. The good Catholic boy couldn't admit that he was homosexual, and I was the ideal cover.

If Ricky had been a friend, I would have had nothing but support and sympathy for his situation. But as a heterosexual woman, I'd rather my partner was not exclusively into men - and I'd rather that he was honest and open in his behaviour towards me. No matter that ours was no great love affair, when I found out that he was cheating on me and he confessed it was with a man, I hit the roof. The gender of his lover was not particularly an issue, but we were supposed to be exclusive, and I was furious at being betrayed.

When I confronted him and he admitted his actions to me, I was eager to break up with him. But he begged me not to, giving me a laundry list of reasons why I shouldn't, and Perry and Cora weighed in heavily on his side, likening our relationship to theirs. It was a stressful situation for me, made all the harder because I was in the earliest stages of a full-fledged nervous breakdown, so I took the path of least resistance - complying.

I didn't love him, or even like him very much, but in all honesty I had nothing better to do than to be his girlfriend and pretend it was genuine. That might sound like a harmless enough arrangement on the face of it, but in truth it was a very stupid thing to do. It was stupid because the more involved we got with each other, the more his family began to expect from us and soon things got out of control.

The best thing about living in Cincinnati was the marvellous nights we spent DJing in our apartment. With mine, Perry's and Cora's record collection combined we had hundreds of records spanning various musical genres. Perry had spinning decks and a huge sound system. For lack of a club or diner to hang out in like we had in St. Louis, we made our apartment into the place we wanted to spend all our time in. Perry was unstoppable once he got on the decks. I tried to learn but I wasn't coordinated enough to make the music transition from one song into the next the way Perry could. I much preferred lying back and listening to Perry's brilliance. He and I were both like machines. His machine made music, mine ate it up with my ears, consuming it like it was life giving. The year in Cincinnati was a feast for my ears and for those memories alone I suppose I'm glad I went.

Despite the fact that I didn't have a licence, Cora generously began letting me drive her car late at night. She understood that I felt hemmed in in the apartment; Ricky had virtually taken over my bedroom and more often than not I wanted space away from him. At twenty-seven he still couldn't quite bring himself to move out of home, but he loved having somewhere to go that made him feel like an adult. My night driving was wonderful. I stayed within the confines of a map that I memorised so that I would never get lost or encounter unknown territory. I never exceeded the speed limit but it always felt like I was floating; coasting silently above the earth at 3am, a mixed tape playing on loop in the stereo. For the first time I realised that driving could be a hobby. If only I could have written at the same time as steering a wheel, I would have been in sensory bliss. I became addicted to those drives, spending all day counting the hours and then minutes until I could escape, when Cora tossed me the keys late that night. When I was driving I was fully surrounded by the sounds of the music playing. I was acutely alert to everything around me, relishing the feeling of executing a beautiful curve on the road seamlessly with only the slightest wrist movement. It gave me time to think, free of any intruding voices or opinions. Sometimes I would drive that circuit until 6am. I never got tired, but I did lose all track of time. The sun caught me unawares, rising when I thought I'd only just begun my drive, and I'd have to head home, not wanting Cora to worry about her car (or less likely, me). I would tiptoe into the apartment and see all three of them sleeping, and I'd climb into my own bed. The drives were the only things that allowed me to sleep. Otherwise, my thoughts were too intrusive, repetitive and painful. The quiet meditation of driving and singing was all that could eventually wind me down. Then I'd sink into the bliss of a few hours' sleep before it was time to go to work again.

Round Seventy One

Finally, endless years of terrible living conditions caught up with me. Too little erratic sleep, too little food, too much pain, almost a decade of smoking and internalising whole worlds of stress while playing punching bag for a few people here and there, does not a healthy person make. Although I'd had the ongoing problem of random physical attacks that would temporarily paralyse me, for the most part I'd been remarkably healthy all things considered. No longer. First I was just more tired than usual, finding it almost impossible to get up for work each day, and giving up my midnight drives altogether, then able to sleep every spare minute. Next I developed a relentless cough. I saw a doctor and bronchitis was diagnosed. I got a prescription and took to my bed but the medicine didn't help, in fact I got worse. The fever overwhelmed my body, the cough wracked my ribs as I gasped for breath; I was so weak I couldn't even hold a drink for myself.

A long and valiant (or stupid) attempt to keep attending work despite being fit for nothing came to an end, and I was signed off work indefinitely. My body turned into a painful shipwreck and my lungs were the iron anchor pinning me down in bed. Sometimes Cora and Perry popped their heads in but I was mainly left alone. For the first few days Cora enjoyed playing nurse for me but as I became increasingly disgusting in my sickness and showed no promise of improvement, she went back to her regular activities. A week or so into this wasting illness she angrily asked me how I intended to pay my part of the rent if I wasn't working. I was too sick to even speak, let alone express my feelings in response to that statement.

Hoping for Ricky to take care of me was something that never occurred to me. Unfortunately he was one of the most self-absorbed people I've ever had the displeasure of knowing. We had no sex life, but we had shared a bed for some time. The most he contributed for most to my illness was a constant nagging that my fever made the bed unbearably hot. Until he was ready to sleep he spent all of his time with Cora and Perry in the living room. As he was quick to point out, the atmosphere in my room was thick and unpleasant with sickness. Therefore I was alone almost twenty-four hours a day.

In the middle of this long, severe illness, I turned twenty. I got a birthday card from Linda that Cora brought to me in bed. When I saw her familiar handwriting on the envelope my heart lurched in my chest. I thought that the fact that she was sending me a birthday card perhaps meant that she wanted to mend fences. I was disillusioned of that fantasy when I opened it. Other than her name, signed "Linda" not "Mama" the only other words were a bible verse she'd written detailing the torments that the unsaved in hell endured. There really wasn't any potential positive spin I could put on that birthday message. It crushed me. A person doesn't send a birthday card detailing your eternal residence down below because they're filled with a desire to save a soul and life. A person does that because they hate the person they're doing it to. I told Cora to throw the card away, lay back down in bed and drifted off back into my feverish sleep, tears rolling down my cheeks.

As my illness carried on, Ricky, who I was beginning to silently label "Stupid Ricky" carried on coming to the apartment every night. I didn't even see him until he came to my bed in the early hours of the morning because I couldn't get out of bed and no one wanted to be in my room, which did reek of sickness and sweat. Eventually he'd come to bed and complain incessantly that I made him too hot. Night after night he got up and opened my bedroom window, despite the snow blowing in. He was happy but it made things drastically worse for me. I tried to speak, to tell him to close it but my voice hardly worked anymore and he turned a blind eye to my gesturing attempts to request he close the window. This wasn't a matter of me being passive. I was physically unable to get up to shut the window. Once or twice every twenty-four hour period I staggered to the toilet and back, several times I collapsed on the way, waking up on the floor hours later. The window was out of my control. Ricky literally couldn't take the heat of being with me, and apparently months of my hospitality didn't merit any assistance in my hour of need. The nights were a living hell during which I shivered, sweated and hallucinated, but never slept anymore. When he woke in the morning to leave for work he did me the courtesy of shutting the window. During the day until it all started over again I faded in and out of sleep. The last time I took my temperature before I can't remember anymore, it was 105 degrees Fahrenheit.

Gently, or so I dreamt, I was roused from sleep by two figures approaching my bed. They were slate grey and their features were soft, not overly defined. Their bodies were rounded, pillow-like, and strong. They reminded me of my Grandparents. They said nothing as they entered my room, but one sat on the side of my bed while the other one lifted me up, its arms supporting my back. The sitting one held a cup to my lips and I gratefully drank the loveliest, purest cup of water I'd ever had. I tried to focus my eyes over the cup at the one holding it for me, to pin down their features. It smiled at me with a look of love and sympathy that made me feel not as alone as I had. I was gently lowered back down to a sleeping position, and before my head hit the pillow they were gone and I was asleep. Over twelve hours later I woke up, and my fever had broken. The window was closed.

The day after my fever broke Stupid Ricky reappeared. He was alarmed at my appearance, as if only just then noticing that his purported girlfriend was knocking on death's door. At last he helped me. He arranged for a doctor's appointment for me that day, and drove me there, panicking as I went in and out of consciousness during the drive. It would have been preferable if he'd helped me see a doctor the month before, and if he hadn't forced me to sleep in a snowy room, but at least something was happening to save me.

The doctor was alarmed at the sight of me when I was half carried into his office. He immediately did several tests and a thorough examination, and within an hour declared that I had a nasty case of pneumonia. He also said that with lungs like mine, I'd do well to leave Cincinnati, whose winters I wasn't fit for, and go somewhere with a hotter, drier climate. "Go to the desert!" he said, "Vegas, New Mexico! Just get out of Cincinnati! Our weather will finish you off in ten winters." It's advice that rings in my head during every English winter I live through, with increasing irony.

Round Seventy Two

My recovery was long, slow and incomplete. When I was more or less 70% better the Wheel of Fortune turned once again, demanding I return to the scramble that was attempting to maintain my existence. Just as I regained enough strength to return to work two afternoons a week Cora and Perry decided they'd had enough of Cincinnati, and they wanted the three of us to get an apartment in St. Louis. I couldn't have been happier to see the back of that city and go home. I was also eager to break my connection with Ricky; it felt like it was weighing me down twenty-four hours a day.

But, like most things, moving back to St. Louis didn't go quite as planned. We were meant to go as a threesome, to a new apartment in St. Louis, living with the same set-up that we had in Cincinnati, the three of us working and paying towards the bills equally. I was thrilled at the prospect of being back in my home city, but no longer as a beggar. I wanted to show every naysayer that I'd always been willing to work hard and I was capable of succeeding. I earned everything I was and had. I was going to hold my head in pride because my living arrangements would be as legitimate as anyone's, and they'd be entirely paid for by me. Of course I'd lived that way in Cincinnati, but everyone I knew hadn't been around to witness it. Success is much sweeter when those who condemned you to failure witness it.

Moving was the perfect excuse to end my rather one-way "relationship" with Ricky. However, much to my shock and dismay, like two giggling, naughty children, Cora and Perry spontaneously invited him to come with us, without even asking me beforehand how I felt about it. He said he was seriously considering it. With my back against the wall I finally, properly broke up with him, telling him I wanted to start fresh at home in St. Louis. He cried a great deal and bemoaned how much he needed me. We remained in contact as friends, mostly out of a sense of obligation on my part and desperation on his.

Cora, Perry and I went to St. Louis for a long weekend to search out an apartment and begin applying for jobs. But no sooner than Perry stepped foot back in his parents' house, he decided he had to move home again – home to his parents. When he told Cora, she decided that if she couldn't live with Perry than she may as well move home to live with her family in Cincinnati. Neither of them told me until the morning of the final day of our four day trip, despite deciding it on the first. They consulted each other and knew we wouldn't be living in St. Louis together, but they still trotted around with me, viewing apartment after apartment, because they didn't want to tell me the truth. It wasn't until I tried to get them to agree on an apartment and realised that they were being suspiciously quiet that I confronted them and asked what was going on. They dropped the bomb that in three weeks they'd each be moving home to their parents, and I'd be on my own finding living accommodation.

I was truly astonished. Having the rug pulled out from under my feet was a familiar sensation but this one was harsh. Years of friendship, descended to that. They knew I had nowhere else to go, they knew I had no family to return to. And they didn't give enough of a shit to at least do me the favour of telling me at the beginning of that trip, when they decided it between themselves. The tireless work I'd done looking for "our" apartment was all for nothing, when all that time I could have been looking for a way to provide for myself. Their delay in informing me only added insult to the injury they did me. Being neglected by family was par for the course but I expected better of the friends I'd known and loved for years.

It took me at least a year before I would speak to Perry and Core again. When Perry did finally contact me and apologise, freely admitting that they'd done a shitty thing and claiming that he and Cora still loved and missed me, I was somewhat beyond expecting better of people, and was content to enjoy their company on a more superficial basis. I responded honestly, saying that I'd be thrilled to be friends again, but I'd never trust him with more than the loan of a record. I had finally had enough of people throwing me under the bus as soon as a little pressure entered a situation.

But Perry's belated apologies were still a long way off. Right then, I needed to find a job and a place to live in St. Louis. I had one day left in the city then almost three weeks back in Cincinnati to secure both of those precious commodities. As soon as Perry and Cora informed me of my new living circumstances I shut them out, searching for the cheapest apartments I could find in the many papers I'd been using. Cora was hysterical in tears because I made no secret of how furious I was with both of them and she could never handle criticism. I shouted at her to pull herself together and drive me around the city until I found a place to live. Miraculously, I secured the very first apartment we visited, likely because I ordered the search with the cheapest place in the dodgiest neighbourhood at the top of the list, knowing my chances of getting a place like that was miles better than being approved for one of the polished complexes three of us had been viewing.

The apartment was on the destitute side of the Loop. The management were satisfyingly ambivalent; unlike most places that required credit checks and an application process, they only required that you present a deposit to be given an apartment; they didn't even ask if I was employed. That was a good thing, because although I'd submitted more than a dozen applications I hadn't heard back from any of them yet. I was gambling that one of those places would hire me before I was actually required to pay rent. There really wasn't anything else I could do.

I returned to Cincinnati totally broke, having given all my money over for the large-but-no-questions-asked-deposit. Having only budgeted to pay for a third of the initial moving costs, I was terrified about how I'd manage. I didn't even own furniture, but that was the least of my problems. Rent, water and electricity dominated my every waking thought. I couldn't bring myself to speak to either of them on the long drive back. Cora offered me a very lame apology, and then promptly ruined it, adding that it was actually more stressful for her to tell me of their decision than it was for me to sort out my living conditions as "I always landed on [my] feet". That was so laughably insane I couldn't deal with her anymore. I suppose you could look at it that way. I always did manage to find somewhere new when I was chucked out of my previous residence. A true luxury indeed. I *was* landing on my feet! I landed on them so many times, so fucking hard, they were breaking for it, along with every other bone in my body. The remaining weeks in Cincinnati were conducted on strictly business-like terms.

Round Seventy Three

Regardless of how badly I bluffed my way into it, that apartment was the first space I ever called entirely my own, and for that reason, I loved it as well as if it had been a palace. In my final week in Cincinnati I received a phone call telling me I got a job at a record store. It wasn't easy to get to from my apartment without a car: St. Louis' public transport was almost non-existent. I managed it by walking miles every morning, and in the night when I was too tired I'd take a bus to a slightly closer location and then a taxi for the rest. On my days off I went to an employment agency to look for higher paid work, such as secretarial, because I immediately knew the job at the record store wouldn't pay for my apartment. I was making $2.00 more than minimum wage, working an average of sixty hours a week and it still wasn't enough to pay for a two room apartment in one of the most dangerous areas of the city.

Rather shamefully and stupidly, I carried on an odd sort of friendship long distance with Ricky, though neither of us pretended to each other that we were in a romantic relationship. In front of others we did act like a rather lacklustre couple, but we both saw other people and we didn't have sex. His reasons for insisting on carrying on with

403

me were... his reasons. His mother loved me and wanted to hear wedding bells and the pitter-patter of Ricky Jr's feet. Ricky's gayness was something of a spanner in the works of her dreams, but I was a perfect cover for that. Appearing to be close to me also appealed to his vanity, and enabled him to continue exuding a macho exterior.

My reasons were honestly far worse than his, morally speaking. There aren't too many things in this book that I still feel remorse or shame for, but the fact that I kept up that pretence with Ricky is certainly one of them. I was hanging on as an insurance plan. He was constantly debating about moving to St. Louis to live with me, and I was beginning to realise I might need a roommate. Since my apartment had only one bedroom, finding a traditional roommate was impossible. At that time in my life, I didn't like Ricky, but I also didn't hate him yet. I wasn't looking for a soul mate anymore; I just wanted a decent life. I was willing, if necessary, to work with him to achieve that, happy in the knowledge that he was getting something out of it that he wanted too.

I'm really not proud of that decision. It was mercenary, which is something I am not, and it is deceptive, another thing I try never to be. I had changed so much over the years. I'd been through so much. So many people had hurt me, cast me off. I wasn't willing to be the victim any more; I was going to work the system to my advantage for once. If having a steady home I could call my own meant I had a sham relationship with someone I could barely tolerate then I'd do it. He was using me and I was using him. As much as I've regretted that decision, I always come up empty when I try to think about what I could have done better. There are of course ways of coping and seeking help that I know of now, but I was ignorant then of even the very thin welfare state available to me. With the tools and information I had then, I acted out of both desperation and necessity.

One hot summer day I took the bus to a job interview in the posh area of University City, near my Dad's house. I knew as soon as I walked into the office building that the place was way out of my league. It was plush, polished, and perfect, and everyone was wearing designer suits. I'd scraped enough money together to buy one cheap skirt, blouse and heels from a charity shop for interviews. I saw myself as they saw me, and I looked shabby. It was a difficult interview to get through. They tried to be polite, but usher me out the door as soon as possible, and I tried not to break down in tears of embarrassment.

When it was over I left the air-conditioned building and the St. Louis heat hit me like a wall. I realised there was no bus for the return route. Why on earth would there be? I'd only been given this interview two hours before I was meant to attend, so I hadn't had time to do any more than work out how to get there. It was almost funny. It was clear that on this occasion, making the extra effort to rush out of the house on short notice had not only been a waste of time, but it also got me stranded several miles from my apartment. I walked to a nearby McDonalds, seeking air conditioning and a payphone, though I wasn't sure just yet who I might call. I ordered a free cup of water and sat at a table for a while to think about how I could get home.

I was bereft, so discouraged and desperately wondering how I would survive just for that day, let alone forever. Somehow, at that moment, the dilemma of how to get home seemed more pressing than any other problem I was facing. I wanted so badly to curl up in my bed and cry that it physically hurt to remain sane. I only had a dollar in change, so a taxi was out of the question. Back at the apartment was a pile of bills I couldn't even bear to open anymore. I wanted to pay them as much as they wanted to be paid. There simply wasn't enough money to pay more than my rent. My phone and electricity were constantly shut off and turned on again, until I began to treat it as something like camping rather than panic. But the way those collection letters are written smarts like a humiliating slap. It's as if they're attacking your moral character because you can't pay, with their outraged claim that you're "refusing" to hand over the money, implying that being poor is the same thing as being a thief. I was sitting in the wealthiest area of the city, surrounded by beautiful skyscrapers and wealthy stockbrokers, and I could not have been a greater contrast. The depression was overwhelming.

Very reluctantly, I decided I had to call my Dad and Karen and ask them for help. Vianne was away, and she was the only other person I knew who lived in U. City. Most of my friends were from Lemay and it would have been a two hour round trip for them, at least. As the phone rang I prayed they'd be kind and help me without giving me too hard a time for it. Karen answered. She told me she was sorry but I'd missed my Dad, who was out. I couldn't possibly have been more relieved! I could speak to Karen without terror of condemnation or interrogation; she was everything that was proper and well bred. I explained my situation to her and asked if she could please pick me up and drive me home. She said she'd be pleased to and she'd be there in five minutes. I waited anxiously, hoping I hadn't made a huge mistake. I might be spared dealing with my father's anger face to face, but I knew Karen would tell him about seeing me, and why later that day. I don't think he has ever loved anyone but Karen and their animals, and I thought he'd be very angry that I caused her an inconvenience. I made a silent vow not to bother them again for at least four extra months so he'd be likely to have forgotten this by then.

I waited for her in the parking lot, and the heat was boiling me alive. A crippling migraine was coming on (though I didn't know it was called that then) and getting to a cool place where I could lay down was becoming essential. I hoped I'd be able to speak to her properly despite the increasing pain I was in.

When she pulled up outside the McDonalds and waved, I sank appreciatively into her Volvo and its air conditioning. The relief was so great I could hardly bring myself to speak. My hands were gripped tightly into fists; I was concentrating on holding off the seizures that (for me) often came on the heels of a severe migraine. I tried to make small talk: about the cats, my job search, anything that sprang to mind. Despite my attempts, she began looking at me with concern.

When we pulled up outside my apartment, she put her hand on my arm before I opened the car door to say my final thanks and goodbye. She asked me what was wrong. It was the wrong time to ask me that, I was feeling far too low physically and emotionally to lie as I normally would have. After almost a minute with my mouth open like a guppy, searching for the words to express what I was going through and what I had been through, I burst into tears. I almost couldn't answer because the truth was so obvious and potentially offensive to her if I expressed it. I was cracking under the strain. I didn't have enough money for food. I was working like a mule and earning pennies. When I wasn't working I was dragging myself around the city looking for better work. My health was falling apart and there wasn't one single person on earth who I could go to for help. I said I didn't know why I was put on this earth if my life was nothing but struggle, pain and toil. Incoherently I babbled and cried.

She held my hand and a few tears rolled down her cheeks as she listened. I stopped myself, with an almost inhuman amount of will power, from saying my father and by extension she was largely responsible for all of this and asking her how she slept at night knowing she was living the comfortable life I'd been born into. Living that life not even ignorant of what my life was like, from my childhood when they knew Carol hit us, to that car ride when I was twenty and having a nervous breakdown and everything in between. I didn't want to hurt her, but I couldn't stop crying, so I stopped speaking.

Karen wiped the tears off her cheeks and pulled her chequebook from her purse. My first thought was that however angry my Dad was going to be for me asking Karen for a ride, he'd be that much angrier if she gave me any money. He'd explicitly told me many times never to ask him for money. I almost didn't want to accept it, but my rumbling tummy trumped my fear of my father. I silently decided I'd add another couple of months on before reminding him of my existence and began to pray he wouldn't call me for the very first time in order to scream at me. The check she handed me was for $100.00, a good strong sum for me. She said she was very sorry I was struggling so badly, and I should go food shopping right away with this money. She said she had never wanted me to go without. I was embarrassed I had to take charity from my father's wife, but still sensibly grateful for the money. Even as I looked at it and pictured how much food it would buy though, I was still depressed. Because food is consumed and when it was gone there wasn't going to be another random $100 cheque to buy more. It was lovely, but it was essentially merely delaying the inevitable, and it certainly went no way towards solving the root problem itself. I thanked her, I thanked her humbly, knowing she was returning to a house where every object was a carefully selected work of art, and knowing all of that should be mine too. I could thank her, I could even love her, but I condemned her. By her grace, I'd eat well for a couple of weeks. But years of my living hell lay on her, her husband's, and his first wife's feet.

Round Seventy Four

I signed up with more job agencies. In one of them I met a very determined woman who claimed she'd never had a client she hadn't been able to place in employment within one month of working with them, if they did as she told them. Cooperation wasn't a problem with me, so I felt hope hearing that, knowing that within a month I'd be in a better job. She sat me in front of a computer and made me type all day long to increase my speed. She praised me for my typing abilities, and then, placing a hand on my shoulder to soften the blow, told me I must never, ever go to an interview without wearing a suit jacket to hide the large white striped scars on my arm. I felt my cheeks grow hot, but nodded and thanked her for being frank with me. When I left her office I bought a suit jacket.

She sent me on a job interview to a company that was two long bus routes away from my apartment. As promised, I wore the suit jacket on top of my blouse, despite the fact that the temperature that day reached 105 degrees Fahrenheit. I went through the hour and a half bus journey wearing that stupid jacket, I was that nervous about my interview that it didn't occur to me I could take the jacket off and just put it on when I arrived rather than boil alive in it. After the buses, I walked to the top of a long road that ran down the length of an industrial estate. The company I was attending was at the dead end of that road; I had a mile to walk. I put one foot in front of the other, hotter than I ever had been in my entire life. About half way down the road a businessman pulled over and asked me where I was going. I gave him the name of the company and coincidentally he was going to the same place. He offered to drive me the rest of the way and I was too grateful to have a seat to collapse on to worry about abduction. I was so exhausted and hot I could barely speak, but nod my thanks. While the distance I walked had seemed endless, I was only in his blissfully air conditioned car for a little over a minute.

My Good Samaritan and I nodded goodbye to each other as we entered reception and went our separate ways. I was greeted by a middle-aged, rather camp receptionist, who I almost instantly bonded with. He looked me up and down and said "You're here for the interview?" I nodded, still unable to speak. "You look like hell!" he said, and I laughed. He told me to sit in the waiting area and rushed off to get me a glass of water.

When I was a little refreshed he said "Um… you might want to go refresh your make-up…" He was quite right, I did look like hell. I exited the bathroom with combed hair and repaired make-up, but I looked nothing like the cool, carefully manicured girl I'd been when I left my apartment three hours earlier. I felt despondent, wondering if I was doomed to another failure. Taking my mind off those thoughts, the receptionist asked me "Why didn't you take your jacket off until you got here?" I was stumped. That was the first time that possibility had occurred to me. I'd been so focused on the need to hide my scars I'd been a complete idiot. I answered truthfully, that I was too stupid to have thought of it. It wasn't a wonderful endorsement for my employment, but he at least wasn't the decision maker.

The sweat was worth it. The company hired me that day to work in their call centre. My income was going to increase more than $3.00 extra an hour to what I was earning at the record store. I was elated.

It was thrilling news! I'd finally be able to support myself, not indulgently, but with enough to feel safe that the essentials would be covered. That was all I wanted. But it was too late. When I returned jubilantly to my apartment, I saw a neon yellow eviction notice taped to my door. My rent had been regularly several days late due to my pay schedule which didn't allow me to build up enough money before it was due out again. The previous two months I'd only managed to pay partial rent because my hours were cut back at work; although I generally worked around sixty a week I was only contracted for twenty. That current months' rent was a week overdue. I read the notice taped to my door with a horrible sinking feeling. It said that I had to vacate the apartment within two weeks or pay the full overdue rent plus several hundred dollars in crippling fines to cover their legal costs. I owed them around $1000 in total. It would have taken me three months' work just to pay those debts, let alone each concurrent month's rent and other expenses. I wasn't going to have that much money in two weeks; I wasn't even due to start my new job for ten days. I'd finally succeeded in finding a well-paying job, but I was still losing my beloved apartment. I was devastated.

The pain of losing that apartment still smarts. I took great pleasure just gazing at the walls, every inch mine, earned, cleaned and paid for by me, in my name only. I'd taken pride in it, I'd felt I'd accomplished something great to be living independently like that. I'd worked frantically to try to keep it, but in the end it wasn't enough. It wasn't that my money went to luxuries. I just didn't earn enough. I'd failed, once again, and I wasn't sure what I was going to do next.

Round Seventy Five

With fortuitous timing (or perhaps not) for some time prior to my eviction notice being served, Vianne had been making a lot of noise about wanting a boob job. Much to her frustration, her mother resolutely refused to fund one, prompting Vianne to get her first part-time job, with the intention of saving up and paying for it herself. But Vianne wasn't any good at waiting.

The night when I sat on the sofa gripping my neon yellow eviction notice, rocking back and forth with my head in my hands, Vianne burst through my front door waving a newspaper clipping. It was an advert for a strip club, and it was pretty clear they'd take anyone who was hot. Vianne was confident that we fit the remit. She'd already booked herself an interview for that same night, and she was at my apartment to beg me to go along with her for moral support. Neither of us had stepped foot in a strip club before and she was afraid to go alone. I was afraid to go with armed guards!

I tried to talk her out of attending the interview, but it was absolutely futile. When Vianne set her mind to something it was damn near impossible to change it. Eventually I realised I may as well be directing my words down a garbage disposal for all that they were getting through to her. She was too hooked by the idea of quick money. I made it clear I didn't approve of what she was doing, but I very reluctantly agreed to go with her. I just wanted to keep her safe if she was determined to go through with it.

Vianne saw the eviction notice in my hands and suggested I interview for the job too, but I said an emphatic NO. I had done a fair amount of outrageous things in my life, but they weren't pointed in that direction. My experiences with Mark, as well as other encounters, had made me prudish in my own way. Something about the fact that I lived alone often gave people the impression I was less inhibited than I actually was. I was an outrageous flirt when I was feeling outgoing, but I generally just wanted to flirt for the sheer fun of it. But, I wanted money as much as anybody – more than most probably. That's why I'd sacrificed comfort and leisure time traipsing about the city looking for a job that offered more than retail. Oh money was crucial to me! But I was not going to virtually prostitute my body for anyone's enjoyment. I couldn't think of anything more humiliating. I told Vee no but she kept badgering me about it once the idea got into her head. I ignored her, and gave my own simultaneous monologue trying to talk her out of it.

We got ready, got in her car and drove to a seriously unpleasant area of St. Louis. There were gun shops, bars, pawn shops and nothing else. Well, nothing else except the local strip joint! The further into the area we drove the quieter and more pensive we each became. When we parked Vianne reached over to the glove box and pulled out a flask of whisky. I laughed at her ingenuity. We both took several swigs, sharing a cigarette and swapping morale boosting reassurances. When we felt appropriately relaxed, we got out of the car and headed to the door hand in hand. We had no idea what to expect.

We were greeted at the door by the female manager, who was expecting Vianne. I introduced myself as merely a hanger on as she eyed me up like a piece of prime beef. At first I was reassured to be dealing with a woman, until I realised this woman was a snake. The interior of the club was dark, dirty, shabby, and full of smoke. To the left of the door was a long bar and to the centre right was the large square stage with poles all over it and a mirrored podium in the middle.

A woman was on the stage. She was completely naked. That shocked me. For some reason I thought they had to cover up the most private parts. But there she was without a single stitch on her entire body, bent over double, facing away from the audience, holding onto a pole. Her buttocks were spread open and she was bouncing her bottom up and down. A man was standing right there in front of her bottom and pussy, his face only inches from her most intimate parts while she danced as if oblivious. He had a small, passive little smile on his face, and his hands were in his pocket. The look on his face said a thousand silent things I wished I hadn't heard. I turned my head away, quickly. It was one of the most disturbing things I'd ever witnessed, and more than ever I didn't want Vianne to do it. The manager paused when she saw the stage had caught our attention, but when we both looked elsewhere, she continued leading us to the office.

I'd interviewed for countless jobs, and this manager was the most overpolite interviewer or indeed woman I'd ever met. After providing us both with chairs she began to stare at us one by one and wax enthusiastically about how beautiful we were. I said a polite thank you, and reiterated that it was only Vianne looking for a job. The manager seemed to take exception to that, as if she was offended because I didn't wish to work there. She asked me to listen carefully while she explained the job to Vianne in case I changed my mind. I nodded politely but was counting the minutes before we could leave, and praying Vianne would say no to the job after seeing with her own eyes what it was. At every opportunity I elbowed her to show my displeasure so all that was left was for me to hope she'd get the point.

The "interview" such as it was, consisted mainly of asking if Vianne was able, willing, and not too squeamish. Then there was a brief discussion of the rules and expectations. Some girls chose to dance nude, some only topless but you'd earn more nude. No touching was allowed, offering lap dances for extra money was encouraged, and any further physical contact with the customers was never to be discussed with other members of staff. In other words, they didn't want to know about any prostitution happening on the side. At the conclusion she smiled and said "Take my advice. Be friendly to the men. No men, no money."

The manager asked Vianne if she was interested. I stared hard at her but she deliberately wouldn't look at me. To my horror, she said yes. Then the manager turned to me. She asked me what I thought, wasn't I happy for my friend that she'd got her new job? I wanted to choke her, and I think she knew that. I didn't say anything. She carried on, "You have a job then, you don't need any more money?" She looked me up and down and smirked. I replied "I have a job. Thank you." She asked me how much I made at this job. It was obviously a rude thing to ask, but I answered her, primarily because I was proud of the huge increase in money I'd soon be earning at my new job. The manager leaned forward and took my hand in hers. I flinched at the touch. She looked me in the eyes and said "You are a very beautiful girl. Life hasn't been kind to you. You will never want for anything again. It's just dancing. Nobody will touch you, I make sure of that. You come in, do your shift, clock off, and go home. I guarantee you'll never earn less than $500 a night. If you two dance together you could double that. I take this club very seriously and when I find a girl who does a great job I'll treat her like my own daughter. Think about it." I was hypnotised by her speech. I was aghast when she said "Life hasn't been kind to you", as if she knew me, wondering what mark gave it away.

I did think about it, for the first time I seriously considered it. I thought very quietly and for an anti-social amount of time, while they both stared at me, waiting to hear what I would say. I thought of my beloved apartment. My beautiful little room that represented freedom, independence and success. I thought of the neon yellow eviction notice and thought, Yes, if I do this now and I earn what she's saying I'll earn, then I'll be able to pay my rent debt in time to save the apartment. Then I'll have a new start at the office job, which thereafter would cover my bills, enabling me to quit work stripping after three weeks. I didn't like it, but the maths and logic seemed irrefutable. Was I or was I not serious about saving my apartment and living without taking from anyone else? As if there was anyone else to take from even if I'd wanted to! I couldn't afford to have the feelings I did. There was no other way for me to come up with such a huge amount of money so quickly. Was I willing to be homeless again when I had the chance to stop it, because doing what it would take to save my home went against my scruples?

Finally I met Vianne's, then the manager's eyes. I said "Okay. Okay, I'll do it." Vianne threw her arms around me and poured thanks and love on me. Over her shoulder I saw the manager. She was smiling at me, a bit triumphantly but not too much so. I understood her very well in that moment. With Vianne, it had been an almost boring, rehearsed sales pitch. With me and my initial refusal, it was a personal triumph.

We shook hands, quickly signed a few forms and Vianne and I left. We agreed that Vianne and I would be back in three days for our first night's work. I couldn't face thinking about doing the actual stripping because every time I imagined exposing

419

myself like that I wanted to be sick. Instead I tried to train my thoughts on my apartment. I was making the most vicious stab at keeping my own home that I could have imagined, short only of penetrative prostitution.

Round Seventy Six

The working night came. Vianne and I got ready together at my apartment. This time when we arrived at the strip club, Vianne produced not only whisky but vodka too. We sat in her car for a long time, drinking, smoking, hugging each other. Finally we got out of the car, more than half drunk, and headed in. The manager greeted us at the door and escorted us through the main room to the girls' dressing room. We passed a row of men sitting at the bar who whistled at us and began discussing with each other the "fresh meat". I worked harder than I'd ever worked before to block out my surroundings.

There wasn't time for second thoughts, nor were there any dancing lessons which I'd been secretly hoping for. I really wasn't sure how to do a striptease. Apparently unlike many girls, I'd never even practised it alone in my bedroom. I'd actually had a relatively boring sex life compared to everyone I knew and most people I still know. When the manager dumped us in the dressing room the other (older) dancers looked at us resentfully. She told the girls to give us a few tips as she left the room. They said

"Take your off clothes, and shake your tits and ass in their faces!" and erupted into laughter with each other. We clearly weren't being welcomed into a sisterhood. Vianne and I had bought our own lingerie for this night, because we didn't want to wear the costumes offered that were shared by all the dancers. Nervously, we changed in a corner of the room. We covertly watched the older girls snort lines of coke. Vianne and I said much to each other with our eyes only, the way only friends of many years can do. We silently agreed that this was not the haven the manager had sold in the interview. We agreed to get out as soon as possible. Then, out loud, I whispered and asked Vianne to leave then, to just get dressed with me and walk out. She said no, that she wouldn't come back again but she wouldn't run scared that night. She begged me not to back out, not to make her do it alone. My loyalty and sympathy with her made me feel inclined that if she was going to go through with it, solidarity demanded I did too.

Within a few minutes of changing our clothes, the manager came and pulled us impatiently towards the stage. Vianne was going first. The manager took us to a jukebox in the corner and told us to punch in the two songs each we would dance to. Vianne let me go first, knowing the way music can shut me off from my surroundings. Scanning the selection, I was appalled at the sort of music people were expected to get off to, but I made do with what was there. I chose Nine Inch Nails "Down In It" and The Cure "Disintegration".

Vianne and I were whispering a few words of comfort to each other when the manager abruptly grabbed Vianne by the arm and led her to the steps on the side of the stage. I felt sick watching her climb them and walk to the middle while her music began. In the first split second that she was up there, Vianne smiled at me, as if to reassure me she was okay. And then I visibly saw her shut me out of her mind. She began to dance like she was born to be a stripper. She always had been the exhibitionist of the two of us.

I couldn't bear to watch her; I saw her in my peripheral vision and I blocked it out. It felt like I was watching her partake in something she couldn't fully comprehend. She looked too young and stupid to be doing this. I glanced at the audience to see their reaction. They loved her. Every one of their faces looked like overfed pigs with no more thought in their head but rutting the youngest female they could find. Another direction I couldn't look at without feeling sick. More than ever before I did not want to do this thing, but as I watched Vianne, I saw her defiant face carry on and I knew she was hurting. I wanted to throw a coat over her and shield her body from dozens of pairs of eyes. I could read her face in a way the men in that audience couldn't, and I saw shame and mortification. I wasn't going to make her go through that alone when we'd got there together. It was time to take my medicine.

When she finally came off the stage, she came to me and hugged me. She whispered in my ear "It's not too bad if you don't look at them." I genuinely felt I could identify (just the tiniest bit) with those who'd climbed the stairs to the guillotine in the French Revolution when I climbed the stairs to that stage, wearing nothing more than panties, thigh highs, heels and a bra. It was the action of moving your own body to climb to your inevitable doom.

I delayed a little too long going onto the stage. The men in the audience began to shout for more and the manager was swearing at me from several feet away. Finally I decided there was nothing for it but to get on with it and get it over with in as business-like manner as possible. Sucking in my breath and drawing on my Nihilistic core, I went out onto the stage without looking back. I walked to the centre of the stage and scanned the audience, looking one by one into so many faces. I thought, "What the fuck am I *doing*?" The music started, and as if on autopilot, I began to dance, making it up as I went along. I tried to picture what I imagined a stripper doing, and do it. As I danced I dropped every item of clothing but my panties, just as Vianne had done, leaving my garter belt to collect dollar bills.

Halfway through the second song, Disintegration I was beginning to feel a little bored. My mind began to wonder while my body carried on doing the things I'd witnessed others do, which the audience seemed to like. My thoughts wandered to the current book I was reading, The Idiot, by Fydor Dostoyevsky. It was part of my never ending quest to understand the strange things that happened to my body. My eyes scanned the crowd I was dancing for, begging for money with my flesh and I thought, "I don't think one man in this building has read that book or is even capable of it. I don't belong here. Yes I'm an idiot!"

When my mind fell briefly unoccupied, a very unattractive man came to the side of the stage and gestured for me to dance over to him, waving some bills in the air. I did as I was told, money being my reason for being there. But I almost wanted to kick that man in the face as I towered above him, for summoning me like a slave. That's what I was though, as long as I was doing that job. Anybody who argues there is equality between strippers and punters is either selling you something, fooling themselves, or hasn't experienced it first hand. I don't expect the men paying for the privilege to be pondering the basic demeaning nature of the transaction, but that doesn't make it untrue. Some people can deal with that arrangement. I tried to. I can't.

Finally my two songs came to an end. I walked off the stage into Vee's arms. We had to put our heads down and rush through the crowd of men blocking our way to the dressing room, grabbing at us and demanding lap dances. Reaching the dressing room we slammed the door behind us. We were silent as we worked as one person to get each other fully clothed and ready to walk out the door as quickly as possible. It wasn't necessary to say the obvious, this place had too much of the amaretto sour about it, too many lines of coke and grasping, dirty men, all things we'd experienced before to our detriment. We had no plans on returning to this new job, but equally knew it would be in our best interest if we simply disappeared, rather than officially quit in a confrontation with the manager and her questionable bouncers.

Again tightly holding hands, we wound our way through the crowd with much difficulty. The manager called after us, inviting us to stay and have drinks. Amaretto Sours no doubt. We called out an "I'm sorry, next time!" and continued to the door. The last thing I saw as we walked out was the manager frowning after us.

Reaching Vianne's car we counted our money. It wasn't going to make a dent in my overdue rent. We laughed a little and cried a little as we drove off. It had been a horrific thing to do. This is another of the few things recorded here that I'm deeply ashamed of to this day. It was an act of desperation; it doesn't represent who I really am at all, but I have to live with its imprint. It hurts to admit to it, but this is what I set out to do when I first began writing this book, and this is what I hold to: to confess all, even the things I would prefer to hide, in order to have my final say

Round Seventy Seven

Having tried and failed at stripping and saving my apartment, I was utterly despondent.

A new, deeper, depression settled within me. A constant sense of there being no such thing as hope settled at the core of me, a sort of quiet acceptance that I would not succeed, that it was not meant for me. All I could hope for was to get through a life with lowered ideals and standards with the minimum amount of pain. I made the only logical choice left to me. I asked Ricky if he was ready to move to St. Louis. He said yes. Without having my apartment to escape to nightly he was finding living with his family too stifling and he wanted a way out. It was a better form of prostitution than stripping. He'd have my company and my identity, but never my body or soul. And after all, it would inevitably fall apart after a while, as all living arrangements did. I was planning on saving every spare penny I could earn – in an office - to prepare me for life after Ricky, even as we signed the lease on our new house.

The house was adorable: a little two-bedroom brick building on the nice side of Lemay. It was owned by good friends of Leah's parents. They were deeply religious and would only rent the house to us if I we were going to be imminently married. I smiled and assured them that we couldn't wait for the date.

Moving to Lemay was going to make it impossible for me to commute to my new job, so Ricky offered to buy me a used car on one of his credit cards. We agreed that I would make monthly payments to him in return for the car, as well as paying my half of the household bills. It was going to stretch my new income considerably, but it was at least a life and it was giving me the keys to gain something more. I needed time, time to earn enough money so I could live with my head held high under my own moral code instead of constantly whoring myself to everyone in my life.   Ricky was interviewing for jobs in St. Louis but was planning on remaining in Cincinnati until he was hired somewhere in St. Louis. In the meantime, he was contributing his part of the rent and bills from the income at his current job in Cincinnati, which he was able to do because living with his parents, he had no outgoing expenses and a substantial income.

I moved on the final day I was allowed to remain in my apartment. It was glorious being back in Lemay, and the house was incredibly luxurious and lovely compared to anything I'd ever lived in. Until Ricky got there it was all mine to do with as I pleased. I felt like a proper grown up.

There was only one problem. I was using Stupid Ricky for a ticket to a house and Stupid Ricky was using me for a cover for his homosexuality and a place to drink a beer in peace. Mutual using does not a bond of trust make. Around six weeks after I moved into the house he was offered a job in St. Louis, meaning it was time for him to finally move. Then he called me and tearfully began to break the bad news, as I listened, numb and speechless. At the last minute, he had decided that still, at twenty-nine years of age, he wasn't ready to leave his family home. He had signed a lease with me two months earlier, and now he wasn't coming. I was furious and full of contempt for him, but after my initial anger passed, I focused on how the house could be financed from then on. Having lived on my own since I was fifteen, I had very little sympathy for a man of nearly thirty weeping that he couldn't cope without his mother's Sunday dinners, especially when he had made a formal commitment to do otherwise. He did actually mention the dinners.

I gave him very little sympathy in that last definitive phone call. My focus was on pinning him down financially, which I had every right to be concerned about. I had his signature on a year's duration lease with me and now he wasn't moving in. The ramifications of that were terrifying to me. I told him to stop crying and think about someone else for a change, to think about what he was doing to me. I told him I expected him to pay one half of all the essential household bills: rent, electricity, water, sewage etc. just as he had originally committed to, whether he was living there or not. Otherwise I would take him to court for the money using the lease as my leverage. He agreed, he even said it was only fair. And then he reminded me that he still needed to be paid back for that car. I almost choked on the irony but replied that as long as he fulfilled his end of the bargain, I would be able to afford mine.

My relief that the charade of us as a couple was finally over was enormous, and suddenly I was in the enviable, if precarious position of being mistress of my own home. I had to depend on Ricky to fulfil his end of the deal, and of course he didn't for very long. But I made the most of the situation and did my best, now working endless hours at the higher paying office job. For the first time in as long as I could remember, I was truly free from everything but the debt of money. I was finally my own spiritual, bodily and romantic mistress, choosing what did and did not enter my home and how I would live my life. I knew success was doubtful in this situation, yet again, because I didn't trust Ricky to pay his half the entire year of the lease. But I was intent on making it last as long as it could, and using the time I had to find my next, and hopefully last, port of call. At first it felt very good living in that house alone.

Then reality hit me and I was standing alone amidst a two bedroomed brick house. It had a living room, dining room, original features; eat in kitchen, mailbox, basement, a six car driveway and garage. A huge front lawn and a beautiful back garden complete with shed and hose. (Trees and bushes) Two ovens, two refrigerators, phone, lawn mower, microwave, neighbourhood watch group, water bills, sewage, drain pipes, a bewildering trash collection schedule, backed up toilets and only myself at the helm of it all. A slow, creeping break in my mind began after I left the Miller's. It grew in strength and size with every moment since then. Finally, the seed was bearing fruit, and it was bitter.

Round Seventy Eight

It was right after Ricky ditched the house on my shoulders that I lost all real semblance to civility, normality and sanity. You know what? It just didn't matter enough anymore to pretend that everything was okay. As I let go of that obligation, the rot I'd been fighting off for most of my life set in. Within two months of moving into the lovely house in Lemay, I went bat-shit crazy. It was the first month in which I had to beg and chase a petulant Ricky for the money he owed me, finally squeezing out only a fraction of his share of the household expenses.

My mind... well, my mind went. I let it go, I gave it permission to go with a smile actually. I remember the moment well. I was standing in the dining room barefoot. A New Order record was playing. I was staring at the cheque that had arrived in the mail from Ricky, doing the maths in my head and wondering how I would pay for that month's bills. I actually heard my mind snap with an audible popping sound. The next thing I knew I was looking up, laying on the floor, and I burst into a mixture of hysterical laughter and crying. This began to happen regularly in moments of still reflection. After a while I'd pull myself together again, and like a well glued Humpty Dumpty would resume attempting to live. I went to work, though I didn't work as efficiently as I otherwise would have; my mind wasn't working properly and I had no ability to hold my focus on anything. It was as if my brain had sprung a leak, and information and memory all flowed straight out of it.

I came home and socialised with friends at my house, which had become the general meeting place for my many acquaintances. Sometimes I'd watch them all laughing and playing in my living room, all of them still living at home, going to college, living lives that were actually going somewhere. I'd feel the urge to demand that they pay towards the house they all but moved into, a dozen of them and more. But I knew that wasn't right, it would only lose me friends, which were the only things of worth left in my life. So I bit my lip and let them use my house as a base until they finally took themselves off to their homes, paid for by parents.

Ricky and I rarely spoke and only about money, typically when I called him to remind him it was due. He became more and more sulky as each month went by, sending a cheque for an increasingly small amount of money. I drove to work in a daze, driving a car he wanted money for. Despite our situation with the house, or rather, because of it, every time I asked him to pay his half he said he would when I paid him my car payment. I painstakingly explained that since every penny I had was paying for the house and often my utilities were being shut off, that I didn't have enough money to make a car payment to him. I explained that if he paid what he had committed to, then I could in turn pay him what I had committed to, as per the budget we'd originally drawn up together.

I contacted several lawyers in an attempt for advice. One seemed to miss the point entirely and say I couldn't take someone to court for breaking up with me. The second said he'd take my case with an upfront fee that I obviously couldn't afford. I was not aware of any kind of welfare that could address my problem. I seemed to always fall between the cracks of one help system or another, never quite ticking all the necessary boxes and therefore always someone else's responsibility. I lost the will to fight. I couldn't form a plan if my life had depended on it. My mind was totally scattered and useless from the accumulated stress of attempting to survive.

I stopped sleeping almost completely. I was so intensely exhausted that I felt that if I allowed myself to collapse into bed, I'd never get up again. So I worked, I socialised, and when everyone eventually left, if they did at all, I kept myself busy in various ways, determined to stay awake so I wouldn't sleep past the hour I was meant to wake up for work. It wasn't a logical system, but I wasn't logical anymore. Not surprisingly, I became sick again. It was another winter, and the pneumonia came back. I missed three weeks from work. I should have stayed off longer but I couldn't afford to. Only part of my essential time off was paid, so I had even less money to cover the house than usual. I refused to care anymore, or beat myself up about the inevitable, but I frantically begged Ricky for more money, pleading starvation and blind panic. Bright red bills poured through my letterbox every day. I had complaints from my neighbours that my lawn wasn't mowed short enough, and Ricky demanding money for the car every time we spoke. All of that and more fell like an avalanche on me. When I attempted to think of a means to extract myself from this situation all I heard was the SHOT in my mind as my brain went to jelly.

One day, about two months after the first shot, I found a psychiatrist in the Yellow Pages who happened to have an appointment available for that same day. In his office, I told him explicitly how I was feeling, explaining the SNAPPING and CRACKING sound I heard in my mind and why, giving him a brief rundown of my life history but focusing on the recent incident of having lost my mind. *SHOT*. He sat and listened patiently, looking quite unfazed, instilling confidence in me.

When I finished he pronounced that there were several psychiatric conditions I might be suffering from, but not to worry, because he knew how to make me feel better. I leaned forward feverishly, wondering how he knew where I could get more money. That was, after all, what would make me feel better. He was thinking along other lines. From a drawer in his desk he pulled out boxes of Lithium, Zoloft, Effexor, and Celexa, and handed them all over to me. I didn't even have to go get a prescription filled! He advised me to start the new regime immediately and I'd soon see a difference. I obliged, though as I accepted them from him I remained disappointed that he wasn't giving me money, or access to money, some kind of social services. Well I was shot, though. Shot. Shot. *Shot*. So why not, not, SHOT?

Round Seventy Nine

Speaking of shot my Dad came to that pretty little bat shit covered house once after one of my bi-annual phone calls. He was there to pick me up, and he was alone. It was the 2nd time in my life that I'd seen him without Karen. She wasn't coming because he wasn't taking me out to eat this time, he was taking me to his shooting range, and she loathed guns. I was excited about the prospect of shooting a gun, knowing it would somehow make me feel better, at least for a while.

My Father taught marksmanship at West Point and has an extensive collection of James Bond style guns, some in a safe deposit box at the bank and others in a safe in his house. I'd never shot before, though I'd handled other people's guns a few times. When we arrived at the range he gave me a long, detailed lecture on gun safety. He told me to listen to every word carefully but he needn't have added that, I was possibly the most eager audience he had ever had. I listened to every word he said raptly, fascinated by each technical detail he relayed to me just as if I were one of his recruits. He showed me how the gun mechanically worked, how to check if it was loaded, how to load and unload it safely. He told me exactly how to move and behave in a shooting alley, and lastly, he demonstrated how to line up my sights and shoot the target I was aiming for. I listened as if my life depended on it, knowing it did. He led me to a lane and deftly hung up the silhouette of a man. He brought his 9mm gun to teach me on,

434

explaining that it would be easiest for someone with a slight form like mine to shoot without experiencing a hard kickback. Finally he handed the gun over, ran the sheet of paper to the back of the room and told me it was time I got shooting.

It was heavier than I expected but I wouldn't have admitted that for the world, and I was careful to show nothing but self-contained calm. The shiver of anticipation that zipped up my spine when I lined up the sights to the centre of the target was exquisite. I let my body go strong but limp to lose the weight of the gun on my arm as he'd taught me, and slowly, then suddenly very quickly, I squeezed the trigger and BANG! Now everyone near us could hear what it sounded like inside my head. A huge smile spread across my face. I lightly bounced the weight of the gun in my hands and felt quite pleased with myself. I set the gun down as my Dad had instructed me to do after I shot, and turned to him for his reaction. For the first time in my life, he threw his arms around me in a genuinely emotional embrace, exclaiming, "Well done! Now do that again!"

I did shoot, again and again, emptying one clip and loading another and reliably hitting my target. It felt like I'd found my calling in life, I so loved the feeling of an exploding gun in my hands. I began to experiment with my abilities to aim, shooting the silhouette in the arm, the brain, the heart, the eye. My Dad saw what I was doing and told me to aim for the crotch. I smiled, as mad as he was then, and did it gleefully. I felt like laughing, I felt light headed and light of care and worry. Never in my whole life had my father been proud of me but he was thrilled over this! He even said that if I'd been one of his recruits at West Point he would have considered me amongst the best beginning shooters. I felt a bit like a Princess, if one crowned in bullets rather than diamonds. There is something comically tragic that the first and only thing my father and I ever bonded over was shooting guns.

I kept taking my turns shooting, but the exhilaration faded when I saw him look at his watch the way he always did when he was done with me. Sadness overcame me again, knowing I wouldn't see him until the next time I reminded him of my existence in approximately six months. I was even sad knowing I wouldn't be able to shoot again without him. I'd enjoyed it immensely. Soon he'd be dropping me off at home, and I didn't want to go back there, where it was all demands and no rest. I wanted to stay there and keep shooting guns until I forgot everything else existed.

I shot the target in the heart again, this time in anger, imagining it was my father. And then a thought occurred to me. I wasn't going to live. I wasn't going to survive this and make things right. There was no way out. I had a way out right then. He'd taught me so well, taught me to shoot, taught me that people were to be sought and culled, taught me to be ruthless like him when I'd started out so sweet and tender. I could still have some justice, though I'd miss out on serving any to my mother. All I had to do was turn around and shoot him, then turn the gun on myself and blissfully end it all. I imagined his face as he saw me aim his own gun at him. I imagined saying thank you to him, and pulling the trigger. I saw myself turn the gun to my head and shoot before the proprietors in the lobby could get in the locked doors of the range. I thought about all of it, playing it out before my inner eyes. And I knew I couldn't do it, it wasn't me. He was speaking, saying it was time to go and return me home. I aimed at the target once again, superimposed a dozen faces over the head, and blew their brains out. He drove me home.

Round Eighty

The day my father took me to the shooting range, he also brought me a box of books that he and Karen had cleaned out. Even he knew me well enough to know I was never without a book in my hands, I read anything I could get my grubby hands on. Looking through the box I found "The Year of the French" by Thomas Flanagan. In case you aren't familiar with the book, it's a novel based on the failed Fenian rebellion against the English in 1789, so called "The Year of the French" because French assistance essentially failed to materialise as expected in Ireland. The book is passionately written, demonstrating the causes propelling the story forward from deeply personal perspectives. It's a fictionalised version of what the Irish suffered under the tyranny of English rule. I made the connection then between the Troubles and the music of Sinead

O'Connor and the Cranberries, beginning to form a larger picture. It sparked my curiosity on the deepest of levels. I wanted to understand how much of the book was fictional license and how much was true, and how modern Ireland was shaped by those events. My long standing envy of my friends trooping from college class from master's classes morphed into a campaign to grab some higher education for myself.

The company I worked for offered a tuition remission program for college education. I had to pay for the class up front, which cost me two weeks without electricity, but as long as I got a C or better I'd be reimbursed at the end of term. My local community college offered a class called "Humanities: Irish Studies". I enrolled for the first bit of formal education I'd had since I was fourteen. I was so happy to be going to school; I excitedly bought a dedicated notebook, folder and pen for the class and kept them in pristine condition. I was chomping at the bit to have somebody else feed my brain for a change.

The first night of class I was understandably nervous. There was just time to have a cigarette before class began, so I loitered at the back of the building where all the other smokers were loosely congregated. Imagine my surprise when I saw Isaiah Miller there, also partaking of a cigarette! By coincidence, he'd enrolled in a different class held the same time as mine. St. Louis is funny like that. It's a city that spreads far and wide with a population of roughly 1.3million people but you can never get away from yourself.

Isaiah and I faced each other awkwardly over puffs of smoke. Once the basic formalities were over neither of us was knew what to say. We hadn't seen each other in a long time. He was married to Jennifer and they had a baby now. Everything about me, from my thinness, my cough and my pallor said I was very unwell. I was still fainting, having seizures and suffering from ulcers but I couldn't have dreamt of paying doctors co-payments, so everything was left untouched. Isaiah looked at me as if I had sunk several levels in society since we'd last parted. It was blatantly evident I wasn't glowing with vibrancy and success. My opinion of him was no higher. He was a spoiled boy who'd been taught not to think for himself. He was born with a silver spoon in his mouth and went along with a pack of lies to pacify his hysterical fiancé. I wasn't going to squirm for him.

He took one of his customary long draws off his cigarette, and then slowly exhaled for dramatic effect. He asked me how I was doing, showing by the smirk on his face that he didn't expect a positive answer. My fingers twitched to avoid slapping that superior look off his face. I could have lied to him, I could have excused my appearance by saying I had the flu and everything in my life was terribly perfect. But I rather fancied that he knew the consequences of his and his wife's actions, so I answered him honestly. I said I was in the middle of a nervous breakdown. I added that I was hopeful for a quick recovery because I was taking a great deal of psychiatric prescriptions. I listed each dose and the time of day I took it, a lengthy explanation.

He took another slow drag off his cigarette, looked at me condescendingly, and said, "What are you going to turn to when that little cocktail stops working for you?

I stared at him hard, trying to infuse as much contempt into my eyes as possible as I stubbed out my cigarette. So many thoughts flew through my mind as I looked at him, happy in the realisation that I truly felt no remaining affection for him. I erupted into laughter and then walked away. We had once been best friends, then brother and sister; now unable to pass a civil ten minutes. It was the perfect introduction to my Irish Humanities class!

Round Eighty One

Despite the inauspicious beginning, my class was good and I liked the teacher very much. He was passionate about his subject and had engaging teaching methods. He was an "Irish American" and although he was not entirely blind in favour of the Irish cause, he did show a barely suppressed antipathy towards the English. Initially I was strongly inclined to agree with him, at least historically speaking, but the more content I read the more confused I became, specifically on modern Irish politics. The history of

Irish/Anglo relations was fairly easy to put in boxes clearly labelled Right and Wrong. Studying what the IRA and Thatcher years were like for both Ireland and Britain was far more perplexing and required more thought.

The most amazing thing I took away from that class was the comprehension gained over how far into the future political actions and movements can reach, events that form causes and effects unfolding over hundreds of years, right into the modern day. History had long been alive and vibrant to me, but the action of chronicling the timeline of Irish history to present day made me feel that every moment that came before the present was just there, waiting behind a door I could open and walk through to examine the contents therein.

I spent hours thinking and writing on the subject of government, studying past and present models, dreaming up new ones and looking at where they'd succeeded and where they'd failed. It began to dawn on me that our world was still in a state of flux, revolution and evolution, although the alterations generally come about more slowly and subtly than historical changes of power and government. We haven't reached the pinnacle of human ingenuity in enlightened government with capitalist democracy. Equally importantly, I realised that I, along with every other human on earth, have a role to play. I might not have been wanted by my parents but I had a purpose, and that purpose was to play my part in the world I lived in, whatever that may be. How history will cast us, villain, martyr, and hero, apathetic, criminal, saint or chump was just a question of time. Most of us will shuffle off our mortal coil without being remembered by the masses, but how we live and the choices we make mattered. That is what history taught me. Nothing teaches the human condition better than studying the people and actions that come before us and comparing them to those in our lives. I asked myself how I wanted to be remembered, how far I would go, and what I could possibly contribute to humanity that would make even a tiny dent in the heap of its need.

One of our assignments in class was to write a paper combining a range of topics relating to Irish history and current affairs. I'd been writing versions of that assignment for weeks in an attempt to understand how I felt about the issue, so I was able to write the paper very quickly and easily.

The week after handing it in, my teacher asked me to stay after class to speak to him for a moment. He told me that my paper was outstanding, and asked me for permission to send it to some colleagues of his in Ireland for their review. They were editors of an Irish newspaper, and he thought there was a good chance they'd like to print my piece. I was stunned. I even wondered for a moment if he was just saying that to get in my pants, but he seemed honestly sincere. It was the most intellectually flattering thing that had ever happened to me. I thanked him profusely and gave him my permission to pass my paper on.

He kept me behind after class again the following week. He told me the name of the newspaper in Ireland, *An Phoblacht*, which I'd never heard of, so I mainly just nodded and listened. I was blown away when he excitedly told me they'd asked him to relay not just a request to print my paper, but a job offer to me. I could start working for them as a training journalist, and they expected great things from me. Even lodgings had been found for me with someone who worked at the paper. It was an overwhelming offer - well, overwhelming doesn't quite do it justice. My teacher told me that he was sure that with my talent I'd quickly do very well at the paper, and strongly pleaded that I consider this remarkable offer. I told him I would think about it but that I needed time. It was strong, unprecedented recognition of my writing, a job offer writing for a newspaper and the possibility of starting life fresh over in a foreign country, all rolled into one mind blowing package. I drove home hypnotised by the questions and possibilities circling in my head.

The following week my teacher asked me if I had made a decision yet, I said no. He reassured me that was alright, he didn't mind waiting. I couldn't vocalise to him why I was unable to decide. My mind had *snapped* after all, and it wasn't very agile and generally becoming increasing slow and rusty in the process of making decisions. The Irish offer was such a puzzle that it exhausted me every time I thought of it; therefore, very neatly, I avoided thinking of it. There were so many unknowns holding me back

443

from saying yes, and simultaneously temptations beckoning me onwards. The most sensible thing to do in that situation seemed to be to remain in place until one sensation or another trumped the rest and indicated which direction to go. I felt uncomfortable sitting in class under the constant pleading gaze of my teacher, and noticing little statements he dropped into his lecture that were clearly aimed at me. So I stopped attending my Irish Humanities class several weeks before it was due to end.

My humanities teacher, as you may imagine, had more invested in me than a community college grade. When I didn't attend class he called me at home several times, leaving messages on my answering machine because I'd stopped answering the phone. First he offered to extend the deadline for the final paper, but I had no intention of writing it. I knew he was planning on sending mine to the newspaper and I felt it would make my situation more difficult. Next he called to tell me he'd given me an A+ despite my non-attendance and no final paper being turned in. I felt guilty and exceedingly muddled, unable to understand why he was doing these things. He called once again, asking me to please tell him if I'd decided about the job in Ireland. I was sick of thinking of the job in Ireland; the dilemma it presented to me ruined my first and only attempt at higher education. With hindsight I'm very pleased I was too apathetic to accept that offer.

Round Eighty Two

Around this time several things of note happened more or less at once. Leah announced her and her then fiancé were returning to St. Louis, moving into another house owned by the same friends of Leah's parents who owned mine. I found it difficult to face Leah, loving her as much as I did and knowing I was about to accidentally screw over her close family friends. I couldn't pay for the house, it was a total mess, and before long I'd have to jump because I make it a point to avoid being pushed. I didn't think Leah would understand, even though she'd understood everything in my life before. This was different, it involved her family. I was already hesitant to face her because of this, but there was one more element that was driving us apart - her fiancé.

I'd been friends with him too as they'd been together for many years. But he was a chronic alcoholic by this point and his personality had totally changed. I didn't think he was good for Leah and I didn't enjoy his company. He didn't want to do anything that didn't involve sitting on a bar stool, and he thought jokes about raping six year old girls were giggle material. I knew better than to pit myself against him when she was deeply in love and planning a marriage, so for the first time since we met, I backed away from Leah. She'd always been the one person who I was totally myself with, even if we weren't physically in the same space all those years. It was a strong sign of how much my life had changed. It was easier to let my much loved Leah go than go through the fight required to make things right with her. I didn't have the strength,

445

spirit or fight in me to say the things I should have said and make the confessions I needed to make. I was too busy drowning under it all.

Round Eighty Three

Vianne moved to Miami. Leah and I were distant and I tried to keep her out of my house so she wouldn't see the state it was in. Cora and Perry and I were friends on only a shallow basis. I was absolutely alone for the first time since I met Eliza all those years before.

Then I made one friend. She worked where I did, and her name was Angel. Maybe she even was an angel for me. She came, helped, and moved on like people say angels do. Maybe we've all been angels to someone at some points in our life, and devils in others.

Ricky had long since stopped sending even token amounts of money. I believe the last monthly cheque I received from him was for $25.00. I tried a couple more times to look into taking him to court but I wasn't able to find legal aid. One day while driving home from work my car died. Hardly a month had gone by without me needing to replace something so I could carry on attending work. But this time the entire engine was shot. It would have cost more to repair it than it cost to buy the car, but that was a moot point anyway as I didn't have enough money to tow it to the mechanics. It was a lemon, but I loved it almost like a friend. Crying, as I seemed to do constantly those many months, I called a friend and left it on the side of the road. I never saw my car again. Ricky still wanted his money. He often threatened me with legal action, to which I replied to go right ahead because then I'd be assigned representation by the state and I could produce our lease as evidence in my favour. He did nothing but make noise.

A friend of mine gave me a used computer, and aged twenty-one in the year 2000 I was introduced to the World Wide Web. It changed my entire life. Leah actually signed me up on a website where you made pen-pals from all over the world in one of her last acts as my dearest friend. It wasn't a dating website. I was in love with the idea of knowing people in faraway places and learning what their lives were like. Initially I had almost a dozen casual email pen pals scattered all over the globe. One of them, from England, called himself "Mr. Nomad". I liked him very much. He intrigued me, possibly because he didn't talk as much as what I was used to. He seemed intelligent, insightful and kind and had a responsible job and his own flat. Eventually the rest of both mine and his pen pals fell away as we spent every spare moment emailing or instant messaging each other. We were falling in love. Very slowly, very cautiously and almost disbelievingly, but we were. It was absolutely unintentional but no less real for that.

What fragments of friends and friendships that were still lingering in my life evaporated when I made it clear I had feelings for someone none of us had ever met. Online dating is incredibly common now, but in the year 2000 everyone still had the expectation that only crazy people did it. They all thought I was mad and he was just another symptom of my deterioration. In one sense, they were right. If I hadn't been so depressed that I didn't want to leave my home or socialise anymore, I wouldn't have been spending my time talking to strangers on the internet. But in another sense they were wrong. My feelings for him were genuine. Perhaps the first thing I loved about him was that he didn't view me as a villain in my life. He made it clear to me over and over again how outraged he was over the things I'd been through. He treated me like something so exquisitely fine, precious and delicate, and he wanted to protect me. If ever we spoke and something bad had happened to me, or I told him one of my secrets or how I couldn't even feed myself I could physically feel him shake with frustration and anger that he couldn't reach across the Atlantic and help me. But it wasn't as one sided as that sounds. He had been through a great deal in his life, and the way he opened up to me made me feel similarly protective towards him. I liked his sense of humour and we had very similar opinions on general happenings and world affairs. Someone was showing me every day that to him, I was above every other concern or person in the entire world. How could I not fall in love with him?

Eventually Mr. Nomad became Matthew, and he and I continued getting to know each other via the internet for several months. On Christmas Day 2000, he called me and we spoke on the phone for the first time. We both thought the other had lovely voices. That Christmas, we decided the foundation we'd built was enough with which to begin a serious long distance relationship. We'd take care of the whole "meeting each other" issue later on. From that point on I considered him my boyfriend.

There wasn't enough money left over for me to participate in Christmas festivities that year. I knew that when January came I'd have to leave my house. There had been too many months where my rent was late or unpaid, and I'd finally been given notice to pay up or leave. Paying up wasn't possible, and damn every bill collector who ever thought I was out shopping while neglecting my bills. Food was a luxury for me.

My new and now only friend, Angel, offered to let me come live in her apartment with her. Her husband was deployed in Iraq and she was lonely, not being from St. Louis and knowing no one there. I was grateful, in a dog tired kind of way. I was numb. Angel had collected me from my house, and once again I'd packed only the most essential things to me. Looking back, there is much more I wished I had been able to take, and many things that I left behind I still miss.

I was fired from my job for poor performance and attendance. I also knew that was coming. Both I and my manager cried as he informed me in a private conference room. We'd been good friends and he knew a little of what I was going through, but company policy was company policy and to be fair I deserved getting sacked. I'd worked so hard for that job but it came too late in my life for me to be able to operate it. I was devastated – I've always taken a great deal of pride in my professionalism. But I was already so depressed that it was only another drop in the ocean. I didn't even try to find another job. It was patently obvious I was in no condition to hold one down. Thankfully Angel was able to support me. I was cheap to provide for. Most of my days were spent lying on Angel's sofa crying and I had no appetite for food.

Matthew and I spoke more and more, and usually on the phone. I had a relapse of the bronchitis I was prone to and he was on the other end of the phone hearing me inch nearer and nearer to pneumonia again. He begged me to tell my father about my health and ask him for help. I replied that Lawrence knew very well about my health problems and living situation and he'd never been willing to help before, so I'd rather not. But Matthew was positive that if only my Dad would see me as sick as I was he would be moved to step in and intervene in my life. He begged me to give him my father's phone number, asking me to do it out of my love for him. I obliged because I was too tired to argue the point, but I knew it was not only pointless, but also potentially harmful to ask my Dad for help.

And so Matthew called Lawrence. I do enjoy imagining my Dad's surprise when he answered the phone and heard a man with an English accent inform him that his daughter was very ill, she needed hospital treatment, was suffering from homelessness malnutrition and a whole host of other things, and he (Matthew) expected Lawrence as my father to do something about it. What an interesting way to meet your future son-in-law, by having him remind you of your parental duties.

To give Matthew his due credit, I'd described my father very well to him, and he was still brave enough to make that phone call. No one had ever before dared remind my father of his responsibilities towards me or my sister. Lawrence and Karen duly came over to Angel's to see me. The apartment was trashed; it had been like that when I moved in and I certainly didn't have the energy to clean it. My father walked in, covered his and Karen's mouth and nose, and stood in the doorway, staring at me lying on the sofa. Angel had answered the door and unbelievably, as soon as Lawrence and Karen came in he told her to leave the room to leave us alone. In her own house – he would never tolerate anyone speaking to him like that in his home. I was mortified by his rudeness and mouthed an "I'm sorry" to Angel as she walked past me into her room. My father has that effect on people, making them obey him even when he has no jurisdiction over the situation.

Karen, who is a nurse, came around to the sofa and asked me a few questions. She gave my Dad a long silent look above my head after I answered above my wracking cough. He shook his head no. Then he said to me that he was disgusted that I didn't have enough pride to live somewhere decent, and I was old enough to get myself to the doctor if I needed one. I rolled my head away from him, so I wouldn't have to see him speak those words. Of course I was old enough. Apparently I'd always been old enough. Maybe I was old enough, but the whole point Matthew tried to make in his phone call to my Dad was that I wasn't capable. It didn't matter, he wasn't willing to help. He summoned Karen and left within three minutes of walking in the door.

It was such a horrible, blighting mistake of a conception, mine. Poor Matthew, like an innocent, was shocked and genuinely alarmed when he heard the account of Lawrence and Karen's visit. It was merely boring and tedious for me to recount.

Round Eighty Four

After I grew a little stronger and was able to leave the apartment for a few hours at a time, Angel and I began going out. We found a coffee house to hang out in, and met several entertaining acquaintances. Several weeks after Lawrence and Karen's visit to Angel's apartment, just after Christmas, we were driving home to her apartment after being at the coffee shop. It was around three in the morning, and it was freezing cold. Fate decreed that one of Angel's rear brake lights was blown out that night. For that traffic violation she was pulled over and the officer gave her a warning to get the light fixed within one week. Then, as procedure dictates, the officer took both our ID's to run them through his computer and see if we had outstanding issues with the law. We both handed ours over without fear, knowing we hadn't done anything illegal.

Imagine my surprise when the officer came around to the passenger door and told me to step out of the car! I actually thought he was mistaken at first. Well, not *just* at first, for quite some time. I did as he asked, but I was confused. I asked him why it appeared he was arresting me. And he was, he was handcuffing me and reading me my rights and I didn't even know what I'd done. I was told it would be explained to me fully when we arrived at the police station. They told Angel to leave, and directed me to the back seat of the police car. She asked them where they were taking me, they replied to the county jail, at which point I almost fainted, so terrified and still unaware of *why*. She promised she'd contact Matthew and find a way to get me out right away. I was totally dazed, I truly didn't know of anything illegal I'd done. They didn't speak to me in the car on the way to the station, and I sat in the back of the car, shaking so hard I was terrified I was going to go into a seizure in handcuffs. I worked monstrously hard to regulate my breathing and calm myself to stop the shaking. I was genuinely afraid that I was too weak and sick to withstand the shock and processing of being arrested, but I had no choice in the matter.

On arrival at the station I was brought in to be booked. The person who was booking me in looked friendly, so I said in as sweet a voice as I could summon, "Please can you tell me why I have been arrested? What have I done?" He glanced at his sheet, read it, and replied, glancing back at me. "Bounced cheque to the government." I searched my mind. I couldn't remember having written any cheques to the government. I asked if there were any other details. He looked again and replied "Car tax" and suddenly it clicked into place. When Ricky had bought me the car I'd paid the tax with a cheque, and then promptly moved from the apartment to the house I was supposed to share with Ricky. I was admittedly ignorant, but in my defence, I was raised ignorant: I only grew older and learned from my own trial and error. I didn't know you were supposed to have your mail forwarded when you moved. It's easy to underestimate how many aspects of running an adult life need to be actively taught, rather than just presuming everyone magically knows how to do it.

I honestly didn't understand banking. I just did the best I could by not spending any money except on urgent essentials. Without the letter reaching me and missing several bank statements lost in the post I really didn't know that cheque had gone unpaid. Sadly it wasn't my only debt, but it was the only one to the U.S. government, so I was in jail. I tried to take that in, wondering what would happen to me. The officer who was booking me in looked at me once again and said "You're not like most people who come through here." I looked back at him, but said nothing, unsure how to rightly reply to that. I could see what he saw. A petite young girl dressed decently and speaking well and softly. I did make a contrast to the predominantly male and rowdy people in the cells near me. But I was still an outsider and a criminal, or he wouldn't be taking my fingerprints. I didn't quite belong with the very good or the very bad: that was my problem.

As soon as my details were taken myself and the rest of the prisoners were rounded up and the police began the process of loading us into a paddy wagon. We were at a local police station and had to be driven to the main one in U.City which doubled as a residential prison. Everyone was handcuffed and we were surrounded by armed police as we walked across the car park. I was shaking from the cold. I was the only woman there. The men, some twenty of them, were loaded into the main compartment of the wagon while I was held, waiting outside with another officer. I wasn't sure why they weren't putting me in, too. Then, to my horror, it became obvious where they were intending to put me.

On the back of a paddy wagon, bolted to and dangling off the back doors, is a compartment typically reserved for the most dangerous criminals, as it's solitary and more securely locked. I was being put in it for my own protection, as I overheard the police loading us into the van say that they couldn't put me in with the men. I didn't want to go in the compartment they were preparing for me. It looked like a vertical

455

coffin and it actually shook with every bounce the wagon made from the many bodies shuffling about inside it. I didn't argue though. I was very different from the last time I had been arrested. This time I just wanted to get through the whole dirty experience as quietly and meekly as possible so I wouldn't be further hurt. Slowly, I climbed the metal steps up to the container. My body wanted to rebel, it seemed to run counter to my own sense of self-preservation to be strapped into that seat by five different points, my hands handcuffed behind my back. That would all have been bad enough on its own, but I was more desperately ill than I could even try to make the police understand. I didn't know how I was going to get through this. Tears began to roll down my cheeks but I cooperatively moved my body into the contraption that would no doubt break it.

The drive we were embarking on was almost an hour long. The male prisoners inside had the benefit of heating and light. In my metal standing box bolted to the back of the wagon it was as freezing as the Missouri winter raging outside and pitch black. I was in more intense physical pain than I could ever remember being in. The cold seemed to eat me alive. My arms were breaking, my legs were strapped in a position that pulled on my bad knee, and a strap across my chest held me to the back wall, my shoulder blades digging into the metal wall behind me. I was effectively like a butterfly pinned on a board.

The cage rattled and shook so much, arguing back with every single bump in the road, that by the time we eventually arrived I felt as if I'd been beaten bloody. There was a window grill between my holding place, and the back of the wagon where all the men were. They knew I was in there, they'd watched me get loaded in. I heard so much on that long drive... So many different ways to rape me, so many insults, so much imaginary cum choking me alive. Someone suggested screwing me with a knife, twisting it up my pussy.

I went to another place. I wasn't even well enough to sob. I just vacated my head, as if willing myself to mentally die and detach myself from my broken body. I had a seizure then, strapped into a position that prevented my body from moving as it was demanding. The pain was unbearable. I had a seizure, unseen, as the words of the male criminals floated through my brain. Eventually the seizure must have ended. I was aware of lying limply within my straps, as limp as it was possible to go. The voices from the next door carriage had quieted. I assumed that my lack of response made them lose interest in taunting me. They all thought they were so fucking hard, threatening to rape me, boasting about who could be more grotesque in the destruction of another human being. They were pathetic, every single one of them. Hard is living through a never ending series of sadistic events and continuing to walk forward with your head held high. Since that day I've suffered much physically, but still nothing compares to the horror of that drive and it's impossible for me to remember it without re-entering that pain.

Finally the van stopped and parked. I couldn't see anything, but I heard movement. I prayed I wasn't going to be hurt further. I listened as the men were unloaded from the back and I began to panic, thinking they might forget I was in the extra container, forget me and leave me there. Finally, after what seemed an eternity, a police officer came and opened the door. He shined his flashlight on my face, blinding me. The light was painful, but perhaps it allowed him to see I was not only no threat but I was also extremely unwell. I could barely speak after the seizure, my words were slurred. I mumbled "seizure". He didn't seem to understand, but he unstrapped me as gently as he could. Being unstrapped was far more painful than being strapped in had been. My muscles had been held in the same horrific position, so cold for so long and even having a seizure within those bonds. Moving again made me cry out in pain.

After making several attempts to move myself it soon became obvious that the police officer was going to have to help me get out. He lifted me down and set me on my feet, and I promptly lost consciousness and fell over. A moment later I came to and there was an officer now on either side of me, half carrying me into the jail. They called to another officer that a medic would need to see to "this one" (although that request never materialised). As I was brought inside, they led me to a cell. I dropped with relief on to the shelf made for sitting on. The officer, who had first tried to get me out of the box knelt and looked me in the eyes. He said "If I take your handcuffs off, you're not going to do anything stupid, are you?" I shook my head no. He unlocked them, and my arms fell free. I screamed in pain. Kindly he rubbed my arms hard, up and down several times, and then he left me there. I was on a shelf hanging off a wall that was meant to be a bed. The bars closed across my cell and were locked. I had absolutely no idea what would happen to me but I wasn't even well enough to devote much thought to it.

After a long rest it occurred to me that I should take some action to get myself out of there. I waved for the attention of an officer and asked him what the terms were for my release, and if I was allowed a phone call. He went away and came back an hour or so later with my answers. In order to be released I'd have to pay the amount that my bounced cheque was for, the fine from the government, and some sort of fee you pay when you're released from jail. And yes, I was allowed a phone call. He escorted me to the phones. I called Angel.

Despite it being a great struggle for me to speak, and not just to speak, but to order my thoughts well enough so that I could say what I needed to, I had to get everything set in motion to get me out of jail. I needed a real bed more than words could possibly express. I explained to Angel the terms of my release. She used her three-way calling service to call Matthew so he was also included in the conversation. The three of us spoke together, I cried a great deal. Mostly Angel and Matthew spoke to each other, while I, in the centre of it all played absently with a toggle on my jacket. I couldn't follow their words, they sounded almost like a foreign language. They agreed it would be best if I went and rested but they stayed on the line with each other to coordinate my release. I made them say it again in many different ways to be sure they understood that I had to go home right then, not in several days or a week. I knew it would cost them money but I needed help worse than I'd ever needed it before and if they ever loved me at all they had to pay now and save me. They reiterated that they understood and Angel would be there right away, they promised neither of them would do a single other thing until I was released. Knowing as well as they did that I was in the middle of a serious and progressing mental and physical collapse, their main goal was for me to stay as calm and comfortable as possible. We said goodbye. As I hung up the phone I felt a pang of grief and panic thinking that they didn't understand what I needed, that I had missed my chance to explain. Thankfully I was just confused, and they'd understood everything perfectly.

The time I spent in jail was awful, but it was nothing compared to the journey there in the wagon. In jail there was supervision, so prisoners couldn't speak to each other the way I'd been spoken to in the wagon. I twitched like a hunted animal every time someone banged my wall or broke out in screams while I waited. I rested on my shelf-for-a-bed and tried to become absent from my mind again, using those same old tried and tested techniques, hoping that Angel and Matthew hadn't forgotten me and they were doing whatever was necessary to get me out.

They were true to their word, and I needn't have worried. Around seven the next morning an officer came and unlocked my door, telling me I was being released. I was disbelieving, overjoyed! As I was escorted out I saw Angel impatiently waiting for me in the entryway. When I reached her, I collapsed into her arms sobbing, incoherently and futilely attempting to explain how much pain I was in. Angel was aghast seeing my appearance; I think that what I'd been through was writ all over my body. She exclaimed in horror and reactively snapped at the police officer who was escorting me out, saying "What on earth have you done to her?" I pulled her arm and asked her to stop, so afraid because I had not yet stepped all the way out of jail. She helped me into her car and drove us home.

When she had last seen me less than twenty-four hours before I had a modestly healthy look about me that had been absent for months. What she saw before her when she collected me from jail was a black and blue, broken toy. Physically, we didn't know where I was going, only that it was going very badly. Mentally, I was gone for some time after the arrest. When we reached home, she called Matthew. I was too unwell to speak to him. She said I was home and safe but dangerously unwell and she was very worried about me.

Round Eighty Five

The time after being released from jail was not so much about recovery as it was survival. Recovery, for me, had become something too great to ask for. Angel kindly carried on supporting me, even insisting it was her pleasure because without me she was lonely living alone in the city. It was completely impossible for me to work, but I didn't want to take advantage of her. So I repaid her with all the love and loyalty I could offer.

Matthew still wanted me, even though I spared him no detail of the state I was in or my perpetual bad luck, which I had come to view as a sort of curse. He bought me a ticket to fly to London and stay with him for two weeks. It was a sort of "no obligations" trip to meet, though we both expected it to go very well. Travel did something to lift my depression a little. If it didn't have an effect on my health, who could complain? I stayed with Matthew at his flat in a town about an hour outside of London. We spent all of the time getting to know each other face to face. It was certainly awkward at times, but the tenderness we felt for each other before meeting remained and grew.

Several nights before I was due to return to St. Louis, I was sitting alone in his living room trying to understand British TV while he washed the dishes in the kitchen. Suddenly Matthew was standing before me, blocking my view of the television. Before

I could register what was happening he was on his knees before me, asking me if I would marry him. He said that he knew we were meant to be together, and he couldn't bear the thought of me returning home, so far away from him and in so much danger. I was humbled.

I had never been proposed to so sincerely before. I wanted to say yes, to please him, to be with him, to grab the opportunity to be a new me, the real me, and explore that with this person. But I wasn't sure. It was too sudden, much more sudden than how I was used to relationships progressing. A yes wouldn't be just a yes to marriage; it would be a yes to moving to England. As painful as life had been in my hometown, I loved it deeply. I asked him for twenty-four hours to think about it before I had to answer. He was understandably frustrated and anxious, but gave me the time I wanted. I felt bad asking it of him, but I didn't want to say yes and then have to retract it afterwards if I realised I couldn't do it.

I thought of nothing else that night, of course, and neither of us got much sleep. By morning I knew I was going to say yes, but I didn't get around to telling him until lunch, reasoning it would be the only time in my life I'd ever be able to make a man squirm that much. When I told him I would marry him, he was overjoyed, and immediately threw himself into organising everything involved with my immigration, and our wedding. Being in America I couldn't easily arrange the wedding itself and I still wasn't well enough to be awake for more than a few hours at a time anyway. I had no head for the red tape of immigration, and was happy to let Matthew do the work and simply tell me where to sign. Matthew came to St. Louis shortly after I returned so we could spend more time together as well as obtain my visa from the Embassy in Chicago.

Late April, 2001, I moved to England for good and that June I was married. Angel and I eventually went our separate ways. There were no hard feelings between us, it was just that she divorced her soldier husband, married someone she'd known for a week and became an itinerant cross country truck driver, so staying in touch became nearly impossible. For over two years I didn't speak to a single human I'd ever known before. I did all I could to shroud myself in quiet.

Just a couple of months after I moved to England, one of my former friends posted nude pictures of me on the still relatively novel internet. Of course it could only have been one of the friends who had regular unsupervised access to my house, one of the friends who was furious when I announced I was moving to England, which narrows it down significantly. It was funny actually. The pictures were taken in total innocence, by my female Miller "cousin". She was getting a degree in photography and needed a model for nudes. I was comfortable being naked with her because she was a girl I was very close to, it was totally non-sexual, and the photographs would never be public.

464

However she did give me a copy of the pictures, which I kept in a cabinet in my old house.

They were posted on the internet to humiliate me and make me look like a slut, irrespective of how they came about. Abusive comments saying I should be gang raped and murdered were left on the website they were published on. I was mortified, it felt like being kicked while I was very much down, and by someone who had claimed to love me. It was bad enough to have my body exposed online without my permission, but what hurt the most was the animalistic hate that was subsequently directed towards me. This happened in the years before people had any sympathy for internet slut shaming. I was totally isolated, and felt that only Matthew was safe. Thankfully, we were able to get the pictures taken down as soon as an anonymous e-mail alerted us to their existence.

There was a limit to the sadism I could endure and it had long since passed. The first two years of my marriage were spent simply getting me to the point where I could get through a day both physically and mentally without falling into the terrors of memories. Without the obligation to work, I was able to sleep as much as I needed for the first time in all my life. I was able to read and write new things, and enjoy music in the privacy of my own home. I took up studying my favourite subjects again. I buried myself in domesticity. I learned the pleasure that can come from cleaning your own

465

bathroom, making your bedroom pretty and eating cooked food. I stroked our cats. I became calm and gradually grew into myself, coming to know my own mind better than I ever had before. It was on that foundation that I began rebuilding my life, the way I had always intended it to be.

The one thing I did not do for the first two years of living in England, was address my past in any way. I couldn't even approach the door labelled "Life Before Marriage" without hearing a distant SNAPPING sound.

Round Eighty Six

Having married at twenty-two, at twenty-four I finally began speaking to Matthew about my past. Up until that point it had been an unspoken agreement between us that I needed time before I could address the twenty odd years of my life before England. It was almost the matter of piecing the chaos together into one coherent timeline that I struggled the most with. I used my memory and the many notebooks full of writings to establish exactly what happened, forensically examining my life like it was a crime scene. I needed to get to a place where I knew my own mind, history, and concept of right and wrong, irrespective of whoever I was surrounded by. And I did.

Around four years after I moved to England, I was finally ready to try to join the two halves of my life, American and English, into one whole. One of the best things that helped me achieve that was reconnecting with Leah. I had missed her enormously during the time we hadn't talked, and healing that rift with her was very important to me, because I love her so much and she never did anything to hurt me. I'm overjoyed to say we are still best friends. The girl who used to wrap me up in Troy's shirt while I rocked and cried, the girl who made me laugh in the face of it all, who laboriously tried to teach me foreign languages over coffee at Eat-Rite is now the woman who is still my best friend and we are still walking through each other's lives together.

I was flawed and I'd made mistakes, certainly. But I was strong, honest, loyal and brave. Most of all I had tried as hard as I could to live a decent life under extraordinary circumstances without throwing in the towel. I didn't kill myself... I chose to survive, which I've often thought was the harder option.

Round Eighty Seven

When I was twenty-seven I was blessed with the most miraculous event in my entire life, from birth to death. My son, Alex, was born. It was a terribly difficult pregnancy, and labour during his premature birth nearly killed us both. But the moment he was put onto my chest – even as I was haemorrhaging and unsure if I would see him the next day, I was filled with such glorious love and happiness that one day I intend to dedicate a year to writing of nothing but that single moment in time. My god, I loved him, and although I never would have dreamt it possible, I love him even more now that he is a ripe little delicious boy of eight. He is my hero. He is my life, my love, my everything.

I would love him even if he bore no resemblance to me at all. But he is in fact, a little version of me in many ways, one who has been allowed to grow up being fed and watered with love. Every shade that passes across his eyes is an unspoken statement to me. He's far more beautiful than ever I was, and in all things generally more angelic, but his soul is made of the same stuff as mine. We know each other's inner thoughts at a single glance. When we sleep together he exhales and I inhale. He is a joyous, singing, honest, dancing, drawing, joking, reading, twirling, boxing, clever, kind, compassionate, activist of a boy. He's amazing. He is intrinsically bound up in the writing of this book. Yes, I'd planned it long, long ago. But when he was three he reminded me of my obligation, and why it existed. After my marriage I was initially so determined to forget everything that I shelved my previous plan to write out what happened to me in one coherent narrative. I'm writing this now for Alex as much as myself. He and his generation, every child, including myself.

Alex was only three years old when I had a neurological collapse. He was terrified, suddenly far too soon confronted with the reality of death taking the one he loves most.

468

I remember him clinging onto me one day in my bed, crying and begging me to get better and never to leave him. I felt a monumental sense of guilt. There is nothing I love as much as Alex and nothing I've ever wanted more than to be the best possible mother to him. For a while I blamed myself for the haemorrhage that nearly destroyed me. If only I had been more careful with myself, if only I'd grown up normally, if only, if only. I felt I had robbed him of his beautiful innocence and replaced it with terror. I sunk into one of the worst depressions of my life.

I was sobbing every day because I thought the loss of my physical ability meant I could no longer be the mother I was supposed to be. Then the depression kicked in and I wasn't even capable of sharing a giggle with him. Then I'd realise my depression was upsetting him and keeping us apart, and subsequently become more depressed causing further time together lost and the cycle would continue. It really was the attitude that I was facing the situation with that made it seem like my loss of health equalled his loss of quality of life.

For the first time since my teens I was very seriously considering ending my life. I was exhausted from the never ending nightmarish pain and the progressive loss of health. But that alone would not have been enough to induce me to kill myself. The real reason I was considering it was for love of Alex. I could never participate in damaging him. If it was impossible for me to live with him without causing him hurt I would have to take myself away, because I love him so much I would spare him from me if necessary. I did not want to be a spectre of death hanging over a beautiful, clever, energetic, funny, growing, blossoming child. I did not want to ever duplicate the hell my parents put me through, in any way.

One sunny October afternoon I was lying on the sofa watching Alex play a game on the laptop. The sun was streaming in the window, and I was contemplating if I should live or die. The night before he'd cried a great deal about my health and it made me feel I couldn't avoid the issue anymore. I finally snapped out of my reverie and actually looked at him. I truly looked at him, bathed in sunshine, as if I'd never seen him before and was just making a beauteous discovery. I was transfixed by how quick and clever he was as I watched his small pudgy hands move deftly across keys and mousepad, solving a puzzle with efficiency and grace. He looked up at me and smiled so sweetly. I smiled back, and I felt that smile to the tips of my toes. I hadn't smiled so genuinely in so long my face hurt from moving the muscles so far upwards. The moment was a ray of sunshine cutting through the rain.

I saw before me the single most important person in the world. I was so impressed by him, and he was *my* baby, *my* little boy. He came from my body. Suddenly I saw everything as if it were in full daylight, when for months I'd viewed life through a grey film. It was astonishing. His eyes darted about the screen, he made tactical

470

movements, sounds of joy when he won, a look of determination on his little face. When had he become so capable? He played like music in motion, he was a flawless creation. The ramifications were astonishing.

I realised in that moment that all that time I was feeling steamrolled by life, being flattened into a one dimensional sick woman, life itself was actually moving on without me. It was time I caught up. I'd spent enough time grieving over my broken brain. Before that I'd spent ten years mostly in shock over the previous twenty. I wasn't kissed awake like Sleeping Beauty, I was smiled awake. I felt like my thirty year old self was meeting my fifteen year old self, and the two merged into the woman they were meant to be. I felt like fifteen was just the day before, and I still had every chance to live.

Pleased that he now knew he had my attention, Alex turned around again and waved to me. I waved back, still smiling hugely. We giggled. He almost seemed to comprehend that I was back; his Mama was back, even if what she could do with her body was different. And I saw how clearly he needed me, more than anyone else would ever need me, and I was fully capable of fulfilling that need. I sat up quickly as if suddenly realising I had so much to do I'd never have enough time to do it all, so I had no time to waste beginning. I had no intention of letting death take me away from Alex without fighting it every inch of the way.

I was so depressed I couldn't see how the problem was self-perpetuating. Yes, I'd lost my health. I couldn't do many of the day to day activities that had previously made up our lives. But he would have preferred to have a cheerful bedridden mother over a sobbing bedridden mother! He still needs me. I have learned to find many creative ways to play with and educate him that are still within my physical abilities, and every day my condition is changing, sometimes with improvement. There is much to hope for.

Since that moment I've learned to handle bad health pragmatically and with an attitude of positivity. But what I'm most proud of is that I parent wholeheartedly, working constantly on instilling hope in Alex even when it seems there might be none. I make many mistakes as a mother and with each one I try to learn where I went wrong so I won't make that particular mistake again. I'm far from perfect and there are several things I particularly wish I could have a "do-over" for, but it isn't for sincere lack of effort. I'm humbled by the unconditional love and inherent bravery and integrity built into my son, and I will do all I can to deserve those gifts. Joyfully, as a mother I no longer belong solely to myself. I am my child's also, his launch pad into the world. I am the mother that I always wished for myself.

When I woke up in that moment of recognition with Alex I felt like I could take the world on all over again, but successfully this time. I was going to use all the wisdom and information I'd hard won over the years. It was going to take time and patience, things I finally have some measure of. After making everything right with Alex I knew the next imperative thing I do was write this book. It was terrifying attempting it. I didn't feel confident enough to presume I could write when I'm not formally educated, and I could not bring myself to believe anyone would be interested in anything I had to say. However I was determined to say it all the same, for the pure satisfaction of doing it, just like my Grandpa and his painting. I realised that writing is very much like walking in a dark room, putting one word ahead of another and altering your course in accordance to the objects surrounding you. How do you eat an elephant? One bite at a time.

No Second Troy

By William Butler Yeats

Why should I blame her that she filled my days

With misery, or that she would of late

Have taught to ignorant men most violent ways,

Or hurled the little streets upon the great,

Had they but courage equal to desire?

What could have made her peaceful with a mind

That nobleness made simple as a fire,

With beauty like a tightened bow, a kind

That is not natural in an age like this,

Being high and solitary and most stern?

Why, what could she have done, being what she is?

Was there another Troy for her to burn?

***

"Professional bouts are limited to a maximum of twelve rounds, most are fought over four, six, eight or ten rounds depending upon the experience of the boxers. Through the early twentieth century, it was common for fights to have unlimited rounds, ending only when one fighter quit or the fight was stopped by police."

I hardly know where to begin now that I'm finished. I don't know you, but I know you have an inner life, great and harrowing. Now, you know me better than many people who have known me in person for years. I think now that we've gone through so much together, I can speak to you informally. You can't think I'd leave you with a "happily ever after" without weighing in on the things I've confided do you? I think the most important thing to address first is why I wrote this book.

Many years ago Troy and I dreamed about the future together, a few lazy days spent in bed chatting and spinning plans. He thought he'd like to try to be a mechanic. I said I wanted to have lots of babies, and he laughed and smiled and said "One day, one day, we'll get a little house" and kissed me with a serene smile on his face. That future never materialised. Mine was a living hell for too many years afterwards. His ended when he bled to death on his bedroom floor.

And so we start with the first and the original reason for publishing my every awful moment: justice, due acknowledgement, and remembrance. No law will convict my parents for neglect. No one has been held accountable for the things that killed Troy. Justice will not land in my lap, so I intend to create it myself. I'm aware this isn't going to be a popular motivation for some people, but it's the truth.

I also hope that people who read this might be a little slower to judge others for their appearance or lifestyle. One thing I have certainly learned is that things are rarely as they present themselves at first glance, both for the bad and good. No one would have ever guessed from Troy's appearance or life that he had half of Moliere's works memorised, or that he could be as tender and sweet as he was. My father is a pillar of society, impeccably dressed, perfectly spoken with graceful table manners. He's also a man who has taken great pleasure in killing, and using poverty stricken women as prostitutes. He completely neglected his own flesh and blood, effectively throwing us into the gutter while moaning about the ills of society. He *is* the "ills of society". When I was a teenager most people would have summed me up and dismissed me as a waste of time. Going nowhere and of no concern to anyone beyond what they might be able to mine from me. But there was much goodness inside of me struggling to manifest itself despite the situation I was born into. And now, here I am years later, a responsible mother, wife, writer, employer and socially active person. People are not disposable, and children are everything. They must be cherished, not abused or thrown to the wolves to fend for themselves.

***

"Protective headgear is not permitted, and boxers are generally allowed to take substantial punishment before a fight is halted."

I would like to send a message to my family, who I have not spoken to in many years. So they all have a mirror. So they see what they created and what they did with it. So they are held accountable for marrying, breeding, marrying again, neglecting, abusing and destroying. The body count isn't finished yet Dad – none of you are finished ticking off your sins. Lie to yourself and the world as much as you want about what you did and who you are. If you so much as come near me, my child, my husband or my house and I will fight you so hard that the energy I have put into writing this will look downright tame. I am warning you: read and stew over your hatred in private as much as you like, but stay away from everything that belongs to me.

My message to Carol is this: I imagine you've had a fake heart attack and been rushed to hospital from the hysterics by now. I hope you're okay? If you get the nerve to face yourself honestly, get some real, straightforward counselling and don't quit as soon as you hear something you don't like. And Carol... really? You really want to say to me "I never made any mistakes raising you and your sister." Really? You really want to say that? I wouldn't say that as a mother, I very much doubt any sane parent would, and I've never laid hands or terror on my child. Throwing him out of the house right after his fifteenth birthday wouldn't occur to me. I'd fight for him, I'd have made myself worthy of his love.

I have no particular feelings but sadness regarding my sister, I certainly wish her no harm.

Was it the generation of children of Vietnam babies, Lawrence? Were you all so off your heads that you couldn't see what you were doing? Why didn't you notice us, were your problems so very big that you couldn't stop and take a moment in real time and see the very real problems in front of you? What made you think it was okay to teach us we were meat to be bought and sold? Shitheads to ignore, knock around and insult? Tools of self-therapy for you even, things to be used? I was meat. I was nothing but meat. Isn't that what a stripper is Dad, you'd know. It's lucky I didn't bump into you that night; that would have been so awkward. How do you feel about the fact that your daughter sold her body in humiliation, under pressure, trying to keep a roof over her head while you and your wife were living in comfort in your precious gated community. Karen, don't worry, I wouldn't forget you.

Whatever it was, you did it. All three of you and countless of your kind. You thought you got away with it; you thought it had been kept between you and yourselves. And it's not now, is it. That sucks. I'm sorry I can't summon sympathy for you.

Ask yourself what I've been up to all these years and sensibly decide that it's wisest to leave me and mine alone. I've lived through this much and more and I will live through you and your embarrassment. If you keep quiet enough maybe no one will put two and two together and realise it's you except us. That's as much as you could expect from me.

***

"Boxing is a combat sport in which two people engage in a contest of strength, speed, reflexes, endurance and will, by throwing punches at each other, usually with gloved hands. Historically, the goals have been to weaken and knock down the opponent."

Ahh. Society. What a shell to crack. I can't ignore it, can I? It is the silent main character in this narrative.

Child abuse, child neglect, paedophilia, suicide, welfare, teenage pregnancy, divorce, mental health issues, alcoholism, war, absentee parents, financial inequality, overrun school systems, failing medical systems, homelessness, racism, homophobia, rape, drugs, police violence, parenting, sexuality, poverty, disability, guns, religion, immigration, revenge et al.

Those are some of the subjects covered in this book, anecdotes taken from one person's life. Many of them centre on the family home; others have to do with our interactions with the systems we live within. The home is a microcosm of society, and the events that take place in it have a direct effect on our interactions with the larger entity of the world society.

If my parents had owned a priceless ancient vase worth millions, they would have guarded it under lock and key. Their daughters were treated as punching bags and given no protection from the greater world. They were careless and cruel with us - human beings they chose to bring into the world. If we think it is acceptable to treat those close to us in such a barbaric way, what does that say about how we treat the wider world? Carol often said that she could not be expected to do any better at parenting because she had the burden of being a single parent. There is no denying that the prejudices and imbalances in society make life a special kind of difficult for single parents, but to say a single parent equals a parent who is bound to be abusive is clearly ridiculous and insulting. There are an extraordinary amount of people who parent under devastating circumstances, each unique. Most of them make loving and dedicated parenting the cornerstone of their lives.

The majority of the events in this book took place around twenty years ago during the 1990's. The world today is an unimaginably different place and thankfully it will never be the same again. Alex can hardly picture a world without the internet and all its digital devices, yet those things did not even exist until my late teens, and even then they weren't terribly widespread.

This book, and my related goals, would not have been possible without the coming of the digital age. When I woke up again in my moment of understanding after my collapse in health, the first thing I did was to begin writing, something I hadn't done in some time. This led almost naturally into blogging and social media, which led to meeting likeminded individuals, which encouraged me to carry on writing and voicing my thoughts. I found other people who were also speaking out, and I learned from them like a sponge, suddenly having access to all of the information I could have dreamt of during my teens. My education began afresh when I landed online. I'm a huge advocate of the internet and what it can do for the progress of humanity.

I'm avidly looking forward to seeing where we are heading on this roller coaster ride. The internet is still essentially lawless, the Wild Wild West. It means we have to police each other and ourselves to a great extent, and in many ways that's no bad thing. It means we have the freedom to debate with our "betters" and expose the injustices we find. It gives us friendships that we might never otherwise have had, friendships that would have otherwise never happened, friendships that change lives with the love, encouragement and solace they give. I love living in the digital age. It is easily one of the most revolutionary times in human history and I feel privileged to have participated in it.

This has not been an easy book to write and indeed it has been worse still for me to read through again upon completion. I am not happy with any of this. I am not happy at the thought of angering people or potentially fighting once again with my family. I have done this to the best of my ability, and mostly while confined to bed with neurological issues. In these days of media exposure it takes bravery to put your name to any independent thought and while I will have that courage and do my job it is not for lack of fear. I have earned a life of peace, I have worked hard for it. I want my family and my home and my privacy and my beloved friends. I am not at all happy with the idea of any random stranger knowing all these awful details about me, I can only hope you all will be kind and I am quite sure that some of you will not be. I hate this book almost in equal measure to the degree to which I was compelled to write it. I am writing this book because I have to. I am publishing it because I have to.

I sit for hours alone in my bedroom watching reruns of M*A*S*H, listening to music and writing. Not so very different then from how I have always been. I think of all of it. I think of my grandpa and his painting. My grandma and her pure devotion. Troy's beautiful face. I can see them as if they're here and I miss them, my heart breaks for them. I want my son to know the good people he came from. And so much more. More even that I held back, more innocent lives lost that I did not mention so that they could rest in peace. I see them all parade before me in this beautiful pageant of light, strife and love, and I write their faces. I miss my sister, whom I could never peacefully get on with. I have nightmares every night of my mother, coming to take me, coming to take my child, I see myself breaking her heart, a monster as she always predicted. And then Dad and Karen. Oh, how Karen will weep to read the truth, and how futilely I always hoped to be loved by them. Their lives will go on with militant grandeur, only a twitch in the jaw to display the ravages of their actions. I see Troy's eyes and remember a certain sweet, indecipherable look in them and I write.

No I am not happy about publishing this book. Whilst writing I shortened the file name to TheLL, or T'Hell. Every time I opened the file to write more I walked willingly into hell, into my memories. I would be happy to never discuss any of this again, yet I know that by publishing I invite comment. I don't ever want my son to read this book, but I know one day, when he is an adult, he will. I want him to know me only as the happy, hardworking and responsible individual I am today. But he will also know the little girl who was abused and the teenager who abused herself.

This is a painful dichotomy to live within, but I am not budging. I set out to write this when I was heartbroken and alone in a diner at seventeen, and that is what I have done. I have known so many good people who have helped and supported me. I have known so many people be hurt. The world is a violent, frightening place at times. I am not important enough, and my family is not important enough, to stop the progress I hope and long for. No matter how I hate it or whatever else I believe, I believe that within the pages of this book lies part of my contribution to that progress. My hot, searing, agonising reminder that we are all absolutely dependent on the milk of human kindness, and that without it we will all suffer tremendously. A reminder too that children are precious. They are everything, and to hurt, abuse or neglect a child is the ultimate misuse of power. My hope for this earth is also my hope for my son, who is my light, and whom I chose to care and nurture the moment I chose to bring him into the world.

So it is that as I am facing the realities of publishing this beast I am taking stock of all within and without. And there is no happiness within me, not over this book. This book was not born to beget happiness, it was born out of necessity, and it would require a whole second book to explore where art and trauma meet, but meet they do, there on grandpa's canvas, here on this page.

Most true progress is made by the thousands of tiny, daily taps of a million individuals rather than a single hard blow. We're all relentlessly chipping away at one mammoth mountain, at the centre of which we will one day meet in fairness, equality and enlightenment. This book is the hammer in my hands. From the moment I came fully awake in the living room watching my three year old son I was filled with a peace that remains with me to this day, a peace I was seeking my whole life. Finally, I understood that I was meant to be, and I have true love. So it seems I can offer you a Happily Ever After after all, even if it's unconventional. I have what I strove so hard to acquire, and as I write these final words, I'm completing my mammoth task. I made it. I want to be remembered for the love I've had in my life, and the hard work I've put into it, and I wish the same for everyone out there, struggling to survive, flourish and make their mark.

Lightning Source UK Ltd.
Milton Keynes UK
UKOW07f2253281115

263721UK00001B/8/P